TRANSPORTATION INFRASTRUCTURE – ROADS, HIGHWAYS, BRIDGES, AIRPORTS AND MASS TRANSIT

SURFACE TRANSPORTATION

FUNDING AND FEDERALISM CONSIDERATIONS

TRANSPORTATION INFRASTRUCTURE – ROADS, HIGHWAYS, BRIDGES, AIRPORTS AND MASS TRANSIT

Additional books in this series can be found on Nova's website under the Series tab.

Additional E-books in this series can be found on Nova's website under the E-books tab.

TRANSPORTATION ISSUES, POLICIES AND R&D

Additional books in this series can be found on Nova's website under the Series tab.

Additional E-books in this series can be found on Nova's website under the E-books tab.

Transportation Infrastructure – Roads, Highways, Bridges, Airports and Mass Transit

Surface Transportation

Funding and Federalism Considerations

David M. Boche
Editor

Nova Science Publishers, Inc.
New York

For permission to use material from this book please contact us:
Telephone 631-231-7269; Fax 631-231-8175
Web Site: http://www.novapublishers.com

Library of Congress Cataloging-in-Publication Data

Surface transportation : funding and federalism considerations / editor, David M. Boche.
p. cm.
Includes index.
ISBN 978-1-61470-855-1 (hbk.)
1. Transportation and state--United States. 2. Federal aid to transportation--United States. 3. Transportation--United States--Finance. I. Boche, David M.
HE206.2.S88 2011
388'.0490973--dc23
2011028021

Published by Nova Science Publishers, Inc. † New York

CONTENTS

PREFACE

Since the early 1980s, the periodic debate over the reauthorization of federal surface transportation programs has been primarily about money and its distribution. In each of the five reauthorizations that took place during that period, the federal fuel taxes and other sources of revenue dedicated to the highway trust were reliably providing the various surface transportation programs with more money year after year. In 2009, this was not the case. For the first time in decades, driving declined significantly, with a concomitant decrease in fuel tax revenues. Going forward the program cannot count on new money from the familiar sources. The law authorizing federal surface transportation programs expired at the end of 2009, but Congress has failed to enact a new authorization. This book examines the surface transportation program reauthorization issues for the 112th Congress; funding and finance; the Donor-Donee State issue of funding equity and federalism issues in surface transportation policy.

Chapter 1 - The law authorizing federal surface transportation programs expired at the end of FY2009, but Congress has failed to enact a new authorization. Surface transportation programs continue to operate on the basis of authority provided in extension legislation.

This situation should not be a surprise to those familiar with the history of the reauthorization process. Especially during the last two decades, reauthorization has become a difficult undertaking. This is primarily due to controversy over how and to whom federal-aid highway funds should be distributed. The most recent law, the Safe, Accountable, Flexible, Efficient Transportation Equity Act: A Legacy for Users (SAFETEA-LU or SAFETEA) (P.L. 109-59), was enacted 22 months after previous legislation had originally expired. Previous reauthorization bills also were enacted well behind schedule.

Chapter 2 - Federal surface transportation programs are currently funded primarily through federal fuel taxes on gasoline, diesel, and other fuels that are deposited in the highway trust fund. Although there has been some modification to the tax system, the basic fuel taxes have not been increased at the federal level since 1993. Prior to the recession that began in 2007, annual increases in driving, with a concomitant increase in fuel use, were sufficient to keep revenues rising steadily on an annual basis. This is no longer the case. Further, future changes in the nation's vehicle fleet as a result of federal fuel economy standards, including increased use of electric hybrid and fully electric vehicles, are expected to suppress future fuel use even if annual increases in vehicle mileage resume.

Congress has yet to address the surface transportation program's revenue issues, except by increasing transport spending from the U.S. Treasury general fund. Many members of Congress have expressed an aversion to raising fuel taxes, and alternative methods of financing surface transportation have not received serious legislative consideration.

Chapter 3 - Few issues in the history of the Federal-Aid Highway Program have raised such heated debate as the argument over how closely the program's payments to the individual states should match the amount of federal highway taxes each state's highway users pay to the highway account of the Highway Trust Fund (HTF). Referred to as the donor-donee state issue, it is expected to reemerge during the debate over the reauthorization of federal surface transportation programs. The current authorization, under the Safe, Accountable, Flexible, Efficient Transportation Equity Act: a Legacy for Users (SAFETEA; P.L. 109-59), expires on September 30, 2009.

Chapter 4 - American federalism, which shapes the roles, responsibilities, and interactions among and between the federal government, the states, and local governments, is continuously evolving, adapting to changes in American society and American political institutions. The nature of federalism relationships in surface transportation policy has also evolved over time, with the federal government's role becoming increasingly influential, especially since the Federal-Aid to Highway Act of 1956 which authorized the interstate highway system. In recent years, state and local government officials, through their public interest groups (especially the National Governors Association, National Conference of State Legislatures, National Association of Counties, National League of Cities, U.S. Conference of Mayors, and American Association of State Highway and Transportation Officials) have lobbied for increased federal assistance for surface transportation grants and increased flexibility in the use of those funds. They contend that they are better able to identify surface transportation needs in their states than federal officials and are capable of administering federal grant funds with relatively minimal federal oversight. They also argue that states have a long history of learning from one another. In their view, providing states flexibility in the use of federal funds results in better surface transportation policy because it enables states to experiment with innovative solutions to surface transportation problems and then share their experiences with other states. Others argue that the federal government has a responsibility to ensure that federal funds are used in the most efficient and effective manner possible to promote the national interest in expanding national economic growth and protecting the environment. In their view, providing states increased flexibility in the use of federal funds diminishes the federal government's ability to ensure that national needs are met. Still others have argued for a fundamental restructuring of federal and state government responsibilities in surface transportation policy, with some responsibilities devolved to states and others remaining with the federal government.

In: Surface Transportation
Editor: David M. Boche

ISBN: 978-1-61470-855-1

Chapter 1

SURFACE TRANSPORTATION PROGRAM REAUTHORIZATION ISSUES FOR THE 112TH CONGRESS*

Congressional Research Service

SUMMARY

The law authorizing federal surface transportation programs expired at the end of FY2009, but Congress has failed to enact a new authorization. Surface transportation programs continue to operate on the basis of authority provided in extension legislation.

This situation should not be a surprise to those familiar with the history of the reauthorization process. Especially during the last two decades, reauthorization has become a difficult undertaking. This is primarily due to controversy over how and to whom federal-aid highway funds should be distributed. The most recent law, the Safe, Accountable, Flexible, Efficient Transportation Equity Act: A Legacy for Users (SAFETEA-LU or SAFETEA) (P.L. 109-59), was enacted 22 months after previous legislation had originally expired. Previous reauthorization bills also were enacted well behind schedule.

The most difficult issue to be considered during reauthorization is how to finance it. The highway trust fund and the revenue sources that feed it have been a reliable mechanism for financing highway and transit programs for five decades, but this is no longer the case. Fuel taxes, which provide most of the money for surface transportation, are unlikely to provide a solid long-term foundation for this desired growth, even if Congress were to raise them modestly. The choice for policymakers, therefore, is to find new sources of income for an expanded program, or alternately to settle for a smaller program that might look very different from the one currently in place.

One perennial subject of debate concerning the highway program is whether grants to individual states are in line with the taxes those states' motorists pay into the highway trust fund—the so-called donor-donee issue. The use of earmarks and possible

* This is an edited, reformatted and augmented version of a Congressional Research Service 7-5700 publication R41512 , dated December 1, 2010.

programmatic reorganization will likely be prominent concerns in committee discussions of reauthorization. Specific programs, such as the Highway Bridge Program, can be expected to receive extensive congressional attention due to public concerns about the condition of the nation's transportation infrastructure. Congress also can be expected to look closely at transit program spending levels and priorities.

Freight issues have also been of growing importance in recent years and figure to get significantly more attention as part of the reauthorization debate.

INTRODUCTION

Since the early 1980s, the periodic debate over reauthorization of federal surface transportation programs has been primarily about money and its distribution. In each of the five reauthorizations that took place during that period (1982, 1987, 1991, 1998, and 2005), the federal fuel taxes and other sources of revenue dedicated to the highway trust fund were reliably providing the various surface transportation programs with more money year after year.[1] In 2009 this was not the case. For the first time in decades, driving declined significantly, with a concomitant decrease in fuel tax revenues. Going forward the program cannot count on new money from the familiar sources.

The law authorizing federal surface transportation programs expired at the end of FY2009, but Congress has failed to enact a new authorization. Surface transportation programs continue to operate on the basis of authority provided in continuing resolutions and extension legislation.[2]

Reauthorization has become a difficult undertaking in the last two decades. The most recent law, the Safe, Accountable, Flexible, Efficient Transportation Equity Act: A Legacy for Users (SAFETEA-LU or SAFETEA) (P.L. 109-59) was enacted 22 months after previous legislation had originally expired. The bill prior to SAFETEA, the Transportation Equity Act for the 21st Century (TEA21) (P.L. 105-178, as amended by P.L. 105-206) was also passed well after previous legislative authority had originally expired. In fact, no surface transportation authorization bill has been enacted on time since the 1970s. Over time, these bills have become increasingly complex in their structure and in their politics as states, other program beneficiaries, and related interest groups compete for constrained federal transportation resources.

SAFETEA has led to controversies over funding parity among the states (the so-called donor-donee debate), its large number of earmarks (exemplified by the so-called "bridge to nowhere"), and the funding problems ahead. Additionally, the structure of the surface transportation programs under SAFETEA and its predecessors has made it difficult for the federal government to respond to certain intermodal transportation needs. These issues could cause Congress to make significant changes to the surface transportation programs in this reauthorization.

PROGRAM STRUCTURE

The surface transportation programs can be difficult to understand. The language of transportation finance—contract authority, obligation limitations, and so on—is unfamiliar even to many who have a basic understanding of the annual congressional budget process. Therefore, this report begins with a discussion of how the surface transportation programs are structured and financed.

The Federal-Aid Highway Program

The modern federal-aid highway program dates to the 1956 enactment of legislation that provided for the construction of the interstate highway system and created the highway trust fund to finance its construction.[3] The program has been reauthorized and expanded on numerous occasions during the last five and a half decades.

The federal highway program is fundamentally a state-run program. The state departments of transportation, within the federal programmatic framework, largely determine where and on what the money is spent (but have to comply with detailed federal planning guidelines as part of the decision-making process). The states let the contracts and oversee the project development and construction.

The flow of federal highway funds to the states to support this spending operates as follows. At the beginning of each fiscal year each state department of transportation is notified of the federal funds available to it to construct and maintain a designated system of roads known as the federal-aid highway system. The states do not get the money up front. Instead, as work is completed the states submit vouchers to the Federal Highway Administration (FHWA) and are reimbursed.[4]

The federal-aid highway program can be viewed as an umbrella term for various separately funded programs administered by FHWA. The programs, which are mostly for construction project spending, receive their funding in two ways: they are either "apportioned" (formula) programs or "allocated" (discretionary) programs.

Core (Apportioned) Programs

Most highway funding is reserved for six major programs, which are usually referred to as the core programs (*Table 1*). They, along with the Equity Bonus Program, accounted for 82.5% of the highway spending authorized for FY2005-FY2009 by SAFETEA. Each of these programs provides funding for specific segments of the federal-aid highway system or other statutorily enunciated activities, such as congestion relief projects. SAFETEA also combined many formerly separate highway safety programs into one Highway Safety Improvement Program.

Although it does not provide direct spending for highways, the Equity Bonus Program, discussed in more detail later in this report, provides additional funds for the six core programs. The equity bonus is the largest single highway program in SAFETEA, accounting for approximately 20% of all available funding. Funds for the core programs and the Equity Bonus Program are apportioned to the states on an annual basis using formulas found in SAFETEA. As a result they are sometimes referred to as the "apportioned" programs.

In addition to the core programs there are a couple of smaller apportioned programs: Coordinated Border Infrastructure Program; metropolitan planning; and the Recreational Trails Program. SAFETEA also creates some formulas within formulas.

Table 1. Core Program Authorizations for FY2009

Program	FY2009 SAFETEA Authorization
National Highway System Program	$6,306,611,031
Interstate Maintenance Program	$5,119,399,081
Surface Transportation Program	$6,576,630,046
Highway Bridge Program	$4,457,421,829
Congestion Mitigation and Air Quality Improvement Program	$1,777,263,247
Highway Safety Improvement Program	$1,296,474,396
Equity Bonus Program	$9,093,265,575

Source: P.L. 109-59, also Financing Federal-Aid Highways, Appendix B. http://www.fhwa.dot.gov /reports/financingfederalaid/appb.htm.

This is most notably the case for the Surface Transportation Program, which has a minimum set-aside for transportation enhancements and a sub-state distribution formula that allocates funds within states.

Allocated (Discretionary) Programs

All remaining highway programs are subject to allocations that are based on criteria established in highway authorization and appropriation laws and/or subject to congressional earmarking. Although all of the programs in this category are smaller than the core programs, there are nonetheless some programs with significant funding. The largest allocated program is for congressionally mandated High Priority Projects (earmarks). This program, which has a five-year authorization of $14.8 billion, is reserved for projects specifically designated in SAFETEA. Two other large earmarked programs, Projects of National and Regional Significance and Transportation Improvements, received $1.78 billion and $2.55 billion, respectively, over the same period. Among the other allocated programs are the Federal Lands Program, the National Corridor Infrastructure Improvement Program, the Interstate Maintenance Discretionary Program, the Bridge Discretionary Program, and the Transportation and Community and System Preservation Program.

The Transit Program

The federal transit program, administered by Federal Transit Administration (FTA) of the U.S. Department of Transportation (DOT), is a collection of individual programs, each with different funding distribution mechanisms and spending eligibility rules. Of the $10.4 billion made available for transit programs in FY2010, the Urbanized Area Formula Program accounted for about 40% ($4.2 billion), and the Capital Investment Program accounted for 45% ($4.6 billion). The Capital Investment Program has three elements: the Bus and Bus Facilities Capital Program, which receives about 20% of all transit capital investment funds; the Rail Modernization Program, which receives 40%; and the New Starts Program, which also has a 40% share.

The remaining 15% of federal transit monies ($1.6 billion) funds several other programs, such as the Other Than Urbanized Area Formula Program (commonly referred to as the Rural Formula Program), the Elderly Individuals and Individuals with Disabilities Formula Program, the Job Access and Reverse Commute Program, as well as state and metropolitan planning, research, and FTA operations.

Other Transportation Programs

There are a number of transportation activities that are outside of the highway and transit programs that are authorized by surface transportation legislation. These include highway safety, motor carrier safety, transportation research, hazardous materials transportation, some elements of rail transportation, and transportation planning activities. Some of these programs are discussed in more detail later in this report.

SURFACE TRANSPORTATION FINANCE

Federal funding for surface transportation has historically been linked to the revenue stream provided by the highway trust fund. The trust fund has two separate accounts—highways and mass transit.[5] The primary revenue sources for these accounts are the 18.4 cent per gallon tax on gasoline and a 24.4 cent per gallon tax on diesel fuel. Although there are other sources of revenue for the trust fund (truck registrations, truck tires, etc.), the fuel taxes provide about 90% of the income to the funds. The transit account receives 2.86 cents per gallon of fuel, and there is also a 0.1 cent per gallon fuel tax reserved for the Leaking Underground Storage Tank Fund, which is not included in the surface transportation programs. The federal motor fuels tax has been increased several times since its inception in 1956. At the time of the last increase, in 1993, some of the receipts were deposited in the Treasury general fund, but since FY1998 these revenues have been directed to the highway trust fund.

Other changes in recent years have modestly increased trust fund revenues. The American Jobs Creation Act of 2004 (P.L. 108-357) provided the trust fund with additional future income by changing elements of federal gasohol taxation. At the time, there were estimates that these changes could provide the trust fund with an additional $4 billion per year. SAFETEA also included a number of tax and other changes in its finance title. The revenue increases in this title were viewed as quite modest and were derived mostly from cutting back on tax fraud and by transferring some Treasury general fund revenues associated with transportation-related activities to the trust fund. It was believed at the time of passage that the changes enacted in SAFETEA, combined with the changes in gasohol legislation enacted in 2004 and enhanced by expected economic growth, would be sufficient to finance the act through FY2009.

The financial estimates associated with SAFETEA have proved to be overly optimistic. The highway account has already required three transfers from the general fund totaling $29.7 billion,[6] without which FHWA might not have been able to pay states for work they completed.[7] In late FY2008, $8 billion was transferred to carry the highway account into the

2009 fiscal year (P.L. 110-318, September 15, 2008). In FY2009 the transfer was $7 billion (P.L. 111-46, August 7, 2009). The Surface Transportation Extension Act of 2010 (P.L. 111-148, March 18, 2010) transferred $14.7 billion more to the highway account.

Historically, the trust fund-based revenue collection system was a reliably growing source of funding for surface transportation, as the trust funds collected more than was been expended to implement the program defined by Congress. This situation has changed under SAFETEA as spending on highways and transit has exceeded both highway and transit account revenues on a regular basis. The Congressional Budget Office (CBO), in its spring FY2009 baseline calculation, showed that, from FY2007 to FY2009, outlays from the highway account exceeded receipts in each fiscal year. CBO's summer 2010 baseline estimate projected a slight surplus for FY2010, with outlays of $32.5 billion against $32.7 billion in revenues.[8] CBO projects the fund to slip back into deficit in FY2011, with outlays of $37.4 billion and revenues of $34 billion.

Congress provided another $14.7 billion transfer from the general fund on March 18, 2010, and CBO now projects that the balance in the highway account will remain above zero through FY2013. However the gap between tax revenues and outlays remains through FY2020. CBO projects that the mass transit account, which received a $4.8 billion general fund transfer in FY2010, will also remain above zero through FY2013.[9]

The recent declines in motor fuel tax receipts are unprecedented. Even during the oil shocks of the 1970s, driving, as measured by vehicle miles traveled, returned fairly quickly to the 2% average annual growth rate experienced since the 1960s. The same thing has not happened since 2007, even though fuel prices fell dramatically from their highs of around $4 per gallon in mid-2008, as the sluggish economy continues to depress freight, leisure travel, and commutes to work. As a rule of thumb, adding a penny to the federal fuels tax provides the trust fund with between $1.6 and $1.8 billion in new revenues. Without an increase in the existing fuel taxes, the mostly fuel-based trust fund taxation system will not be able to support increased surface transportation spending over the next few years. The immediate choice for policymakers, therefore, is to find new sources of revenue for the trust fund, or alternately, to settle for a smaller surface transportation program that might look very different than the one currently in place.

However Congress chooses to address the short-term funding issue, it will need to address the viability of the trust fund mechanism over the longer term. In recent years, Congress has acted to mandate higher fuel-economy standards for gasoline-powered cars and to encourage development of hybrid and battery-powered vehicles. As these more fuel-efficient vehicles come to make up a larger share of the U.S. vehicle fleet, consumption of motor fuels may decline even if driving increases. If it wishes to maintain or increase the size of the surface transportation programs, Congress may need to explore alternatives to the motor fuels tax as possible sources of funding.

The difficult outlook for motor fuel tax revenues clouds the outlook for surface transportation reauthorization. In the past, steady revenue growth enabled Congress to meet the competing demands for funding in each reauthorization. TEA21 benefitted from a run-up in fuel usage during the boom years of the late 1990s that was at least partially the result of the popularity of sport utility vehicles during the period. SAFETEA did not have quite the same financial backing, but the authors of the act were nonetheless able to find sufficient new revenues to expand the programs. The next reauthorization bill, as the above discussion indicates, lacks a ready source of cash to support expansion—a situation that will define the upcoming legislative debate much more than issues such as program structure and infrastructure needs.

The American Recovery and Reinvestment Act of 2009 (ARRA, P.L. 111-5)

The ARRA contained significant funding for activities normally funded through federal surface transportation legislation. It provided $27.5 billion for federal-aid highways, $8.4 billion for public transit, $1.5 billion for a new Surface Transportation Discretionary Grant Program, and $8 billion for high-speed rail. All money provided by the ARRA is from the general fund and carries no requirement for state or local matching funds. This one-time infusion represented a bit less than one year's funding for the existing surface transportation programs, although it was distributed differently. High speed rail, for example, is a very small program under SAFETA, but received a large share of funds in the ARRA. By giving states an additional source of surface transportation funding, the ARRA may have made the need for reauthorization of SAFETEA somewhat less immediate.

The SAFETEA Legacy

In public, the SAFETEA debate focused on the donor/donee issue and a later, more public, controversy over earmarking. The actual process of crafting the law, however, was complicated by the political need to satisfy the large number of interest groups supporting specific programs, most of which are funded from the highway trust fund but do not involve building highways.

Donor/Donee

The donor/donee debate concerns the efforts of individual states to achieve or maintain as large a share of the total distribution federal highway funds as possible. A donor state is one whose highway users pay more in revenues to the trust fund highway account than it receives in federal highway assistance. Conversely, a donee state receives more in assistance than it contributes to the trust fund. The debate is generally driven by representatives of donor states, who frame their arguments in terms of "equity" in the distribution of federal highway funds. The donor/donee state distinction, however, is far less straightforward than it appears. Federal fuel taxes are not actually collected at the state level, so determining whether a state is a donor or a donee requires a complicated mechanism that attributes fuel usage and associated revenues to individual states.[10]

In the last three surface transportation authorization bills, the donor/donee issue was resolved only by the availability of more money and the creation of a process to distribute it. In SAFETEA, this process, called the Equity Bonus Program, is the largest single highway program. For FY2008 and FY2009 SAFETEA promises that each state will receive a funding share of the major highway program allocations equal to at least 92% of the revenue share its highway users pay into the highway trust fund, an increase from the 90.5% promised under the prior legislation, TEA-21. The Equity Bonus Program, however, is so complicated that effectiveness of the guarantee is unclear. For FY2010 Congress based the distribution to the six core formula programs on their FY2009 totals. There was no equity bonus calculation for FY2010.

The transfer of $29.7 billion in general fund revenues to the highway account complicates the donor-donee framework as a basis for analyzing transportation funding. This is because payments into the general fund have nothing to do with highway tax payments but, because of the transfers, do support the flow of funds to the highway programs. For FY2007 through FY2009 each of the 50 states received more federal highway funding than it contributed to the highway account.

Earmarking

When the Intermodal Surface Transportation Efficiency Act of 1991 (ISTEA; P.L. 102-240) passed in 1991 it included 548 individual highway earmarks with a total value of $6.2 billion. In 1998, TEA21 incorporated 1,883 highway earmarks adding up to $9.6 billion. In SAFETEA, earmarking expanded exponentially, with over 5,600 earmarks accounting for $21.7 billion in the highway title of the act alone. With a few highly publicized exceptions, there was very little debate about the benefits or drawbacks of the individual earmarks in the bill.

Following the 2010 congressional elections, proposals to abolish the earmarking of individual projects have received increased interest. An earmark-free reauthorization could increase the attention given to program structure, funding formulas, and eligibility criteria, as Members attempt to assure the flow of transportation funds to their congressional districts or states.

SAFETEA Funding

SAFETEA provided $286.4 billion in guaranteed spending authority for the six-year period FY2004-FY2009. This was a significant nominal increase over the level in TEA-21, which provided $218 billion over the six-year period FY1998-2003. In reality, however, SAFETEA was barely a five-year bill by the time of its passage late in FY2005. A more useful representation of SAFETEA is that it provided $244 billion in spending authority from FY2005 through FY2009. (*CRS contacts: Bob Kirk and Will Mallett*)

Table 2 shows that all major programs affected by the legislation received significant new funding (the exempt obligation category is provided for equity bonus and emergency funding purposes and does not reflect a program per se). Spending increased in each year and total spending in FY2009 was almost 23% higher than spending in FY2005.[11]

Table 2. SAFETEA Guaranteed Obligations FY2005-FY2009 ($ billions)

	FY2005	*FY2006*	*FY2007*	*FY2008*	*FY2009*	*Total*
Highway Obligation Limitation	34.422	36.032	38.244	39.585	41.200	189.484
Exempt Highway Obligations	0.739	0.739	0.739	0.739	0.739	3.695
Highway Safety and Motor Carrier Safety Obligations	0.742	1.189	1.217	1.239	1.270	5.656
Mass Transit Obligations	7.646	8.623	8.975	9.731	10.338	45.313
Totals	*43.549*	*46.583*	*49.175*	*51.294*	*53.547*	*244.148*

Source: P.L. 109-59, see also http://www.fhwa.dot.gov/safetealu/fundtables.htm for highway amounts and for transit see http://www.fta.dot.gov/index_6536.html.

ISSUES SHAPING THE CURRENT REAUTHORIZATION DEBATE

The reauthorization process will involve detailed consideration of the way in which surface transportation programs are funded, organized, and managed. A handful of fundamental issues, however, will influence the way in which the eventual legislation is constructed.

- *National goals and purposes.* Today's surface transportation programs have their origins in the creation of the interstate highway program (1956) and the collapse of public transit systems (early 1960s). In the intervening decades, it has become difficult to discern how federal surface transportation spending relates to national needs, as the vast majority of the funding is granted to states and localities based not on maximizing the national return on transportation investment, but as an entitlement to be spent largely as state and, to a lesser extent, local authorities think best. Changing the existing decision-making process, however, could involve a transfer of authority from state and local authorities to the federal government.
- *Productivity and performance management.* With the operation of surface transportation programs left largely to states and localities, federal officials often have a poor understanding of the efficiency and effectiveness with which federal funds are being used. States and localities have, in many cases, very robust processes in place to measure and analyze their programs.12 However, these mechanisms are largely internal, and their diversity makes it difficult to compare performance across the country. Federal performance standards might make such comparisons easier, potentially allowing the federal government to direct funding to the state and local governments with the most efficient and effective programs. Once imposed, however, such measures might be "gamed" by state and local officials in ways that negate their value. Even if Congress should decide to enforce performance measures by funding penalties, it is possible that the effect of such penalties would be counteracted by funding guarantees in the bill.

- *Structural issues.* SAFETEA created two commissions to study the structure and the financing imperatives of the surface transportation programs. One of these, the National Surface Transportation Policy and Revenue Study Commission, called for a major reorganization of the federal surface transportation programs into 10 new program areas, often across existing programmatic modal boundaries.[13] A report issued by the George W. Bush Administration entitled "Refocus, Reform, Renew: A New Transportation Approach for America," included several proposals for new and reorganized surface transportation programs, with a heavy emphasis on expanding the role of market forces and the private sector in the provision of surface transportation infrastructure.[14] Numerous think tanks, research organizations, and transportation groups have called for organizational changes in the way federal surface transportation programs are administered.[15]
- *Revenue issues.* The two commissions established in SAFETEA both recommended increases in the motor fuel tax to meet the immediate funding needs of surface transportation programs. Both urged an eventual shift to charges based on vehicle miles traveled as a longer-term funding source. VMT charges represent one type of user fee, but alternatives such as tolls and weight-distance taxes, which are already imposed in some instances on trucks, also might be employed to force road users to pay the costs of surface transportation programs.[16]
- *Alternative funding mechanisms.* Public-private partnerships, in which private companies take responsibility for construction, operation, and/or maintenance of particular transportation projects in return for a flow of payments from government agencies or project users, have been widely encouraged as a means of decreasing reliance on the trust fund.17 Other proposals for expanding alternative funding include federal grants or loans to state infrastructure banks; increased authority to lend to local agencies under the Transportation Infrastructure Finance and Innovation Act (TIFIA); increased reliance on Grant Anticipation Revenue Vehicles (known as GARVEE Bonds) and the private activity bonds authorized by SAFETEA; and creation of a national infrastructure bank, as proposed by the Obama Administration in its FY2010 and FY2011budgets.
- *Reducing program size.* If Congress chooses not to make changes that would increase the flow of revenue into the highway trust fund, it will face a choice between continuing to authorize annual general fund expenditures for surface transportation and reducing the programs' size. It could shift some programs currently funded by the highway trust fund, such as the Appalachian Roads Program, to general fund status. It might reduce matching ratios (90:10 for interstates, 80:20 for most other roads, varying proportions for transit projects) in order to spread the available federal funds more broadly. More dramatically, it could limit surface transportation funding to programs that it determines fulfill clear national needs, and devolve other responsibilities to the states.

HIGHWAY ISSUES

Funding Equity Among States

The donor-donee debate has historically been one of the major hurdles that authorizers must overcome during the periodic reauthorization of federal surface transportation programs. The last several reauthorizations have resolved the disagreements over equity by creating a separate arrangement, currently known as the Equity Bonus Program, under which nearly all states are entitled to highway funding above and beyond that provided for in the funding formulas in specific programs. Under the Equity Bonus Program, FHWA is directed to allocate sufficient funds to ensure that each state receives a minimum share return on its highway payments—92% in FY2008 and FY2009. The calculation is more complicated than this figure suggests, as certain surface transportation programs are not included.

The Equity Bonus Program includes a number of "hold harmless" provisions to guarantee minimum state shares of funding, based on certain thresholds. These thresholds include state population, population density, highway fatality rates, median household income, and state fuel tax rates. In part, these criteria appear to have been devised to assure the bill would get at least 60 votes in the Senate. The Equity Bonus Program also sets an annual percentage floor, relative to a state's TEA-21 average apportionment, beneath which no state can fall. The money is distributed to the states by increasing the amounts apportioned to the core formula programs.

There was no equity bonus calculation for FY2010. The FY2010 distributions were simply based on FY2009 overall funding distributions.

The distribution of the equity bonus had a number of unanticipated consequences. One of these is its interaction with High Priority Program earmarks used by Members of Congress to define their project priorities through the authorization process to their state DOTs. High Priority Program earmarks do not add significant amounts of money to a state's share of highway spending, because states whose earmarks are small tend to receive relatively larger equity bonus distributions than states that receive relatively large earmarks. This means that the total amount received by a state tends to be roughly the same whether or not it receives a large dollar total of earmarks. A corollary of this situation is that the more of a state's total funding is derived from High Priority Program earmarks, the less is ultimately available to the state for the federal-aid highway core formula programs, on which state departments of transportation depend to fulfill their state transportation plans.

The equity bonus distribution also negates the imposition of some penalties that are designed to discourage certain activities of the states. For example, a state that transfers some of its Highway Bridge Program funds to other programs is penalized by having its deficient bridge cost-to-repair total reduced a like amount in the next year's formula calculation. The purpose of this was to encourage states to reserve their Highway Bridge Program funds for bridges. However, the equity bonus distribution in effect gives back what the penalty takes away.[18] The equity bonus overlay combined with the extensive ability given states to transfer funds across programs may undercut the effectiveness of the programmatic structure in achieving the national surface transportation goals specified by Congress.

Since 1982 the equity provisions in surface transportation have been changed many times, and there is a high probability that changes will be discussed in the current reauthorization. Among the possible changes are:

- Increasing the share of its highway tax revenue that is guaranteed to each state above the current 92% level. However, the closer the guaranteed percentage comes to 100% of the total program the more difficult an increase becomes. Bringing the percentage guarantee closer to 100% would probably require a weakening of some of the "hold harmless" provisions that protect certain donee states from losing share. The hold harmless provisions exist primarily due to the practical politics of getting authorization bills through both houses of Congress, so eliminating them may raise political concerns.
- Expanding the scope of the equity provisions. This would require a growth in program size to fund a larger equity overlay unless the underlying core program formulas were rewritten to bring the initial program apportionments more into line with the goals of an increased percentage return guarantee.
- Eliminating the counteracting impact of the equity bonus distribution on the highways program penalty provisions. This could be accomplished by imposing the penalties after rather than before the distribution of the equity bonus funding. However, this could affect some states' guaranteed percentage shares.
- Eliminating the equity provision altogether and allowing program formulas to determine the distribution of highway funds to the states. One way of doing this would be to modify the core formula programs so that they are all entirely weighted at or near 100% on states' annual contributions to the highway account. Most donee states would probably oppose such a change.
- Providing an equity guarantee for transit funding. Roughly 80% of the Federal Transit Administration's budget comes from the fuel taxes paid by highway users. This funding could also be subject to a rate-of-return guarantee. While such a scenario might be attractive to some donor states not already receiving significant transit assistance, there are other donor states which might not benefit from a transit equity distribution. Further, any inclusion of transit in an equity bonus scenario is likely to be opposed by heavily urbanized states and states with large transit systems.

The equity debate is complicated by the fact that significant amounts of general fund money have been transferred to the highway trust fund. Although much of transferred funding reflects interest payments on the trust fund's unexpended balances, such interest not paid directly by highway user fees. Other funds have been transferred to the highway trust fund for a variety of reasons, such as compensation for lower ethanol tax rates. Further transfers may be necessary in the years ahead. The larger the general fund share of federal highway spending, the harder it is to argue that states should get a return based on their highway users' payments, raising the question of whether the Equity Bonus Program is an appropriate source of funding.

Earmarking

Large-scale earmarking was a prominent and controversial feature of SAFETEA. Earmarking has not, however, always been a significant feature of surface transportation bills. Until the late 1980s, earmarks amounted to about 1% of authorized federal-aid highway spending.[19] By way of comparison, SAFETEA earmarked almost $22 billion or roughly 11% of the $199.5 billion highway construction title of the bill. A 2007 DOT report found that earmarking can reduce the states' core transportation programs, lead to funding of low-priority projects ahead of higher priority, non-earmarked projects, and result in funding of projects that do not meet eligibility requirements.[20]

Following the 2010 congressional elections, proposals to abolish the earmarking of special projects have received increased interest. Certain transportation groups which were largely silent on this issue during the last reauthorization debate are now taking the position that earmarking needs to be controlled and limited.[21] An earmark-free reauthorization could increase the attention given to program structure, funding formulas, and eligibility criteria, as Members attempt to assure the flow of transportation funds to their congressional districts or states without earmarking.

Highway Programmatic Structure

According to the National Surface Transportation Policy and Revenue Study Commission established under SAFETEA, the federal government has 108 separate surface transportation programs.[22] Of these, 62 involve highways, 20 concern transit, and the remainder are scattered among other activities. The commission recommended combining all of these programs into 10 broad intermodal programs. It may be difficult, however, for Congress to consolidate programs to that extent. There are numerous potential and competing organizing rationales, and each existing program has specific stakeholders whose support for the overall surface transportation program is associated with the continuation of the mission the program was created to carry out.

The federal-aid highway program gives states a great deal of control over the selection, planning, and construction of federally funded highway projects. This flexibility might, for example, allow a state to shift money from the Highway Bridge Program to the Surface Transportation Program, even though it might have unmet needs in the original program area. This flexibility also has allowed transfers between highway and mass transit programs. Programmatic restructuring that restricts state flexibility could be a source of contention during the reauthorization process.

Congress may also wish to consider project eligibility changes. For example, broadening project eligibility within the Congestion Mitigation and Air Quality Improvement (CMAQ) Program could allow more projects designed to increase road capacity on the grounds that increased capacity would improve traffic flow in congested areas. There may be interest in creation of new programs, such as a program to address bottlenecks in major freight corridors.

Rather than refining or restructuring the various formula programs within the highway program, Congress might opt to replace the existing formula programs with block grants provided directly to the states. This might reduce federal administrative overhead, although it could weaken the ability of Congress to set spending priorities consistent with its determination of national needs.

Bridge Policy

In December 2009, roughly 71,000 bridges were designated by FHWA as "structurally deficient."[23] The Highway Bridge Program is the primary federal program to fund the replacement or rehabilitation of structurally deficient or functionally obsolete bridges. Funds are apportioned to the states by formula based on each state's relative share of the total cost to repair or replace deficient highway bridges. Each state is guaranteed at least 0.25% of total program allocation, and no state may receive an allocation greater than 10%. The federal share is 80%, except that for interstate highway system bridges the federal share rises to 90%.

If Congress chooses to retain a distinct bridge program, the rate of repair and replacement of deficient bridges and the funding needed to support any proposed acceleration of that rate would be major issues. The authorizing committees may hear proposals to limit the use of Highway Bridge Program funds for spending on non-federal-aid highway system bridges and to change bridge inspection standards. There are also concerns that linking funding to a state's number of deficient bridges creates a perverse incentive for states to keep their deficiency rates high. A GAO report found that the program lacks focus, performance measures, and sustainability.[24]

TRANSIT ISSUES

The federal government provides support for transit agencies' capital investments and operating costs. Although federal transit programs direct most funding to capital investment, transit agencies have some discretion over the use of their federal funds among capital and operating purposes. The mass transit account of the highway trust fund is the source of approximately 80% of federal transit program monies, with the remaining 20% drawn from the general fund of the U.S. Treasury. Although the transit account is in somewhat better financial shape than the highway account, it is also projected to go into deficit within a few years. Despite uncertainty surrounding this projection, it is clear that current revenue into the transit account will not sustain Federal Transit Administration programs and activities at current levels through another four- to six-year authorization period. Within this context, there are both funding and programmatic issues that could arise during reauthorization.[25]

The prospect of constrained federal transit funding is occurring in conjunction with financial problems in the transit industry itself. The immediate causes are flat or declining government assistance at the state and local levels due to budget conditions and lower patronage due to a high unemployment rate. But financial problems in public transit are a long-term issue, primarily caused by declining transit system productivity, that results in an increasing requirement for government support from all levels of government. Fares and other operating revenue were only 26% of capital and operating funding sources in 2008. For that reason, Congress may want to consider whether modifications in the federal transit program might boost ridership at a lower cost per rider to the government.

Transit Funding Issues

How much to spend overall on transit is the main issue in the upcoming reauthorization. Various interest groups have argued that America is under-investing in transportation infrastructure, including public transit infrastructure, and called for a significant increase in federal infrastructure investment.[26] Both DOT and the congressionally created Surface Commission have estimated that the capital cost to maintain and improve transit systems in the United States is substantially more than is being currently spent on transit systems by all levels of government.[27] Because many transit agencies currently face severe budget problems, there also have been calls for more federal support of operating expenses.[28]

Support for increased federal spending on transit is by no means unanimous. The growth in transit capacity has outpaced the growth in ridership at the national level, and the physical condition of transit systems has generally improved over the past decade. Nor is there agreement on the proper level of transit spending relative to highway spending; while transit receives approximately 14% of federal highway and transit capital expenditure, only about 2% of all trips and 5% of commuting trips are made by this mode. Given that a significant proportion of federal transit funding, roughly 80%, comes from taxes paid by highway users, the relationship between highway outlays and transit outlays is a sensitive issue.

Federal Fuel Tax

One way to increase transit funding would be increase the proportion of funds coming from the general fund. An alternative would be to raise the federal fuels tax and dedicate 20% of any increase to the transit account, as has been the case since 1983. Calculations based on CBO projections indicate the fuel tax would need to be raised by 10 cents per gallon (with 2 cents per gallon dedicated to the transit account) to close the gap between revenue and expenditures in the transit account for FY2011, assuming no growth in the program.[29]

Federal Matching Share

A potential way to make the federal transit dollar stretch further would be to lower the federal matching share. A larger local match might help ensure that only the most important projects are supported by state and local officials. On the other hand, if the federal government provides a much lower share of the cost of transit projects than of highway projects, state and local decision-makers might favor highway projects regardless of the potential demand for public transit.[30]

PPPs and Innovative Financing

SAFETEA provides limited support for private participation in developing transit projects through public-private partnerships (PPPs) and other types of innovative financing.[31] In reauthorization, Congress likely will consider ways to encourage a larger role for the private sector. While some PPPs have been highly successful, their overall contribution to meeting transit financing needs is likely to be relatively small, as the possibilities for generating new revenue streams from transit operations are limited to situations in which new services encourage land development near transit stations. (PPPs may be more readily used for roads, bridges, and tunnels on which vehicle tolls will provide a source of new revenue, but even then it may be unrealistic to expect private funding to supply more than 5% - 10% of needed funds).

Transit Structural Issues

Congressional discussion of possible ways of restructuring federal public transit programs is likely to explore alternatives to the present configuration of programs. One way to reorder federal priorities would be to focus more resources on major capital investment for the rehabilitation and expansion of transit service in places that are best served by this mode, primarily the densely populated parts of large and often heavily congested cities. This might entail expansion of the programs that make up the transit capital investment program—the New Starts Program, the Rail Modernization Program, and the Bus and Bus Facilities Capital Program—while cutting back on formula grants that are spread more broadly and go for smaller and more routine types of expenses. This change would likely result in a concentration of resources in a few large cities where transit usage is relatively high, an effect that has obvious potential political problems.

Alternatively, Congress may decide that the era of retrofitting large and medium-sized cities with new transit rail systems is largely over, and that resources should now go to supporting and rehabilitating existing systems. This could entail a reduction in spending on the New Starts Program, currently about 18% of the federal transit program, and more support for the other capital programs and the formula grants programs. The effect of these changes on the distribution of funds would depend on the shares of funds dedicated to the Rail Modernization Program, which affects relatively few cities, and to buses and formula programs, which provide support in a much larger number of localities.

A third way to restructure the federal transit program would be to eliminate the capital programs altogether, to be replaced with a block grant that might be distributed based on transit ridership or population. This would allow state and local governments to decide how best to allocate transit funding support among existing and new services. Funds distributed according to transit ridership would reward areas that commit their own resources to providing transit service. The distribution of funding in this way would depend on how this new program is structured, but might encourage states and localities to react to the changes by aggressively promoting transit ridership.

A fourth alternative would be to fold most of the transit programs into a broader "metropolitan mobility" program that would distribute federal surface transportation funding to large urban areas, say those of one million people or more, on a mode-neutral basis. It would then be up to states and localities to decide how to allocate the money to transit and highway infrastructure.

Small Cities and Rural Areas

Because most transit ridership is concentrated in a few large cities, most formula funding goes to the largest urbanized areas. Whether and how much the federal government should assist small city and rural mass transit systems may be an issue in the current reauthorization.

Paratransit

The demand for and cost of paratransit has grown rapidly over the past two decades, placing added pressure on state and local government transit budgets. Paratransit is typically provided by vans rather than buses and serves passengers with limited physical mobility. A number of federal transit programs exist to help states and localities provide paratransit service, and funding is also available from the federal government outside the transit program. Nevertheless, transit agencies are likely to ask for more federal money for paratransit in reauthorization. One consideration, given the social service nature of paratransit services and their generally poor fit with regular bus and rail services, is whether FTA should administer paratransit funding at all.

Transit Industry Productivity

Regardless of whether federal transit funding is tightly constrained or not, but especially if it is, Congress may want to consider a number of options for encouraging transit industry productivity.

Performance Measurement

As noted earlier, there have been many proposals for incorporating performance measures as a central tenet in the distribution of surface transportation program funds. This includes federal transit program funds. The main reason for using performance measurement incentives would be to reward transit agencies for providing more and better service per dollar of public support.

Competition

In most cases, public transit service is a monopoly; even where transit vehicles are operated and maintained by private companies, a local transit agency almost always selects and subsidizes a single operator for that purpose. Reauthorization could include language encouraging more competition in the provision of transit service. This might entail requiring transit agencies to competitively bid transit service provision and/or to allow private operators to provide new services to compete with public transit agencies. Many of the barriers to competition are in state or local laws and regulations that give monopoly power to regional transportation agencies, and it would be possible to make the elimination of these barriers a condition of federal funding. One consideration is the possibility that competition could allow private operators to "cherry pick" routes and services, operating profitable routes at rush hour while leaving public agencies to sustain services on less dense routes or at less popular times.

Work Rules

Some advocate loosening work rules in the transit industry in an effort to boost productivity. This might, for example, include renegotiating union contracts that often do not allow transit agencies to employ part-time workers or to require split shifts to cover rush-hour demand peaks. It might also include changes in federal labor protections in the transit sector, originally established in Section 13(c) of the Urban Mass Transit Act of 1964 (P.L. 88-365).

Fares

Another potential way of reducing the need for public assistance is to increase fares to more accurately reflect the cost of providing a particular service. This occurs at present with some services, such as the distance-based fares on the Washington, DC Metro, but most transit systems charge a flat fare regardless of distance or time of day. The reauthorization might encourage transit systems to collect variable fares, particularly as newer electronic fare payment technology makes it relatively easy to do so.

Congestion Pricing

Pricing automobile use, particularly in congested periods, might reduce the need for government assistance to public transit. One way to do this is to institute highway tolls, particularly ones that vary based on traffic levels. This might encourage some drivers to switch to transit and may provide a source of funds to enhance transit service. Such road pricing schemes usually make the most sense in severely congested regions where good transit options exist. Congress way want to consider whether congested metropolitan areas should adopt comprehensive congestion management schemes that incorporate highway pricing and transit.

FREIGHT ISSUES

Up until the world economy began to slow late in 2007, the immediate concern of freight carriers and shippers was congestion. Major ports and land gateways experienced a notable run-up in import volumes in the early years of the last decade, and certain highway segments had persistent traffic bottlenecks. Congestion frustrates a freight carrier's ability to provide reliable scheduling. Unreliability is costly because it requires shippers to carry buffer stock, reducing an efficient "just-in-time" logistics strategy to a "just-in-case" strategy. The concern for the capacity of the system to keep pace with rising freight volumes is borne out by a steady rise in freight tonnage prior to 2008. From 1997 to 2007, truck ton-miles increased by 19% while rail ton-miles increased by 31%.[32] These modes are also using their respective infrastructure more intensively. Between 1980 and 2007, truck travel grew by 98% while lane miles of public roads increased by only 5% and railroad tons originated increased by 30% while the miles of railroad track decreased by 40%. DOT projects that total tons transported will grow 73% by 2035.[33]

Freight Transportation Planning

Doubts about whether the nation's transportation infrastructure will keep pace with the projected growth in freight traffic have led to calls for stronger federal leadership in developing a systematic approach to addressing freight transportation needs. A national transportation plan that identifies key freight corridors and gives priority to funding these corridors would be a departure from the current planning process, which relies heavily on state departments of transportation and metropolitan planning organizations to plan and select which transportation projects to fund in their jurisdictions. Local action to eliminate a freight bottleneck may merely relocate it to another community, without reducing the unpredictability of travel time across an intermodal network that is North American in scope.[34]

Unlike commuter trips, which generally begin and end within a metropolitan area, freight trip lengths often exceed the jurisdiction of a single metropolitan planning organization or even a state. Thus, these planning institutions have difficulty taking a corridor or an "end-to-end" approach in addressing freight improvements. They also may have a disincentive to do so because, while they bear the costs of improvements, the economic benefits may accrue nationally. Some hub cities have a preponderance of freight that is merely passing through rather than serving local producers or retailers. Land border ports of entry, gateway seaports, and interchange points in the rail network, in particular, must live with the negative effects of freight traffic that is largely serving distant locations.

At the national level, freight transportation may not be able to compete with other pressing priorities. At the local level, however, especially at major freight hubs like Los Angeles, freight transportation may be a priority because residents recognize the pollution and congestion caused by truck traffic and thus support projects to streamline freight movement in the area. Because freight issues vary dramatically from one hub or region to the next, it can also be argued that they are best addressed at the state and local level. For instance, air cargo hubs such as Memphis or Louisville face different problems from large railroad hubs like Chicago or St. Louis, and seaports are tackling different problems than land border crossings like Laredo or Detroit. Rural areas may be more concerned with preserving short-line rail access to the transcontinental rail network and the (not unrelated) issue of upgrading roads to accommodate heavy trucks carrying agricultural and mineral products. Also, local desires to retain jobs that are tied to freight activity and to improve the quality of life may be sufficient incentive for state and local transportation planners to address freight bottlenecks.

One possible way for Congress to facilitate a wider geographic perspective in planning freight-related transportation improvements is to make funding for nationally or regionally significant projects contingent on state and local coordination. The I-95 Corridor Coalition, an association of state DOTs and transportation authorities from 16 states from Maine to Florida, is one model of freight planning from a corridor perspective. In pursuit of its goal of improving traffic movement on I-95, the coalition is investigating rail and waterborne modes as alternatives for freight transport to mitigate congestion on the highway.

Freight Funding

Concerns about capacity limits and financial shortfalls have led to several proposals for imposing user charges dedicated to funding projects that would improve goods movement. Proposals include assessing a container fee, a freight waybill tax, or an intermodal terminal facility charge. Selection of a fee mechanism entails trade-offs involving equity, efficiency, and administrative simplicity. In addition, some freight interests have conditioned their support for new user fees upon assurances that the money will be dedicated only to net new capacity on new projects. This may be a difficult condition to meet, particularly in congested metropolitan areas where additional highway construction would be unpopular.[35]

Targeting Freight Investment

If Congress were to create a separate funding program for freight transportation improvements, it could steer funding toward certain inefficiencies in the national surface transportation network. Trucks, and therefore highway infrastructure, are vital for efficient goods movement because they carry 65% of the tonnage and 75% of the value of domestic cargo. FHWA has found that the preponderance of truck delays are at urban freeway interchange points and that steep grades, signalized intersections, and lane drops were other problem areas.[36] Some states are evaluating the feasibility of segregating truck traffic from automobile traffic on highways with heavy truck traffic, either on short segments or on long-distance routes connecting to a seaport or other freight hub.

All air cargo begins and ends its journey in trucks as does almost all intermodal rail and containerized seaborne cargo. Intermodal shipments, the fastest growing segments of goods movement in the United States, consist of higher-value goods and are closely tied to international trade. The "intermodal connector" roads linking ports, airports, and rail terminals to the interstate highway system tend to be relatively short segments, generally less than two miles in length, but DOT studies have found that they often suffer from poor pavement condition and substandard geometrics (narrow lanes, small-radius curves) because the roads often were not originally designed for the heavy truck traffic they handle.

In some cases, transfers between ports and railroads and between railroad networks still require a container to be drayed, or trucked, in order to make the interchange. In Chicago (and to a lesser extent in St. Louis, Memphis, and New Orleans), where the eastern and western rail networks converge, and at many seaports, drayage generates significant truck traffic that co-mingles with commuter traffic on beltways and arterials. At certain of these locations, additional "on-dock" or "near-dock" rail terminals and "steel-wheel" interchanges might lessen heavy truck traffic on urban roads. The development of "logistics parks"—clusters of warehouses built around a rail terminus—are essentially an effort by the railroads to re-consolidate product distribution centers that have been scattered by circumferential highway building, and may also offer opportunities to reduce drayage. Congress may want to consider whether the federal government should support such private undertakings in order to limit wear and congestion on urban roadways.

Even though almost all U.S. freight railroads are private enterprises, Congress has authorized some public investments in freight rail infrastructure. Most of these, such as grants to improve rail lines serving rural communities, are quite small, but the federal government has also contributed to large-scale efforts to eliminate grade crossings and separate rail lines in Los Angeles and Chicago. Rail users, particularly intermodal customers who demand faster, more reliable, and more precise scheduling than other rail shippers, want railroads to accelerate investment in passing sidings and double tracking to better accommodate freight trains traveling at different speeds. Congress may be asked to consider options such as a federal tax incentive to spur investment in railroad facilities or a dedicated trust fund for freight rail infrastructure. The federally supported expansion of commuter rail service will play a role in this discussion, as commuter trains may occupy track capacity that otherwise would be available for freight service.

Congress may also consider steering funding toward projects that mitigate the negative affects of increases in freight traffic. Some localities have experienced significant increases in freight train traffic, resulting in prolonged blockages of rail-grade crossings. If Congress chooses to direct additional funding to grade-separation projects along heavily used rail corridors, the share of the cost borne by railroads will be a major point of debate.

HIGHWAY SAFETY

Highway safety in the United States has improved in recent years. The number of annual fatalities has been stable for most of the last decade at a little over 40,000, though 2009 saw only 33,808 highway deaths, the lowest number since 1950. As the number of vehicle miles traveled has increased over this period, the fatality rate (the number of fatalities adjusted for exposure to the risk of dying in a crash) has declined. In 2009 it was 1.13 per 100 million vehicle miles traveled,[37] down from 1.27 in 2008 and far below the figure of 5.3 in 1965. However, DOT failed to reach its goal of reducing the fatality rate to 1.0 by 2008 (which would have required a reduction in fatalities to around 30,000).[38] Moreover, since the 1960s, when the United States had the best safety record of any country, several other countries have achieved lower fatality rates.

Most of the fatalities occur to three groups:

- passenger car occupants (69%, or about 23,382 deaths in 2009);
- motorcyclists (13%, or 4,462 fatalities in 2009; and
- pedestrians (12%, or 4,092 fatalities in 2009).

Highway Safety Countermeasures

Countermeasures to improve highway safety can be divided into three general categories: changes to roadways, changes to vehicles, and changes in driver behavior. Changes to roadways are the responsibility of FHWA, which distributed $1.3 billion to the states in FY2010 under the Highway Safety Improvement Program. Changes related to vehicles and drivers are the responsibility of the National Highway Traffic Safety Administration (NHTSA) and, in the case of commercial vehicles and drivers, of the Federal Motor Carrier Safety Administration. In FY2010 Congress gave NHTSA $246 million for its own operations and for research, and $620 million for grants to be provided to states to improve highway safety with an emphasis on altering driver behavior.

Driver Behavior Incentive Programs

Driver behavior is the primary factor in the vast majority of fatal crashes, so programs directed at altering driver behavior are considered to offer the greatest safety impact. The driver behaviors which are most significantly related to traffic fatalities are driving while impaired,[39] speeding,[40] not wearing a seat belt,[41] driver distraction,[42] or in the case of motorcyclists, not wearing a helmet.[43]

In SAFETEA, Congress established or renewed programs providing grants to states that take specified actions to promote the use of seat belts and to reduce the incidence of drunk driving. In some cases, the incentive programs have achieved limited success: for example, in the case of the program that provides grants to states that allow law enforcement agents to stop and ticket motorists for not wearing seat belts, the number of states qualifying for grants increased from 21 in its first year to 29 in its fourth year. In the case of the program that provides grants to states to adopt measures to reduce drunk driving, all fifty states and the District of Columbia qualified for grants in the first year; in the fourth year, as the number of measures required in order to remain eligible rose, four states and the District of Columbia failed to maintain their eligibility. In some cases, there are questions about the eligibility measures set forth in SAFETEA for the program; for example, the program that provides grants to states to improve motorcycle safety excludes promoting the wearing of a motorcycle helmet—demonstrated to be the single most effective motorcycle safety measure—as an eligible use of program funding, while measures that are eligible, such as motorcyclist training programs and programs to promote motorist awareness of motorcyclists, are of unproven value in reducing fatalities.[44]

Highway Safety Issues in Reauthorization

Highway safety programs tend to be less controversial than construction grant programs, because the amounts of money at stake are much smaller. Nonetheless, Congress will likely be asked to consider significant changes to federal safety programs.

Consolidating the Application Process

There are currently five separate NHTSA incentive grant programs, and states have complained that the application process is unnecessarily difficult. Each program has a separate process, all the program applications are due between June 15 and August 1 each year, and each application requires significant attention from relatively small state traffic safety offices. Congress may be asked to direct NHTSA to consolidate or simplify the application processes.

Increased Flexibility in the Use of Incentive Grant Funding

One of the incentive programs in SAFETEA allows states to use the funds for any safety-related expense that is eligible for federal funding, but most of the programs require the money to be used for a limited range of eligible activities. In some cases, the restrictions are even more limiting: motorcycle safety program grants can be used only for safety training provided to motorcyclists, motorcyclist awareness programs aimed at motorists, and public awareness and outreach programs. Officials in Montana told GAO that they would like to use some of the funds to build new motorcycle training sites or expand existing sites, but the grant does not allow that.[45] Congress may be asked to give states greater flexibility in use of highway safety funds.

Switching from Incentives to Sanctions on States

Sanctions, in the form of withholding of federal funds, have been found by some studies to be more effective than incentives in gaining state compliance with federal goals.[46] States generally oppose sanctions, but even so the Governors Highway Safety Association testified that it would vigorously oppose any effort to repeal an existing sanction requiring states to make purchase and public possession of alcohol illegal for those under age 21.[47] That sanction, established by Congress in 1984, was preceded by an incentive program which failed to induce many states with lower minimum purchase ages to change their laws.

Linking Grants to Performance

Most of the eligibility criteria for the various incentive programs are actions—passage of laws and implementation of programs—rather than measures of results.[48] Thus, states can receive safety grants under these programs without demonstrating improved highway safety.

One possible reform would link the receipt of a grant, or the size of a grant, more closely to a state's performance. Such a change, however, might require data that are not currently available; for example, not all states are able to calculate motorcyclist vehicle miles traveled, which is necessary to measure changes in the rate of motorcyclist fatalities. Past surface transportation reauthorizations have included federal support for data collection related to highway safety. For example, Congress provided funding for improvements to states' traffic safety information systems in SAFETEA.

MOTOR CARRIER SAFETY ISSUES

Congress tends to treat commercial vehicle safety issues separately from passenger vehicle safety issues, as matters related to commercial vehicles and their drivers come under a specialized agency, the Federal Motor Carrier Safety Administration. Increases in federal limits on the size and weight of commercial trucks may be among the most controversial proposals related to safety, as they would increase the productivity of the trucking industry but might have adverse effects on safety as well as on roadway life. Congress may choose to explore the potential of in-vehicle technologies, such as driver-fatigue warning systems and lane departure warning systems, to promote safety. Inspections of commercial vehicles are considered important in promoting compliance with federal safety requirements, but there is concern that the resources available to support inspections do not allow inspections to be done on more than a fraction of the commercial vehicles, making the risk of discovery of noncompliance low.

A separate set of issues concerns the behavior of commercial drivers. Previous laws have funded efforts to prevent drivers from driving while drugged or with serious medical conditions that may impair their driving. GAO, however, found that it was easy for drivers to avoid detection because many collection sites did not follow regulations intended to maintain the integrity of urine tests.[49] GAO also found that drivers who failed a drug test were able to continue driving without submitting to the required return-to-duty process by hiding their past drug history from employers, many of whom did not conduct thorough background checks. Among the measures that Congress may wish to consider to deal with this issue are the establishment of a national database for drug testing, additional funding for inspectors, and additional authority to impose fines for failure to comply with federal requirements.

Research, Development, and Technology Deployment

The federal surface transportation program supports research in many areas, from system efficiency and passenger safety to environmental degradation stemming from transportation projects. FHWA has the largest research budget of the DOT agencies, while NHTSA, FTA, and the Research and Innovative Technology Administration also have significant roles.

Title V of SAFETEA authorized $411 million annually for research. Of that, $196 million went to the surface transportation research program; $110 million to research on intelligent transportation systems (ITS); $70 million to support research at university transportation centers; $27 million to the Bureau of Transportation Statistics; and $27 million to training and education programs.

Congress is likely to face questions about the adequacy of transportation research funding; under SAFETEA, federal spending on surface transportation research is approximately 0.9% of total federal expenditures on highways, and some advocates contend that a higher share will have a payoff in terms of reduced costs from crashes, congestion, and environmental damage.

Congress also faces competing claims for how transportation research funding should be used. In SAFETEA's research title, Congress earmarked more funding than the total amount that was authorized by the title, with the result that individual research programs and projects received less funding than each was authorized in order that the available funding could be stretched to cover all the designated programs and projects. No unearmarked research funding was available for some FHWA projects, such as the biennial conditions and performance reports, that in previous years had been funded with such moneys. In 2008 Congress addressed these funding shortfalls by enacting the SAFETEA Technical Corrections Act (P.L. 110-224), which added additional funding to all of the research programs. The lack of peer review in the allocation of research funding has also surfaced as a concern.

Environmental Issues

Environmental Compliance

During past reauthorization debates, environmental requirements have drawn attention due to both the impact that surface transportation projects can have on the environment and the impact that compliance with environmental requirements can have on project delivery. Previous reauthorization legislation has attempted to address environmental compliance issues by authorizing funding for projects to mitigate or minimize environmental impacts associated with surface transportation and by specifying procedures intended to expedite compliance with certain environmental requirements. The upcoming reauthorization process may include debate over ways to speed the environmental compliance process and fund certain regulatory requirements.

Reviews under the National Environmental Policy Act

Before final design, property acquisition, or construction on a highway or transit project can proceed, FHWA and FTA must comply with all applicable environmental review requirements, including those of the National Environmental Policy Act of 1969 (NEPA, 42 U.S.C. 4321 et seq.).[50] NEPA requires all federal agencies to consider the environmental impacts of their proposed actions. To ensure that environmental impacts are considered before final decisions are made, NEPA requires the preparation of an environmental impact statement (EIS) for any federally funded project that significantly affects the quality of the human environment. If the level of significance of a proposed project is unclear, the agency must prepare an environmental assessment in order to make that determination. Projects that do not individually or cumulatively have a significant social, economic, or environmental effect, and which DOT has determined from past experience have no significant impact, are processed as categorical exclusions.

DOT regulations require the final NEPA documentation to demonstrate that a project will be in compliance with all applicable environmental laws and related requirements.[51] This means that, for any given transportation project, any environmental study, review, or consultation required by law should be conducted within the framework of the NEPA process. According to FHWA, legal requirements most frequently applicable to its projects are the Endangered Species Act of 1973 (16 U.S.C. 1531 et seq.), National Historic Preservation Act (16 U.S.C. 460 et seq.), Clean Water Act (33 U.S.C. 1251 et seq.), and "Section 4(f)"of the Department of Transportation Act of 1966 (40 U.S.C. 303). To meet the requirements of these laws, various agencies, such as the U.S. Fish and Wildlife Service, the Advisory Council on Historic Preservation, the U.S. Army Corps of Engineers, or the Environmental Protection Agency (EPA) may be required to participate in the NEPA process. That participation may involve performing scientific analysis or issuing permits.

SAFETEA, and TEA-21 before it, both included legislative changes intended to streamline the NEPA process.[52] Debate continues on the impact that environmental compliance requirements have on transportation project delivery, with more efficient interagency cooperation frequently identified as an area in need of improvement. Additional provisions intended to expedite NEPA reviews may be debated in the upcoming reauthorization process.

"Section 4(f)" Requirements

Another requirement generally carried out within the context of the NEPA process is compliance with Section 4(f) of the Department of Transportation Act of 1966.[53] Section 4(f) requirements apply to the use of publicly owned parks and recreation areas, wildlife and waterfowl refuges, and publicly or privately owned historic sites of national, state, or local significance. The law prohibits the use of a Section 4(f) resource for a transportation project unless there is no "prudent and feasible" alternative, and requires all possible planning to minimize harm to the resource. When a proposed project would use a Section 4(f) resource, a separate "Section 4(f) evaluation" must be prepared and included with the appropriate NEPA documentation.

SAFETEA amended Section 4(f) to allow for the use of parks, refuges, and historic sites if that use results in "de minimis impacts." SAFETEA also required DOT to issue regulations clarifying factors to be considered and standards to be applied in determining whether alternatives are "prudent and feasible." Due to the continued prohibition on most uses of

Section 4(f) resources, further changes to the requirements may be debated during the upcoming reauthorization process.

The CMAQ Program

The Congestion Mitigation and Air Quality Improvement (CMAQ) Program was created in by ISTEA in 1991, and was reauthorized in TEA-21 and again in SAFETEA. It provides funds to states for transportation projects designed to reduce traffic congestion and improve air quality, particularly in areas of the country that do not attain National Ambient Air Quality Standards. In particular, it authorizes funding for programs and projects intended to reduce carbon monoxide, particulate matter, and ozone. CMAQ funds are apportioned in accordance with a formula based largely on a state's population and pollution reduction needs. During the reauthorization process, there will likely be debate regarding the level of CMAQ funding and possibly the types of projects eligible for funding.

From FY2005 to FY2009, the CMAQ program provided over $8.6 billion to state departments of transportation and local transit agencies. Specific types of projects eligible for CMAQ funds include, but are not limited to: programs for improved public transit; traffic flow improvement programs that reduce emissions; and programs to control extended idling of vehicles.[54] SAFETEA required states and metropolitan planning organizations to give priority in distributing CMAQ funds to diesel engine retrofits and other cost-effective emission reduction and congestion mitigation activities that provide air quality benefits. SAFETEA also expanded eligibility requirements to specifically allow certain types of projects to qualify for CMAQ funding.

SAFETEA also directed DOT to evaluate and assess a representative sample of CMAQ projects, in consultation with EPA, to determine their impacts on air quality and congestion levels and to ensure the effective implementation of the program. Further, SAFETEA directed DOT to maintain and disseminate a database describing project impacts. In response to SAFETEA requirements, in October 2008, FHWA released a report that studied the effectiveness of 67 CMAQ-funded projects.[55]

Conformity of Transportation Plans and State Implementation Plans (Sips)

Under the Clean Air Act, areas that have not attained one or more of the six National Ambient Air Quality Standards must develop State Implementation Plans (SIPs) demonstrating how they will reach attainment. As of September 2010, at least 47 areas with 119 million people were subject to the SIP requirements. Other areas are likely to be added to this list in the next few years, as more stringent air quality standards for ozone and particulate matter take effect.

Section 176 of the Clean Air Act prohibits federal agencies from funding projects in these areas unless the projects "conform" to the SIPs. To demonstrate conformity, a transportation improvement program (TIP) must show that the projects to be undertaken will not lead to an increase in emissions that would delay attainment of air quality standards. New highway and transit projects cannot receive federal funds unless they can make this demonstration.

There are some exceptions: highway safety projects, rehabilitation and reconstruction of transit facilities, purchase of replacement buses and rail cars, noise attenuation projects, and pedestrian and bicycle facilities are all allowed to proceed whether or not an area's conformity has lapsed. But the threat of a conformity lapse and the potential "loss" of highway funds[56] has been a powerful incentive to get local officials to focus on air quality considerations as they plan transportation projects. In surface transportation reauthorization, Congress may weigh the benefits of conformity in achieving air quality goals against the burdens it imposes on proposed transportation projects.

Climate Considerations

If the United States is to address climate change, legislation and regulations will need to require significant reductions in emissions of "greenhouse" gases (GHG)[57] from transportation sources. Transportation accounts for about one-third of U.S. emissions of the leading greenhouse gas, carbon dioxide (CO2),[58] and about 27% of total emissions of the six major GHGs typically considered.

CO2 is largely a product of combustion: the carbon in fuel (be it gasoline, diesel, natural gas, or whatever) combines with oxygen in the atmosphere when the fuel burns. Thus, the principal method of reducing CO2 emissions from transportation sources is to burn less fuel. Emissions can also be reduced by substituting fuels that contain less carbon. In the case of motor vehicles, this would mean substituting natural gas or other lower-carbon fuels for gasoline and diesel fuel.

In the Energy Independence and Security Act of 2007 (EISA, P.L. 110-140), Congress required both improved fuel economy for new cars and trucks and a lower carbon content in renewable transportation fuels. The law required that new motor vehicles attain an average improvement of 40% in fuel economy by 2020 with incremental improvements between now and then, and that future renewable fuels have a lower carbon content on a life-cycle basis. The Obama Administration has now advanced the schedule for EISA's fuel economy standards, with full implementation scheduled by 2016.

Surface transportation reauthorization offers the possibility to look at transportation emissions in a broader context, and could provide incentives for systemic changes that might lower the carbon footprint of the transportation sector. Electrification of truck stops to reduce idling, congestion mitigation, high occupancy vehicle lanes, funding for pedestrian and bicycle facilities, preferences for lower carbon vehicles in FTA grants, incentives to shift freight and people to lesscarbon-intensive modes, and incentives for "smart growth" are among the potential policy options.

Alternative Fuels and Advanced Technology Vehicles

Current laws provide subsidies to promote the use of alternative motor fuels. For example, while gasoline, regardless of its ethanol content, is taxed at 18.4 cents per gallon, every gallon of ethanol blended into gasoline is subject to a credit of 45 cents per gallon. (This credit is set to expire at the end of 2010.) Therefore, the effective tax rate on a 10% blend of ethanol in gasoline is 14.9 cents per gallon. A credit of 50 cents per gallon for natural gas, hydrogen, and other alternative fuels, along with tax credits for biodiesel and renewable diesel, expired at the end of 2009. These various incentives were enacted as provisions in energy and economic legislation. However, there may be interest in using surface transportation reauthorization to extend them.

With interest growing in the environmental effects of alternative fuels, there also may be interest in modifying the fuel credits to reflect their performance on environmental measures.

SAFETEA and various energy laws include incentives to promote alternative fuel and advanced technology vehicles. For example, the Energy Policy Act of 2005 established tax credits for the purchase of alternative fuel and hybrid vehicles, many of which expire at the end of 2010. FTA bus programs provide additional matching funds to transit agencies that purchase alternative fuel and advanced technology buses, including advanced diesel buses, beyond those available for conventional buses. Congress may wish to use reauthorization to modify these incentives to focus more on their energy efficiency or environmental performance.

To expand the use of alternative fuels and advanced technology vehicles, infrastructure to support them must also grow. Just as there are incentives for the purchase of new vehicles, there are tax credits for retail stations to install refueling infrastructure. As part of the surface transportation reauthorization debate, there may be interest in providing additional incentives, including grants, for tax-exempt entities such as transit agencies to install additional refueling infrastructure, especially if those stations are accessible to the public.

End Notes

[1] John W. Fischer, Specialist in Transportation, retired, coordinated the original version of this report.

[2] Surface transportation bills authorize a wide variety of federal transportation programs but are often referred to as "highway" bills because the highway program constitutes a significant majority of the bill's funding provisions.

[3] This section provides a brief overview of the organization of the federal-aid highway program. For greater detail see http://www.fhwa.dot.gov/safetealu/index.htm.

[4] The reimbursable nature of the federal-aid highway program is to prevent fraud, waste and abuse. No federal outlays are made until work is done.

[5] The "highway account" is a term of convenience. In legislation it is referred to as the "Highway Trust Fund (other than the Mass Transit Account)."

[6] The third rescue package, P.L. 111-147, also transferred $4.8 billion to the mass transit account.

[7] *Transportation Weekly*, "DOT Prepares for Next Highway Trust Fund Default," May 20, 2009. p. 1.

[8] Information supplied by CBO as part of its summer FY2010 Baseline, August 19, 2010. The revenue figure for FY2010 does not include the $14.7 billion in general fund transfers made that year.

[9] Ibid.

[10] For a detailed discussion of the Donor/Donee debate see CRS Report RL31735, *Federal-Aid Highway Program: "Donor-Donee" State Issues*, by Robert S. Kirk, available upon request.

[11] A summary of funding for major programs and activities is at http://www.fhwa.dot.gov /safetealu/fundtables.htm.

[12] For example: Poister, Theodore H. "Performance Measurement in Transportation: State of the Practice" Resource Paper. Transportation Research Board. Conference Proceedings 36. Washington, D.C. p. 81-98. Available at http://onlinepubs.trb.org/onlinepubs/conf/CP36.pdf.

[13] http://www.transportationfortomorrow.org/final_report/.

[14] http://www.fightgridlocknow.gov/reform/reformproposal08.pdf.

[15] *Financing Transportation in the 21st Century: a Report of the Intergovernmental Forum on Transportation Finance*, the National Academy of Public Administration (Washington, 2008), 95 p. *The Transportation Challenge: Moving the U.S. Economy*, (Washington, National Chamber Foundation, 2008), 116 p. *ARTBA Recommendations for SAFETEALU Reauthorization* (Washington, American Road & Transportation Builders Association, 2007), 72 p. *Performance Driven: A New Vision for U.S. Transportation Policy,* (Bipartisan Policy Center, 2009). *A Bridge to Somewhere* (Brookings Institution, 2008). *The Route to Reform,*

Transportation for America. *AASHTO Authorization Policy* (produced as a series of topic papers) (October 2008). 230 p.

[16] See CRS Report R41490, *Surface Transportation Funding and Finance*, by John W. Fischer, Robert S. Kirk, and William J. Mallett.

[17] Most observers believe that tolling and PPPs combined can only provide from 5% to 10% of system needs.

[18] *Highway Bridge Program: Clearer Goals and Performance Measures Needed for a More Focused and Sustainable Program*, "GAO-08-1043," (Washington, GAO, 2008), p. 22.

[19] "In-Depth Analysis: Earmarked Highway Projects: Their History, Their Nature and Their Role in Highway Legislation," *Transportation Weekly*, April 10, 2002, 3. See also *A Primer on Lobbyists, Earmarks, and Congressional Reform*, By Ronald D. Utt, (Washington: Heritage Foundation), Backgrounder no. 1924, 2006, 21 p. For a discussion of spending earmark definition see CRS Report RL34462, *House and Senate Procedural Rules Concerning Earmark Disclosure*, by Sandy Streeter.

[20] Department of Transportation, *Review of Congressional Earmarks Within Department of Transportation Programs*, "Report no. AV-2007-066," 2007, 1-31.

[21] http://www.transportation.org/sites/policy_docs/docs/viii.pdf.

[22] Surface Commission. p. 15. found at http://www.transportationfortomorrow.org/final_report/pdf/volume_1.pdf.

[23] See CRS Report RL34127, *Highway Bridges: Conditions and the Federal/State Role*, by Robert S. Kirk and William J. Mallett.

[24] Government Accountability Office, *Highway Bridge Program: Clearer Goals and Performance Measures Needed for a More Focused and Sustainable Program*, (September 2008), available at http://www .gao.gov/new.items/d081043.pdf.

[25] See CRS Report RL34171, *Public Transit Program Issues in Surface Transportation Reauthorization*, by William J. Mallett; and CRS Report RL34183, *Public Transit Program Funding Issues in Surface Transportation Reauthorization*, by William J. Mallett.

[26] For example, American Society of Civil Engineers, "Report Card for America's Infrastructure 2005"; and National Chamber Foundation, *Future Highway and Public Transportation Financing, Executive Summary* (Washington, DC, 2005).

[27] U.S. Department of Transportation, Federal Highway Administration and Federal Transit Administration, *2008 Status of the Nation's Highways, Bridges, and Transit: Conditions and Performance* (Washington, DC, 2009); and National Surface Transportation Policy and Revenue Study Commission, *Transportation for Tomorrow* (Washington, DC, 2007).

[28] Alec MacGillis, "Legislation Fuels Rift in World of Mass Transit," *Washington Post*, June 11, 2010, p. A16;

[29] CRS calculation based on Highway Trust Fund projections provided by the Congressional Budget Office, August 19, 2010.

[30] In certain circumstances, especially in the new starts program, the federal share can be lower.

[31] See CRS Report RL34567, *Public-Private Partnerships (PPPs) in Highway and Transit Infrastructure Provision*, by William J. Mallett.

[32] BTS, *National Transportation Statistics,* Table 1-46b, U.S. Ton-Miles of Freight (BTS Special Tabulation), November 2010. A "ton-mile" is one ton of freight shipped one mile and thus reflects both the volume shipped (tons) and the distance shipped (miles).

[33] FHWA, Office of Freight Management and Operations, *Freight Facts and Figures, 2009,* pp. 11 and 19; Association of American Railroads, *Railroad Facts 2009* (Washington, DC), pp. 28 and 45. Rail volume projections could be influenced by the future of coal-fired power generation.

[34] Not only does NAFTA freight cross U.S. land borders but so too does a portion of U.S. overseas freight.

[35] See for example a speech by a Senior Vice President of UPS at the Intermodal Association of North America, Expo 2007, "Agenda for Action: Avoiding National Gridlock," Atlanta, Georgia, November 12, 2007.

[36] FHWA, *An Initial Assessment of Freight Bottlenecks on Highways*, October 2005, http://www.fhwa.dot.gov /policy/ otps/bottlenecks/index.htm. A "lane drop" is where a multi-lane highway narrows to fewer lanes.

[37] NHTSA, H*ighlights of 2009 Motor Vehicle Crashes*, DOT HS 811 363, August 2010.

[38] DOT revised their timetable in 2006, shifting the target date for achieving a fatality rate to 1.0 to 2011.

[39] 10,839 driving fatalities—32% of all motorist fatalities in 2009—involved a driver who was legally impaired, i.e., having a blood alcohol content (BAC) of 0.08 or more. NHTSA, H*ighlights of 2009 Motor Vehicle Crashes,* DOT HS 811 363, August 2010.

[40] Driving too fast for conditions or exceeding the posted speed limit has been estimated to be a contributing factor in one-third of fatal crashes. DOT, *Speed Management Strategic Initiative*, 2005, p. 1.

[41] NHTSA estimates that if seat belts had been worn by all passenger vehicle occupants over the age of 4 during 2008, an additional 4,152 lives could have been saved. NHTSA, *Lives Saved in 2008 by Restraint Use and Minimum Drinking Age Laws*, DOT HS 811 153, May 2010.

[42] NHTSA's definition of distracted driving includes a driver using electronic devices (cell phones, GPS, audio systems), reading, eating, performing personal care (using razor, painting nails, applying cosmetics), lighting a cigarette, talking, or being distracted by children. NHTSA reported that 16% of fatal crashes in 2009 involved driver distraction, up from 10% in 2005, resulting in 5,474 fatalities in 2009. NHTSA, *Distracted Driving 2009*, "Dot HS 811 379, September 2010.

[43] Nationwide use of motorcycle helmets in states that comply with federal safety regulations was 67% in 2009, but in the 30 states where helmets are not required, usage was 55%. NHTSA, *Motorcycle Helmet Use in 2009—Overall Results*, DOT HS 811 254, December 2009. Requiring all riders to wear a helmet—a universal helmet law—has been estimated to reduce motorcyclist fatalities by 20% or more. National Cooperative Highway Research Program, *Effectiveness of Behavioral Highway Safety Countermeasures*, Report 622, 2008, p. 41.

[44] NCHRP, *Effectiveness of Behavioral Highway Safety Countermeasures*, Report 622, 2008, p. 7.

[45] Government Accountability Office, Traffic Safety Programs: Progress, States' Challenges, and Issues for Reauthorization, GAO-08-990T, July 16, 2008, p. 18.

[46] Sarah F. Liebschutz, The National Minimum Age Drinking Law, Publius, V. 15, No. 3, Summer 1985, pp. 49-50, cites a report by the U.S. Advisory Commission on Intergovernmental Relations which noted that for provisions in two laws—the Highway Beautification Act of 1965 and the Federal Emergency Highway Energy Conservation Act of 1974—Congress had first enacted incentive programs which over several years had resulted in only about half the states adopting the provisions; Congress then switched to sanctions, which quickly resulted in most if not all the rest of the states complying.

[47] Statement of Christopher J. Murphy, Chairman, Governors Highway Safety Association, before the House Subcommittee on Highways and Transit, House Committee on Transportation and Infrastructure, July 16, 2008, p. 8.

[48] Exceptions to this include the seat belt performance grant, under which a state can qualify either by having a mandatory seat belt law or by maintaining a seat belt use rate of 85% or better, and the motorcycle safety grant program, whose eligibility criteria include reductions in fatalities and crashes.

[49] GAO, *Motor Carrier Safety: Improvements to Drug Testing Programs Could Better Identify Illegal Drug Users and Keep Them off the Road*, GAO-08-600, May 2008.

[50] An "environmental review" refers to a requirement to show evidence of formal consideration, evaluation, or analysis of the impacts of a proposed federal action. Most often, the use of the term is in reference to the process of complying with NEPA requirements. However, depending upon the project at issue, an environmental review may refer to the process of complying with provisions of any applicable environmental requirement.

[51] 23 CFR 771.133.

[52] For details on SAFETEA-LU's NEPA-related provisions and DOT's response to those provisions, see FHWA's "SAFETEA-LU Environmental Provisions and Related Information" Web page, available at http://www.environment.fhwa.dot.gov/strmlng/es2safetealu.asp. 53 Section 4(f) of the DOT Act was originally set forth at 49 U.S.C. § 1653(f) and applies to all DOT projects. A similar provision, found at 23 U.S.C. § 138, applies specifically to Federal-aid highways. In 1983, as part of a general recodification of the DOT Act, 49 U.S.C. § 1653(f) was formally repealed and codified in 49 U.S.C. § 303 with slightly different language. This provision no longer falls under a "Section 4(f)," but DOT has continued this reference, given that over the years, the whole body of provisions, policies, and case law has been collectively referenced as Section 4(f).

[54] See FHWA's Interim Program Guidance "The Congestion Mitigation and Air Quality Improvement (CMAQ) Program under the Safe, Accountable, Flexible, Efficient Transportation Equity Act: A Legacy for Users," October 31, 2006, available online at http://www.fhwa.dot.gov/environment/cmaq06gm.htm.

[55] See "SAFETEA-LU 1808: CMAQ Evaluation and Assessment," available on the FHWA "Congestion Mitigation and Air Quality (CMAQ) Improvement Program" Web page at http://www.fhwa.dot.gov /environment /cmaqpgs/.

[56] Highway funds are not actually lost in a conformity lapse. As noted, many types of project are exempt from the requirement and go forward as planned. Other projects face a temporary suspension of funding until they submit a conforming TIP. Generally, the officials involved refer to this temporary and partial suspension as "losing" their federal highway funds, which undoubtedly speeds their efforts to remedy the situation.

[57] Greenhouse gases are pollutants that trap the sun's heat, with effects on the earth's climate.

[58] CO_2 accounts for more than 80% of U.S. GHG emissions.

In: Surface Transportation
Editor: David M. Boche

ISBN: 978-1-61470-855-1

Chapter 2

SURFACE TRANSPORTATION FUNDING AND FINANCE*

John W. Fischer, Robert S. Kirk and William J. Mallett

SUMMARY

Federal surface transportation programs are currently funded primarily through federal fuel taxes on gasoline, diesel, and other fuels that are deposited in the highway trust fund. Although there has been some modification to the tax system, the basic fuel taxes have not been increased at the federal level since 1993. Prior to the recession that began in 2007, annual increases in driving, with a concomitant increase in fuel use, were sufficient to keep revenues rising steadily on an annual basis. This is no longer the case. Further, future changes in the nation's vehicle fleet as a result of federal fuel economy standards, including increased use of electric hybrid and fully electric vehicles, are expected to suppress future fuel use even if annual increases in vehicle mileage resume.

Congress has yet to address the surface transportation program's revenue issues, except by increasing transport spending from the U.S. Treasury general fund. Many members of Congress have expressed an aversion to raising fuel taxes, and alternative methods of financing surface transportation have not received serious legislative consideration.

These financial issues have delayed reauthorization of federal surface transportation programs. In the past Congress has reached agreement on reauthorization only when it could count on sufficient revenues to meet many of the competing demands for funding. With efforts to reauthorize the existing, but already expired, surface transportation program at a standstill, the programs authorized by the Safe, Accountable, Flexible, Efficient Transportation Equity Act: A Legacy for Users (SAFETEA-LU or SAFETEA) (P.L. 109-59) continue to operate as a result of extension legislation and cash infusions to the trust fund from the U.S. Treasury general fund.

* This is an edited, reformatted and augmented version of a Congressional Research Service 7-5700 publication R41490, dated November 10, 2010.

This report focuses on possible revenue sources for surface transportation infrastructure. It begins with a brief discussion of the problems associated with the trust fund financing system and then explores possible immediate and longer-term solutions to the financing problem. Some of the major issues discussed in this report are:

- Raising motor fuel taxes offers a simple short-term solution to the revenue issue, but is not a long-term solution due to likely future declines in fuel consumption.
- Proposals such as replacing current motor fuel taxes with a fuel sales tax or a fee based on vehicle miles traveled (VMT) pose their own problems, and in any event will require overcoming numerous administrative and political barriers.
- The trust fund system itself may be a barrier to increased or more effective federal transportation spending, and its continuation in its current form could be reconsidered.
- The general aversion to taxation in the current economic climate has drawn attention to private and nontraditional funding sources, such as tolls, leveraging private capital through pubic-private partnerships (PPPs), existing federal loan guarantees, and creation of a national infrastructure bank. These nontraditional funding mechanisms could potentially make an important but somewhat limited contribution to overall national infrastructure needs.

INTRODUCTION

Almost every conversation about surface transportation finance begins with a two-part question: what are the "needs" of the national transportation system and how do we pay for them? This report is aimed almost entirely at discussing the "how do we pay for them" question. The report accepts the premise that some level of additional financial resources will be needed to build and maintain transportation infrastructure. The report does not speculate as to what this level of additional finance would be, nor does it suggest that meeting these needs should be an exclusively federal undertaking.[1]

Congress remains deadlocked on the entire issue of surface transportation reauthorization. The last major reauthorization, the Safe, Accountable, Flexible, Efficient Transportation Equity Act: A Legacy for Users (SAFETEA-LU or SAFETEA) (P.L. 109-59) occurred in 2005 and expired at the end of FY2009. All programs authorized by SAFETEA continue to operate only as a result of extension legislation. Draft authorization legislation discussed since 2009 by various congressional committees will expire with the adjournment of the 111th Congress, and the extent to which such legislation will be a priority in the 112th Congress is unclear.

Over the last few decades Congress has been able to agree on long-term reauthorization of federal surface transportation programs only if significant funding increases could be included in the legislation. Program growth was accommodated by the increasing revenues flowing into the highway trust fund as a result of steadily increasing motor fuel use and of occasional increases in federal fuel taxes. As will be discussed subsequently in this report, the steady growth in trust fund revenues came to an end in 2008.

The reauthorization debate provides an opportunity for Congress to revise federal transportation policy. The authors of the last authorization had planned for this debate, setting up two commissions to advise Congress on changes to the surface transportation program and its funding mechanisms. At this juncture, however, the unpromising outlook for highway trust fund revenues complicates efforts to expand federal support for surface transportation and to secure approval for new transport programs through the reauthorization process.

THE HIGHWAY TRUST FUND PARADOX

There is considerable discussion associated with the current state of the highway trust fund. A recent article began with the following statement: "The federal transportation finance system is broken and will be short on cash for the foreseeable future."[2]

Other commentators have described the trust fund as being in crisis, inadequate, or antiquated. Each of these descriptions would seem to suggest that the trust fund is no longer a viable funding mechanism for transportation. In reality, however, this is only partially the case. What is really at issue is that trust fund revenues are no longer growing on a reliable basis. These revenues, therefore, cannot meet the perceived additional needs of our nation's surface transportation system.

For over 50 years the federal transportation programs and their linked user-fee financing systems were the envy of the federal assistance world. The highway trust fund, created in 1956, was a reliable source of funding for the vast majority of federal surface transportation programs. As motor fuel usage increased steadily, the trust fund provided annual increases in funding, even though the rate at which the federal government taxed motor fuel was increased only infrequently. But the history of significant annual growth in the fund appears to have come to an end. Since FY2008, the revenue flowing into the trust fund has been insufficient to pay for the surface transportation programs enacted by Congress, thus requiring that Congress provide additional resources from the U.S. Treasury general fund to keep the programs solvent.

The highway trust fund comprises two separate accounts—highways and mass transit. The primary revenue sources for these accounts are the 18.4-cent-per-gallon federal tax on gasoline and a 24.4-cent-per-gallon federal tax on diesel fuel. Although there are other sources of revenue for the trust fund, such as truck registration fees and a truck tire tax, fuel taxes provide about 90% of the income to the fund. The transit account receives 2.86 cents per gallon of fuel taxes. Separately, there is also a 0.1-cent-per-gallon fuel tax reserved for a fund to mitigate leaking underground fuel storage tanks, which is not part of the transportation program. Since the trust fund was created in 1956, motor fuels taxes have increased four times, in 1959, 1982, 1990, and 1993. The last two increases were initially partially reserved for deficit reduction purposes, with significant sums being deposited in the Treasury general fund account. By FY1998, following several years of congressional debate, all fuel tax collections were again being deposited in the trust fund.

Since the 1993 tax increase, additional changes to the taxation structure have modestly increased trust fund revenues. The American Jobs Creation Act of 2004 (P.L. 108-357), for example, provided the trust fund with increased future income by changing elements of federal gasohol taxation. In 2005, the finance title of SAFETEA included a number of tax and other revenue-raising changes designed to bolster the trust fund, mainly by addressing tax fraud. SAFETEA also provided for the transfer of some general fund revenues associated with transportation-related activities to the trust fund. It was believed at the time of SAFETEA's passage that the tax changes, a $12.5 billion unexpended balance in the trust fund, and, most importantly, expected economic growth would be sufficient to finance the program through its expiration at the end of FY2009. This prediction proved to be significantly off the mark.

To make up for the shortfalls resulting from the overly optimistic forecasts associated with SAFETEA, the highway account has already required three large general fund contributions and could, if the current annual piecemeal funding system continues, require further annual general fund payments. In FY2008, $8 billion was transferred from the general fund to the highway account to carry it through the end of fiscal year (P.L. 110-318, September 15, 2008). In FY2009, the transfer required was $7 billion (P.L. 111-46, August 7, 2009). Most recently, as a result of the Hiring Incentives to Restore Employment (HIRE) Act (P.L. 111-147), $14.7 billion in general fund monies was transferred to the highway account and, for the first time, a general fund transfer of $4.8 billion was deposited in the transit account.

SAFETEA created a framework in which spending on highways and transit has exceeded both highway and transit account revenues on a regular basis. Data provided by the Congressional Budget Office (CBO) in its summer FY2010 baseline calculation shows that the highway account had outlays of $37.6 billion in FY2009 against receipts of $30.3 billion.[3] In FY2010, outlays of $35.1 billion were expected to be matched by only $31.6 billion in revenues. CBO does not project an improvement in this situation. The general fund infusions, however, will keep the trust fund actuarially healthy at least into FY2013, assuming outlay rates do not exceed projections. In this regard, spending on transportation infrastructure associated with the American Recovery and Reinvestment Act of 2009 (ARRA; P.L. 111-5), financed from the general fund, is probably depressing outlays from the trust fund. ARRA funds were made available without a requirement for a state or local matching contribution. As a result, CBO believes states are spending ARRA funds first and delaying projects using trust fund financing.[4]

Trust Fund Prospects

The era of automatic trust fund growth appears to be over. This means that the trust fund will be an adequate source of funding for an expanded surface transportation program only if there are new sources of revenue or cuts in outlays, or both.

The revenue declines of the last few years are unprecedented historically. Even during the oil shocks of the 1970s, driving, as measured by vehicle miles traveled (VMT), returned fairly quickly to the 2% average annual growth rate experienced since the 1960s. The same has not occurred since 2008, even though fuel prices are now far below that year's highs of around $4 per gallon. The main cause of the reduction in revenues appears to be the sluggish economy, which has suppressed growth in personal incomes and also weakened demand for freight shipments.

Over the longer term, other forces are conspiring against the trust fund mechanism. Most importantly, an ongoing change appears to be under way in the U.S. vehicle fleet. In 2007, Congress enacted new fuel economy standards, and the average fuel efficiency of cars and trucks will rise over time as new, more efficient vehicles enter the fleet.[5] Increased sales of hybrid vehicles, electric vehicles, and alternatively powered vehicles will weaken the link between driving activity and motor fuel tax revenues. As a result of these changes, fuel use could decrease on a relative basis even if driving increases.

As a rule of thumb, adding a penny to the federal motor fuels tax provides the trust fund with between $1.6 billion and $1.8 billion in new revenues. An increase in the existing fuel taxes would provide immediate relief to the trust fund. The prospect of reduced motor fuel consumption, however, means that higher taxes on motor fuels probably will not be adequate to support increased surface transportation spending beyond the next decade. Policymakers, therefore, face a choice between finding new sources of income for the existing or expanded surface transportation program or settling for a smaller program, which might look very different from the one currently in place.

Revenue and Revenue-Related Studies

The reauthorization debate is not stalled due to a lack of ideas. Prior to the enacted reauthorization deadline of October 1, 2009, numerous studies looked at the strengths and weaknesses of the surface transportation program. SAFETEA created two commissions, one to study primarily the program structure and the other the financing imperatives. The former, the National Surface Transportation Policy and Revenue Study Commission, issued its report, entitled *Transportation for Tomorrow*, early in 2008.[6] The report called for a substantial increase in overall federal transportation spending, a major reorganization of the federal surface transportation program into 10 new program areas (often across existing programmatic boundaries), and, controversially, a dramatic increase in the federal fuel tax, as well as possible new taxes and fees from a number of potential sources. The second commission, the National Surface Transportation Infrastructure Financing Commission, completed its work in February 2009.[7] The most notable among its numerous recommendations called for an immediate 10-centper-gallon increase in the federal fuels taxes, indexing of these taxes for inflation, and a move to a financing system based on vehicle miles traveled in the years ahead.[8]

The Bush Administration provided its thoughts on reauthorization in a July 2008 report entitled "Refocus, Reform, Renew: A New Transportation Approach for America."[9] The report placed heavy emphasis on how market forces and the private sector could play an expanded role in financing and providing surface transportation infrastructure. The report did not, however, call for new federal taxes for the program.

Additional studies and documents touching on reauthorization have been prepared by a wide spectrum of think tanks, research organizations, and transportation groups. Among these are the National Academy of Public Administration, the U.S. Chamber of Commerce, the American Road and Transportation Builders Association (ARTBA), the American Association of State Highway and Transportation Officials (AASHTO), the Bipartisan Policy Center, the Brookings Institution, and Transportation for America.[10] Most of these studies make revenue as well as programmatic recommendations.

SALES TAXES

The federal motor fuels tax, since its origin, has been structured as an excise tax on each gallon of fuel. The same is true of most states' motor fuel taxes. In a few states, however, motorists pay both a fixed cents-per-gallon excise tax on motor fuel purchases and an additional sales tax on the total purchase price of the fuel.[11] In four states, California, Georgia, Michigan, and Utah, all of the proceeds of taxes on motor fuel are reserved for transportation purposes. In a few other states some portion of the state sales tax on fuel is made available for transportation purposes, though sometimes only in special circumstances.

AASHTO has proposed the idea of shifting the federal motor fuels tax to a sales tax, based on the value rather than volume of motor fuel sold.[12] According to AASHTO, an 8.4% tax on gasoline sales and a 10.6% tax on diesel sales would produce revenue roughly equivalent to current excise tax collections. Underlying the AASHTO proposal is the expectation that fuel prices will rise in the future, as forecast by the Energy Information Administration of the U.S. Department of Energy. The sales tax rates could be adjusted in future years, if necessary, to keep up with inflation in construction costs. The proposal was designed to be "revenue neutral" at the outset so that it would not be characterized as a tax increase.

This is not the first time sales taxes have been promoted as an alternative to a fixed excise tax. After the fuel shocks of the 1970s, a significant number of states sought to make up for what turned out to be a temporary decline in fuel tax receipts by moving to forms of variable-rate taxation of motor fuels.[13] In some cases these taxes were sales taxes; in others the excise tax rates were automatically adjusted by some mechanism such as the Consumer Price Index. Some states placed floors on their tax rates; others did not. Over a 20-year period most of these taxes disappeared, having not lived up to expectations in terms of revenue generation. When fuel prices fell dramatically in the 1980s, tax revenues in many cases fell quickly and states were not always able to react promptly, exacerbating their transportation funding problems.

The sales tax would be at best an interim solution to the long-term problem of finding a way to pay for transportation infrastructure because, like the current motor fuels tax, it relies on fuel consumption to fund transportation programs. To the extent that improved vehicle efficiency or adoption of hybrid or electric vehicles leads to long-term declines in fuel usage, a sales tax on fuel may not lead to increases in trust fund revenues. In addition, a sales tax calibrated to produce a desired amount of revenue in an environment of high motor fuel prices would significantly underperform if fuel prices were to be lower than anticipated.

DISTANCE-BASED (VMT) CHARGES

Both of the study commissions created by SAFETEA recommended charging drivers based on vehicle miles traveled to fund federal surface transportation activities. The Financing Commission supported its recommendation for VMT charges as follows:

> A federal funding system based on more direct forms of "user pay" charges, in the form of a charge for each mile driven (commonly referred to as a vehicle miles traveled or VMT

> fee system), has emerged as the consensus choice for the future. The Commission cast a wide net, reviewed many funding alternatives, and concluded that indeed the most viable approach to efficiently fund federal investment in surface transportation in the medium to long run will be a user charge system based more directly on miles driven (and potentially on factors such as time of day, type of road, and vehicle weight and fuel economy) rather than indirectly on fuel consumed. At the same time, this choice for the federal system provides a foundation for state and local governments that choose to use it to develop their own mileage-based systems that piggy-back on the federal system in order to raise their share on needed revenues in ways that spur more efficient use of the system. The Commission believes that such a system can and should be designed in ways that protect users' privacy and civil liberties, that incorporate any necessary cross-subsidies (for instance, to benefit the national network or to meet social equity objectives), that do not interfere with interstate commerce, and that support goals for carbon reduction. Moreover, greater use of pricing mechanisms, including both targeted tolling and broad-based VMT pricing systems, may spur more efficient use of our highway network and, by shifting demand to less congested periods of the day or to other modes, may in turn enable more efficient investment, thus reducing the additional capacity that needs to be built.[14]

Fees based on vehicle miles traveled have been discussed in the transportation world for years, and have been the subject of extensive studies by the Transportation Research Board (TRB)[15] and other groups. The conclusions reached by these studies almost universally suggest that a transition to a VMT system of financing is desirable and feasible. These same studies, nonetheless, suggest that the transition to a VMT system will take time, and identify numerous obstacles to implementation. The most common recommendation in these studies is that the transition process begin on a pilot basis, to gain experience prior to potential national adoption.

VMT charges could, but need not, entirely replace motor fuel taxes. Certain classes of vehicles might remain subject to fuel taxes even after a VMT charge is put into place. It is also possible that the VMT charge might be used in addition to other revenue-raising measures discussed in this report.

Distance charges are viewed by economists as being a superior form of user charge. Although the fuel tax is often referred to as a user fee, it is better understood as a proxy for a user fee because fuel use does not directly correspond to the quantity (miles) of infrastructure consumed. A Toyota Prius hybrid and a gasoline-powered sport utility vehicle making the same trip, for example, use the same amount of infrastructure (highway miles), but pay different taxes based on the fuel efficiency of the vehicles. With a VMT charge, by contrast, the amount paid would be directly related to the amount of road miles used. Adding vehicle weight into the equation might result in a charge that more fully incorporates infrastructure use by reflecting the pavement wear attributable to the vehicle as well.

Distance-related charges have a long history in the transportation sector. A few states impose weight and distance taxes on trucks, despite long-standing complaints that these fees can be difficult to collect and enforce. (Notably, several states that once had weight and distance taxes have repealed them.) Many toll roads base their toll structure on miles traveled and the number of axles on a vehicle, which is used as a proxy for weight. In the aviation world, outside the United States, weight- and distance-based fees are the backbone of air traffic control system financing. The barrier to implementing distance-based fees in the surface transportation environment has always been finding an efficient means of measuring usage and collecting the corresponding fees.

An additional attraction of VMT charges, at least to some proponents, is that they can be adjusted to reflect the full costs of using a particular segment of infrastructure. For example, the VMT charge can be set at a higher level on a heavily used urban highway and lower on a lightly used rural road. It can be varied by time, traffic level, or some other measure to reflect congestion on a road segment as it occurs, giving drivers price signals that might encourage them to change their driving patterns to avoid crowded roads or rush hours. In principle, VMT charges could be set high enough to preclude the need for new highway construction or highway improvements by moving travel to time periods when the existing highway has excess capacity.

The technology to assess and collect VMT charges either already exists or will exist shortly. The widespread adoption of high-capacity electronics in new vehicles, combined with cellular communications technologies and integrated global positioning systems (GPS), are viewed as the framework of a robust VMT collection system. What is lacking at the moment, however, is a clear set of technical standards to enable the collection and processing of the information generated by this technology on a uniform basis. There are also cost, privacy, and administrative hurdles that will need to be addressed. None of these issues is viewed as a deal breaker by proponents of VMT charges. It remains to be seen, however, whether the driving public can be convinced to share the enthusiasm for a VMT-based system.

The in-vehicle communications infrastructure required for VMT charges could be used for other purposes as well. It might allow drivers to pay for tolls and parking. In theory, it might allow those who drive infrequently to purchase insurance on per-mile basis rather than paying annual premiums to insure a vehicle that is used little. The data a VMT charging system would generate could also enable transportation agencies to make more effective planning, construction, and maintenance decisions.

VMT Issues

Privacy

The same technology that makes VMT charges possible is probably the major barrier to implementation. To many, a VMT charge just sounds like "Big Brother" will be watching, constantly monitoring citizens' movements. As a Florida newspaper editorialized,

> It's not the government's business to know about everyone's whereabouts. A VMT pilot program in South Florida will use a tracking device to log drivers' mileage. Impose the VMT, and Big Brother, for all intents and purposes, will be in the back seat. Tracking your comings and goings isn't akin to installing cameras at intersections to catch red-light-runners who threaten anyone's safety, an effective measure we heartily endorse that saves lives. It's a gratuitous intrusion into drivers' lives. And an intrusion that policymakers need to steer clear of.[16]

Research suggests that it is the GPS tracking involved in some proposed collection schemes that causes individuals the most discomfort.[17] Alternative technologies would allow tracking of vehicle mileage without the use of GPS. A well-known pilot study in Oregon relied on a periodic odometer reading of each vehicle, which could be done at some fixed interval by visiting a special facility, or else during refueling at a gas station equipped to record an electronically transmitted odometer reading. Another approach would use cellular linked technology, such as a weekly automated contact between a vehicle and a collection center, to collect mileage information without disclosing details about individual travel. These less sophisticated reporting systems, however, would be less suited to implementing the variable pricing mechanisms touted by some as a major advantage of a VMT system.

Depending on the collection technology required for a VMT system, drivers of older vehicles could face the need to install potentially costly equipment. A VMT system could avoid this problem by allowing owners of older vehicles to continue to pay fuel taxes until they replace their vehicles. This, however, would increase the complexity and administrative cost of the system.

Pricing

VMT charges are easily described as tolls, leading some critics to characterize VMT charges as a national toll system that would supplement, rather than replace, fuel taxes. This is why proponents of VMT charges have gone out of their way to suggest that a VMT system should be revenue neutral; that is, the rate charged per mile has to be roughly equivalent to the fuel tax paid by an average driver in the course of driving one mile. According to some studies, this would probably mean a fee of around 1 cent per mile initially.[18]

Individual drivers, however, do not necessarily pay "average" fuel taxes. As a result, the suggestion that a VMT charge of around 1 cent per mile will be revenue neutral is, from an individual driver's perspective, a potentially dubious claim. Many drivers may be unable to determine whether a VMT charge at 1 cent per mile will cost them more or less than the current fuel tax. Some vehicle owners, such as those who have paid a premium to buy a hybrid vehicle that uses little fuel, may face higher costs with a VMT system—and may object to paying the same charges as an individual driving a fuel-inefficient SUV.

Such concerns introduce issues of social equity into the VMT rate-setting process. In theory, economists generally agree that drivers should pay the full "social cost" of their vehicles, but there is little agreement about what those costs are. Attempting to reward certain classes of vehicles with lower charges might raise further barriers to public acceptance of VMT charges.

Setting initial charges at the revenue-neutral level poses a further problem. One argument for moving to VMT charges is that fuel taxes are providing insufficient funds for transportation infrastructure. If a VMT charge is to provide additional revenue, then by definition it cannot be revenue neutral. In that case, the initial charge would need to be higher than 1 cent per mile. Although the rate could be set low initially and raised over time, there is nothing to suggest that raising a VMT rate on a periodic basis will be any easier politically than raising the fuel tax has been. The obvious solution for this problem would be to index a VMT charge to the Consumer Price Index or some construction cost index, but this would have the same political issues as indexation of fuel taxes, an idea that has not been enacted by Congress.

Transition Costs/Complexity

A major advantage of the federal fuel tax system is its low cost of collection. Less than 1% of revenues is devoted to collection. In part this is due to the relatively small number of places where the fuel tax is collected: it is paid not at the fuel pump, but at the so-called "first point of distribution," normally a refinery or a tank farm. This collection system has been developed over time to reduce the opportunity for fraud and theft. It also saves money, because it is much easier administratively to collect taxes from a few rather than many locations and firms.

A VMT charge portends a far broader collection system. Depending on the technology employed, the number of collection locations could be extremely large. Experience in Germany, where trucks using the autobahns pay VMT charges, suggests that the cost of collecting a VMT charge could be 6% or more of collections, although that might decline over time.[19]

Administratively, billing is a major challenge for a VMT charge collection system. It can, of course, be automated. For example, an autonomous vehicle-based system could take periodic mileage readings and use a linked credit or other account to deposit the appropriate fee in a collection center that is also automated and linked to the appropriate revenue authority. This represents, however, a huge technological challenge. There were almost 244 million privately owned vehicles in the United States in 2008, not counting 7.7 million motorcycles.[20] Each of these vehicles is a potential tax collection point.

Obviously the transition from a tax collected at a few places to a fee collected at many places creates efficiency issues. Also relevant in this context are questions about a possible rise in avoidance and fraud, both of which, in the history of the fuel tax collection, occurred at a higher rate when more collection points existed. These complexities would need to be overcome for a VMT charge to become an efficient source of revenue.

Public Support

The driving population of the United States is mostly unaware of the VMT discussion. Where the idea has been aired, as was the case in the Florida example cited earlier, the reaction has not always been positive. In one survey, 61% of those queried about adopting a VMT tax were opposed to it.[21]

One major transportation group, the American Trucking Association, has declared its opposition to a VMT-based system of transportation finance. Primary among its reasons is the likelihood that trucks will remain dependant on diesel fuel long after other types of vehicles have transitioned to hybrid, electric, and other technologies. The group prefers an increase in the federal tax on diesel fuel, with the caveat that the increased revenues be used for transportation projects that benefit the trucking industry.

Marshaling public support for a shift in the method of raising transportation revenue will be challenging. Although there has been some acceptance of VMT charges in the small number of pilot programs launched to date, there is no larger public call for a change in the method of financing transportation outlays. The public is largely unaware of the underlying trends that have stimulated interest in a move away from fuel taxes. The transition may be a slow process that will require many pilot programs, using different types of technologies, to determine what is ultimately publicly acceptable. An alternative approach would phase in VMT charges starting with non-fossil fuel vehicles. As these vehicles would not otherwise be paying any taxes specifically for transportation, a VMT charge in lieu of a fuel tax might meet with public acceptance.[22]

VMT and Non-Highway Programs

Since 1982, when the transit account within the highway trust fund was established, there has been an unwritten truce between highway and other transportation interests not to reopen the debate over funding non-highway programs from the trust fund so long as total federal transportation spending continued to increase. With trust fund revenues no longer soaring, the question of appropriate uses of the trust fund is likely to arise again.

The move to a VMT charge would reopen this debate. If the VMT charge were collected strictly from motorists and applied only to highway financing, it might reasonably be characterized as a user fee, even if, as noted above, the amount paid by each individual driver would be unlikely to correspond precisely to the social cost of that user's driving. If instead the amounts collected were distributed among various transportation modes (which is the case to some degree in the current trust fund-based system), the VMT charge might appear more as a tax.

From a policy perspective, the question of whether a VMT charge is perceived as a user fee or a tax is an important question. Transit, bikeways, and a wide range of alternative transportation activities have had growing access to federal funds collected from highway users over the last three decades. Supporters of these programs assert that the programs benefit society by reducing congestion and pollution, curbing fuel consumption, and strengthening dense urban areas. Any debate over shifting from fuel taxes to VMT charges would reenergize the highway versus transit debate, as Congress would almost certainly have to consider the uses to which any VMT revenues would be put.

OTHER OPTIONS

In addition to the revenue initiatives discussed in detail in this report, a wide range of additional proposals has been put forward. These proposals largely originated from the work of the two SAFETEA congressional commissions and of groups such as AASHTO and TRB.[23] Among these are the establishment of freight-related taxes or fees such as a freight waybill tax, container fee, or terminal facility charge. These revenues could be used to address freight bottlenecks. Similarly, some portion of customs duties, which are deposited in the general fund, could be made available for freight-related port-of-entry infrastructure. Further, some believe that transportation in general, and perhaps the trust fund specifically, should benefit from any revenues generated by a broad-based carbon tax that might be imposed primarily for environmental reasons.

AASHTO has compiled an expansive list of potential revenue sources, including those mentioned above. An AASHTO table showing these alternatives and estimating how much revenue each potential source could produce for surface transportation over a six-year period is reproduced in *Table 1.* It should be emphasized that the estimates are suggestive rather than precise forecasts of what each revenue source could produce. Also, there are variables attached to each estimate that are not delineated. For example, the number of annual auto registrations could turn out to be higher or lower than AASHTO assumed for purposes of revenue estimation.

If Congress chooses not to impose new taxes and fees as part of the reauthorization process, it could still expand the surface transportation program with general fund monies.

This would reduce the highway and transit programs' dependence on the trust fund, but also would weaken the historic link between the revenue derived from taxes and fees paid by highway users and spending on the nation's highways and bridges.

Finally, Congress could ultimately choose to reduce the highway program's size. It could, for example, relegate some programs currently, but not historically, funded by the trust fund, such as the Appalachian Roads Program, to general fund status. It could also consider reducing the existing program matching ratios (90:10 for interstates, 80:20 for most everything else, with the notable exception of the transit "new starts" program where the matching rates vary dramatically) to levels in place in the 1980s or earlier (75:25 or 70:30), thereby spreading the available trust fund revenues more broadly.

THE FUTURE OF THE TRUST FUND

Any of the financing alternatives discussed above—higher motor fuel taxes, sales taxes on motor fuel, VMT charges—could easily be used to sustain the existing federal financing mechanism, the highway trust fund. But if Congress considers changes in the sources of highway financing, it may also wish to consider alternatives or supplements to the existing trust fund structure.

The trust fund was set up as a temporary device that was supposed to disappear when the interstate system was finished. It has endured, and its breadth of financing has expanded well beyond the interstates. But it is certainly not essential to a federal role in transportation finance. Congress routinely funds large infrastructure projects, such as those constructed by the Army Corps of Engineers, from general fund appropriations. Before 1956, it funded highway and other transportation projects using annual appropriations. As recently as the 1990s, significant highway programs such as the Appalachian Highway System were funded from the general fund.

One alternative would be to refocus the trust fund only on highway-related programs integral to the national network,[24] such as the interstates, the national highway system, key bridge infrastructure, and the Federal Lands Highway Program.[25] This would leave transit and other surface transportation programs to be funded exclusively by annual appropriations of general funds.

Such a change would have political implications. Since the early 1990s, transit and cycling advocates, environmentalists, and a wide range of other groups have become full-fledged supporters of the surface transportation program, as it has benefited their interests. The expanded coalition supporting the surface transportation program played an important role in the hard-fought political battles of the mid-1990s that gave the trust fund accounts special status as separate accounts in the budget. This special status, in turn, broadened support for large spending increases in each of the last two reauthorization bills.

From a congressional perspective, restricting the trust fund to highways would be difficult as well. In 1998, budget changes occurred which gave the highway account and the transit account special status within the annual congressional budget similar to that enjoyed by the Social Security trust fund. This occurred over objections by the appropriations and budget committees, which had previously exerted far more control over transportation spending then they do today.[26] Control over the majority of trust fund programs now rests primarily with congressional authorizing committees. Removing transit and other non-highway transportation from the trust fund would raise questions about congressional committee jurisdiction over these programs.

Another alternative would be to eliminate the trust fund structure, thereby doing away with its complicated budget framework of contract authority, obligations, and apportionments. The purported advantages of the trust fund are that it prevents appropriators from spending trust fund revenues on non-transportation programs and that it encourages Congress to fully spend amounts collected from system users on an annual basis. Eliminating the trust fund would force surface transportation to compete with other federal programs for funding each year, possibly leading to less spending on transportation. The events of the last three fiscal years, however, suggest that Congress is willing to spend money on surface transportation regardless of the revenue source. Congress has authorized substantial contributions of general fund monies to the trust fund. Additionally, funds provided by the American Recovery and Reinvestment Act (ARRA) have also involved large expenditures from the general fund for transportation purposes.

There could be advantages to moving away from trust fund financing of surface transportation. One of the most intractable arguments in every reauthorization debate concerns which states are "donors" to transportation programs and which are "donees." The donor-donee dispute is unique to the federal highway program, and occurs only because of the ability to track federal fuel tax revenues by state. This issue would likely disappear if transportation-related taxes were deposited into the general fund instead of the trust fund. Treating fuel taxes as just another source of federal revenue would also dampen the long-standing link between road user charges and program spending. This would provide Congress with greater flexibility to allocate funding among various transportation modes and between transportation and non-transportation uses.

Eliminating the trust fund might also focus more attention on the costs and benefits of individual surface transportation programs. Most trust-fund outlays take the form of formula grants over which states have a great deal of spending discretion. Especially within the highway program, money can be transferred among projects relatively easily. While there are many federal requirements attached to trust fund expenditures, there are relatively few performance-oriented goals that the states are required to meet in selecting projects to be undertaken with federal monies.[27]

Getting rid of the trust fund in and of itself will not cause states to choose better projects, but it might allow for the injection of performance measurement into all federally supported surface transportation activities. Eliminating the trust fund might also allow for creativity in thinking about the provision of transportation infrastructure across the modal boundaries that now define much of federal transportation spending. Historically, important parts of the U.S. transportation infrastructure, such as the transcontinental railroads and the Panama Canal, were authorized by specific congressional enactments rather than grant programs. Reconsidering the trust fund structure might give Congress and the President the opportunity to come up with a new way to fund infrastructure needs.

Table 1. Revenue Options for Consideration (all revenue estimates in $ millions)

Funding Mechanisms	Mechanism Yield (2011)		Illustrative Rate	Revenues 2011	Average Annual Revenues 2011-2016	Total Revenues 2011-2016
Annual Drivers License Surcharge	$1.00 Surcharge =	$222	$5.00	$1,110	$1,165	$6,993
Annual Highway Miles Traveled Fee (All Light Duty Vehicles)[a]	1 cent/VMT =	$6,538	2 cents	$13,075	$28,413	$170,478
Annual Highway Miles Traveled Fee (All Trucks)[a]	1 cent/VMT =	$977	3 cents	$2,931	$3,401	$20,406
Annual Registration Fee (Light Duty Vehicles)	$1.00 Fee =	$261	$10.00	$2,613	$2,741	$16,448
Annual Registration Fee (Trucks)	$1.00 Fee =	$4	$15.00	$66	$66	$399
Container Tax	$1 per TEU =	$605	$15.00	$9,076	$10,658	$63,946
Dedicated Income Tax—Personal	0.1% of current taxes =	$1,130	1.0%	$11,301	$11,881	$71,285
Dedicated Income Tax—Business	0.1% of current taxes =	$383	1.0%	$3,832	$4,029	$24,172
Diesel Tax Increase	1 cent/gal =	$386	15 cents	$5,794	$6,052	$36,309
Gas Tax Increase	1 cent/gal =	$1,379	10 cents	$13,795	$14,030	$84,183
Harbor Maintenance Tax	0.1% Tax =	$1,236	2.0%	$24,725	$26,323	$157,939
Heavy Vehicle Use Tax Increase	10% Increase =	$97	15.0%	$15	$169	$1,017
Imported Oil Tax	$1.00/Bbls =	$4,217	$1.00	$4,217	$4,356	$26,138
Sales Tax on Auto-related Parts & Services	1.0% of Sales =	$2,567	1.0%	$2,567	$2,823	$16,938
Sales Tax on Gas	1.0% of Sales =	$2,987	8.4%	$25,091	$30,945	$185,671
Sales Tax on Diesel	1.0% of Sales =	$868	10.6%	$9,198	$11,484	$68,903
Sales Tax on New Light Duty Vehicles	1.0% of Sales =	$2,337	1.0%	$2,337	$2,571	$15,427
Sales Tax on New and Used Light Duty Vehicles	1.0% of Sales =	$3,515	1.0%	$3,515	$3,837	$23,021

Funding Mechanisms	Mechanism Yield (2011)		Illustrative Rate	Revenues 2011	Average Annual Revenues 2011-2016	Total Revenues 2011-2016
Share of US Customs Revenues	1% of Receipts =	$333	1.0%	$333	$381	$2,288
Tire Tax on Light Duty Vehicles	$1.00 Fee =	$1,960	$3.00	$5,880	$6,168	$37,009
Ton Freight Charge—All Modes	1 cent/ton =	$164	25 cents	$4,111	$4,432	$26,592
Ton Freight Charge—Truck Only	1 cent/ton =	$113	25 cents	$2,835	$3,057	$18,340
Ton-Mile Freight Charge—All Modes	1 cent/ton-mile =	$43,497	0.5 cent	$21,748	$23,446	$140,678
Ton-Mile Freight Charge—Truck Only	1 cent/ton-mile =	$12,731	0.5 cent	$6,365	$6,862	$41,174
Truck/Trailer Sales Tax Increase	1% of Sales =	$219	5.0%	$1,095	$1,529	$9,174
Truck Tire Tax Increase	10% Increase =	$33	10.0%	$33	$477	$2,863
US Freight Bill—All Modes	1% of Sales =	$7,612	1.0%	$7,612	$8,206	$49,236
US Freight Bill—Truck Only	1% of Sales =	$6,608	1.0%	$6,608	$7,124	$42,745
Total Revenues				$191,878	$226,629	$1,359,772

Source: Provided by AASHTO.

[a] VMT fee estimates refer to miles traveled on the interstate system.

TOLL FINANCING OF FEDERAL-AID SYSTEM HIGHWAYS

During much of the history of federal aid to highways, toll financing was prohibited, discouraged, or relegated to a minor role.[28] Given this, the small share (5%) of overall highway finance provided by tolling is not surprising. The Federal-Aid Highway and Federal Highway Revenue Acts of 1956 (70 Stat. 374; P.L. 84-627), which provided for the construction and financing of the interstate highway system, reaffirmed the prohibition of tolling of federal-aid highways. Thirty-five years later, however, the Intermodal Surface Transportation Efficiency Act of 1991 (ISTEA; P.L. 102-240) opened non-interstate system highways to tolling, subject to certain limitations (including requiring public jurisdiction over privately owned toll facilities). Both the 1998 Transportation Equity Act for the 21st Century (TEA-21; P.L. 105-178, as amended by P.L. 105- 206) and SAFETEA included tolling provisions which changed the legal treatment of high-occupancy vehicle (HOV) lanes, established pilot projects for tolling of a limited number of interstate system routes, and provided for the use of congestion pricing in some instances.

Significant growth of nationwide toll revenues would require the building of more tolled facilities, conversion of free roads and bridges to toll roads, increases in toll rates on existing toll facilities, or increases in traffic. Augmenting toll road mileage is difficult to accomplish: FHWA statistics identify 5,238 tolled miles of roads, bridges, and tunnels as of 2009,[29] a net increase of only 517 toll road miles, or 11%, since 1990, despite the relaxed federal tolling prohibitions.[30] Nor have the changes in Title 23's highway tolling provisions in the last three authorization bills led to an increase in toll receipts as a share of total revenues. Since FY1991, toll revenues have kept pace with the combined total of other sources of highway funding. Although toll revenues grew in nominal terms, from $7.75 billion in FY2005 to $9.3 billion in FY2008, they accounted for approximately 5% of total funds available in each of the last four fiscal years.[31] This is only slightly above the annual average since FY1955.[32]

The recent inability of the current combination of federal highway user taxes and fees to provide sufficient revenues to support even the SAFETEA baseline has encouraged consideration of policy changes that could include the expansion of toll financing. Toll road financing can be used to build projects that, under pay-as-you-go financing, would otherwise be delayed as a state waits for the needed amount of federal grant funding. Another advantage of tolls is that they can provide the flow of funds necessary to attract private financing of road projects or to support public-private partnerships (PPPs) and other innovative financing techniques (such as those discussed later in this report).

Tolls can be advocated as a form of user charge, even though a few jurisdictions use highway toll revenues for non-highway purposes, notably mass transportation. Unlike VMT charges, tolls are broadly familiar to the driving public. (Currently, 31 states have at least one toll road, bridge, or tunnel.) A few toll road operators have attempted to manage congestion by setting higher tolls during the most congested hours or adjusting the charge throughout the day to keep traffic in the toll facility flowing freely.

Table 2. Active Federal Tolling Programs

Program	Intent
Section 129 Exceptions to the Freedom from Tolls Provision	Authorizes federal participation in the construction of a toll road, bridge, tunnel or ferry; reconstruction of existing toll facilities; reconstruction of a toll-free federal-aid highway (other than on the interstate system) and conversion to a toll facility; and preliminary studies to determine toll facility feasibility. Facility must be publicly owned or, if privately owned, under contract to a public authority.
High Occupancy Vehicle (HOV) Facilities	Section 1121 of SAFETEA allows states to charge tolls on vehicles that do not meet the occupancy requirements for HOV use (including HOVs on the interstate system).
Interstate System Reconstruction and Rehabilitation Toll Pilot Program	Allows tolls on three pilot projects in different states to reconstruct an existing interstate system highway and convert it to a tolled facility. Originally passed in TEA-21.
Interstate System Construction Toll Pilot Program	Allows tolls on three projects by a state or compact of states to construct new interstate system highways.
Value Pricing Pilot Program	Provides funds for local transportation programs to try value pricing approaches to managing congestion, including the use of tolling.
Express Lanes Demonstration Program	Allows 15 demonstration projects to use tolling on Interstate Highways to manage congestion, reduce emissions, or finance additional interstate system lanes to reduce congestion.

Source: FHWA. Title 23 U.S.C. § 129, 301. P.L. 109-59, Sec. 1604.

Tolling of Federal-Aid Highways under Current Law

The conversion of most federal-aid highways, bridges, and tunnels to toll roads is permissible under current law, subject to certain limitations. The major exception is the prohibition of tolling of the interstate highway system. The interstate system exception is important from a policy perspective because it is those routes that most often carry a volume of traffic sufficient to make toll financing economically viable. *Table 2,* below, briefly describes active federal tolling programs.

The programs of the largest scope are the Section 129 exceptions (which have been in place since 1991) and the HOV lane tolling provision. The others are programs of pilot projects to encourage and test the use of pricing to manage congestion or pilot projects to provide experience in converting interstate highways.[33]

Toll Financing Issues

Congress, if it chose, could expand the role of tolling in federal highway policy in several ways. A policy requiring, for example, that most or all new construction on the federal-aid system be toll-financed might relieve the demands on other sources of revenue.[34] An even broader alternative would be to allow states to toll any federal-aid highway. Such authorizations might, or might not, encourage further use of tolls that vary by time of day or by degree of congestion.

Another approach would make more or all interstate system highways eligible for conversion to toll roads. The interstates carry high traffic volumes relative to other roads and are often congested in urban areas. Only 7% of urban interstates are tolled. Both of the commissions established under SAFETEA[35] recommended allowing expanded tolling of interstate highways. Such a policy would overturn the "freedom from tolls" provision of the 1956 Act, and might be open to criticism that tolling of roads that were built or improved with highway trust fund revenues is double taxation.

One issue in the expansion of tolling is the extent to which state and local governments may use increased toll revenues to substitute for other spending, reducing the net impact of more expansive federal tolling policy. If its aim is to increase total spending on transportation infrastructure, Congress may wish to require that state and local governments not simply use revenues from tolls on federal-aid highways to replace current transportation outlays.

How tolling would interact with a national VMT charge could become an issue if a VMT charge is imposed. It might be possible to use the VMT collection system to collect tolls on certain roads, although this could raise the issue of double taxation. The issue could also become moot should the driving public come to view a VMT charging system as a national toll set at an identical per-mile rate on every road, if such a collection structure were adopted.

Most toll facilities in the United States are controlled by public authorities, many of which have been in continuous operation since the 1950s. Private-sector involvement in toll financing of public roads has received increased attention, especially with the growing number of public-private partnerships (PPPs). A policy encouraging both private investors and public authorities to pursue toll road projects could be considered.

Obstacles to the Expanded Use of Tolling

Raising tolling to greater prominence in federal highway policy faces significant obstacles. Overcoming general public hostility to tolls and garnering political support may be the greatest obstacle to tolling projects.

Tolling in the United States is primarily a state and local issue, as there are no federal toll roads. For a state or local entity to toll a federal-aid highway, certain federal requirements must be adhered to, including the negotiation of a toll agreement with the Federal Highway Administration (FHWA). Some states already rely on tolls as an important source of income. Five states (Florida, New Jersey, New York, Pennsylvania, and Illinois) receive over 10% of their annual highway revenues from tolls.[36] On the other hand, there are 19 states that have no toll facilities and others that have only bridge or tunnel tolls. Because toll facilities by their very nature are local, public acceptance of toll facilities can vary by location. The fact that decisions about tolling are made locally may limit the impact of changes in federal tolling policy.

At the local level, expanding tolling faces a number of challenges beyond general public hostility.[37] Revenue projections from planned toll facilities generally do not cover project costs, and some states find it hard to garner public support for toll projects that also require public subsidization. For projects with private partners, often either a public subsidy is needed or the competing free facilities must be converted to toll facilities for the projects to make business sense. Other challenges include securing the authority at the state level to consider a range of tolling options and public concerns about diversion of traffic, especially trucks, from the tolled roads to adjacent free roads.

Views on the Growth Potential of Toll Revenues

Few systematic estimates of the growth potential for toll revenues exist. A 2006 TRB report, *Future Financing Options to Meet Highway and Transit Needs*, estimated that an aggressive use of the tolling and pricing opportunities in SAFETEA could generate an average additional $1.1 billion in revenue per year during 2010 to 2017, reaching an additional $2.4 billion for 2017.[38]

Another TRB publication, also published in 2006, *The Fuel Tax and Alternatives for Transportation Funding*, argued that an aggressive program of "toll conversion and new toll road development following the models of the HOT networks and FAST lanes proposals might raise additional revenue equal to the tolls already being collected on U.S. highways."[39]

Some more recent commentaries, however, have expressed caution in projecting revenues from high-occupancy toll (HOT) lanes and other tolled express lanes, warning that "HOT lanes are not necessarily big generators of revenue ... most projects—particularly HOV-to-HOT expansion projects—barely cover ongoing expenses for management and operations, much less offset the capital costs."[40] Another article examining the value pricing experience of I-15 in San Diego found that it generated only enough revenues to cover operating costs, pay for the California Highway Patrol to enforce vehicle occupancy rules, and provide a small amount to support bus services on I-15.[41] In 2008, AASHTO president Pete Rahn testified before the House Transportation and Infrastructure Committee that "[e]ven the most optimistic forecasts project that this revenue source [tolls] would only meet seven to nine percent of investment needs nationally in the future."[42]

Since most planned tolling projects in the United States would use express toll lanes that parallel "free" regular lanes, the revenue question is an important issue for federal policymakers. Annual national toll revenues totaled $9.3 billion for FY2008, up from $6.6 billion in FY2004. The revenue increase appears to be due more to traffic growth and increases in the rates charged by toll authorities than to increased miles or lanes of tolled roads. The big generators of revenue continue to be the long-standing toll facilities. The *Fuel Tax* special study also concluded that adding tolls to all lanes of selected heavily traveled intercity routes could raise revenue, but would raise less than anticipated because public opposition would lead state legislatures to adjust other fees to partially offset the tolls.[43]

VALUE CAPTURE

Value capture represents an attempt to cover part or all of the cost of transportation improvements from landowners or developers who benefit from the resulting increase in the value of real property. Value capture revenue mechanisms include tax increment financing, special assessments, development impact fees, negotiated exactions, and joint development.[44] As the Government Accountability Office (GAO) noted in a recent report, the federal role in value capture strategies may be limited.[45] It is worth describing those strategies here, however, to provide a fuller picture of the ways in which more commonly used funding and financing mechanisms may be supplemented or supplanted.

Value capture is not a new idea. Land developers built and operated a number of streetcar systems in the late 19th century as a way to sell houses on the urban fringe, for example. Much of the recent experience with value capture has been associated with public transit. GAO found in its recent study that the most widely used mechanism is joint development, in which a real estate project at or near a transit station is pursued cooperatively between the public and private sectors.

An example might involve a transit agency leasing air rights over a station to a developer in exchange for a regular payment.

GAO found that joint development has generated relatively small amounts of money for transit agencies.[46] For example, the Metropolitan Atlanta Rapid Transit Authority expected about $4 million from such deals in FY2008, about 1% of its $374 million operating budget. However, less widely used strategies, such as special assessment districts, are estimated to generate significant amounts of funding for specific projects. A special assessment district in Seattle produced $25 million of the $53 million (47%) needed to fund the South Lake Union streetcar project.[47]

There has been less use of value capture in highway projects, but this appears to be changing. Texas, for example, has authorized the creation of transportation reinvestment zones to help fund highway projects. Special assessment districts have been set up in several states, including Florida and Virginia, to fund highway projects. In Virginia a special assessment district was used to help fund the expansion of Route 28 near Washington Dulles International Airport beginning in the late 1980s.[48]

PUBLIC-PRIVATE PARTNERSHIPS

Growing demands on the transportation system and constraints on public resources have led to calls for more private-sector involvement in the provision of highway and transit infrastructure through what are known as "public-private partnerships" (PPPs). Private involvement can take a variety of forms, including design-build and design-build-finance-operate agreements. The focus here is on private financing and other ways in which PPPs can lessen demands on public-sector funding. The opportunity to own or lease assets that could have the potential for generating stable, medium-level revenues over the long term has attracted private-sector interest. Typically the "public" in public-private partnerships refers to a state government, local government, or transit agency. The federal government, nevertheless, exerts influence over the prevalence and structure of PPPs through its transportation programs, funding, and regulatory oversight.

Private Financing

PPPs offer a means of financing highway and transit infrastructure. They may be viable when there is an anticipated project-related revenue stream from a source such as vehicle tolls, container fees, or, in the case of transit station development, building rents. Private-sector resources may come from an initial payment to lease an existing asset in exchange for future revenue, as with the Indiana Toll Road and Chicago Skyway, or they may arise from a newly developed asset that creates a new revenue stream. Either way, a facility user fee is often the key to unlocking private-sector participation and resources.

In some cases, private-sector financing is backed by "availability payments," regular payments made by government to the private entity based on negotiated quality and performance standards of the facility. For example, major improvements to I-595 near Fort Lauderdale, FL, are being made by a private company that will design, build, finance, operate, and maintain the facility for 35 years with availability payments made by the Florida Department of Transportation (FDOT). Toll rates on the new express lanes will be set by FDOT, and revenue collected will be retained by the state.[49] The financing includes a federal TIFIA loan (see discussion below) and state funds.

Tolled highways are particularly attractive assets for private financing. Of course, the public sector can build toll roads, raise tolls on existing facilities, or, in some cases, even institute tolls on existing "free" roads, bridges, and tunnels. Two factors purportedly enable PPPs to attract more capital to highways than the public sector alone can muster.[50]

First, a privately operated toll road can be financed with both debt (bond) and equity financing. Because equity investors have an opportunity to share in the profits, they may be less conservative than traditional municipal bond investors in selecting which projects to finance. Private concessions are often for terms longer than traditional municipal bond maturities of 25, 30, or 40 years, and with an assured income stream over a longer period the concessionaire may be able to raise additional capital. One estimate suggests that, under public control, the Chicago Skyway would only have supported at most $800 million in traditional revenue-bond financing, compared with the $1.83 billion received by the city for the 99-year concession.[51]

Second, toll facilities are thought to be more successful when operated privately because tolls can be raised in line with costs and demand. Due to political pressures, public agencies often have difficultly raising tolls, a factor that not only reduces revenues, but also affects an agency's ability to borrow money to initiate construction. The private sector would be more able to generate funding if lenders think it more likely that decisions about toll rates will be based primarily on business considerations.[52] The private operator usually does not have complete freedom to set tolls because toll rates are often regulated under leasing agreements. Nevertheless, proponents of private-sector involvement argue "long-term toll road concessions ... are not simply a private-sector version of a public-sector toll agency. They are a new and important innovation in U.S. highway finance."[53]

How much private investment is available for transportation infrastructure, such as toll roads, is open to question. Prior to the recent economic crisis, the former Secretary of Transportation, Mary Peters, repeatedly stated that there is at least $400 billion of private-sector capital available for infrastructure.[54] One independent review of the evidence has suggested that this was a credible number, with funds available, after leveraging existing capital, ranging from $340 billion to $600 billion.[55] However, this approximately $400 billion of private capital was available to be invested anywhere in the world and in any type of infrastructure,[56] casting some doubt on how much might flow to highways and transit in the United States.[57] The economic crisis that began in 2007 likely reduced the amount of private capital available for U.S. transportation projects, at least temporarily, although more money may become available as credit conditions improve.[58]

While PPPs are likely to attract new private investment in highway and transit infrastructure, the amount of capital is likely to be relatively modest when viewed in the context of total highway and transit infrastructure spending.[59] Because transit is revenue negative, that is, its costs are greater than its operating revenues, it is likely that transit PPPs will never generate a significant share of investment. It may be unrealistic to expect PPPs to generate more than 7% to 9% of the future needs of highway and transit infrastructure nationally. Private-sector financing generated through PPPs probably ought to be seen as a supplement to traditional public-sector funding rather than as a substitute.

State and local governments have significant demands for funding in many different areas, and there is no assurance that the resources generated from transportation PPPs will be reinvested to finance transportation infrastructure needs. Asset leases, in particular, provide a mechanism to generate large sums of money that could be used to fund a wide range of social or other governmental services. That is why the leasing of existing roads might be considered "revenue extraction," whereas concessions involving the provision of new toll roads are "added value."[60]

This concern has been realized in the case of the Chicago Skyway, discussed earlier, as some of the lease payment has been used for non-transportation purposes. The city of Chicago contends, however, that it has created a reserve fund that generates in interest revenue what the road did in toll revenue, and notes that excess toll revenues from the Skyway were previously directed to the city's general fund.[61] GAO has stated that the city's credit rating improved when it reduced its general obligation debt using lease revenues, thereby reducing the future cost of borrowing.[62] The possibility remains, nevertheless, that future facility users may face higher tolls if the money generated by asset leases is used for non-transportation needs.[63]

Diversion of resources may also be of more general concern in that new private resources attracted to transportation infrastructure may substitute for public resources in the sector, not add to them. With competing demands for public funds, it is possible that with increases in private funding, state and local governments will divert public resources to other public programs with no net gain in transportation outlays. In a study of the effect of federal highway funding increases on state highway funding between 1982 and 2002, GAO observed a substitution effect, particularly between 1998 and 2002, when a 40% increase in federal capital spending was accompanied by a 4% drop in state and local capital spending.[64]

Nearly all toll road privatization discussions face the issue of paying back any federal funding spent to build or improve the facility that is up for lease. In the cases of the Indiana Toll Road and Chicago Skyway, toll facilities that were leased to private investors, federal money was not an issue, as the facilities were not built with federal funds. Many existing toll facilities, however, were built with federal aid. Congress could allow waiver of the payback provisions under certain circumstances, but careful scrutiny may be needed to ensure that privatization does not give the private investor a windfall thanks to earlier government investment.

Other Resource Benefits of PPPs

As well as the potential for additional capital, PPPs may generate new resources for highway and transit infrastructure in at least two other ways. First, PPPs may improve efficiency through better management and innovation in construction, maintenance, and operation, in effect providing more infrastructure for the same price. Private companies may be more able to examine the full life-cycle cost of investments, whereas public agency decisions are often tied to short-term budget cycles. In the case of the Hudson-Bergen Light Rail in New Jersey, procured under a designbuild-operate-maintain contract, the U.S. Department of Transportation (DOT) estimates saving of 30%, or about $345 million, over the more traditional design-bid-build procurement method.[65] Such cost reductions may not materialize, however, if the public sector has to spend a substantial amount of time on procurement, oversight, dispute resolution, and litigation. For example, the California Department of Transportation has had a number of costly disputes with its private partners.[66] Furthermore, GAO argues that most state governments do not have the capacity to manage PPP contracts.[67]

Second, PPPs are meant to reduce government agencies' costs by transferring the financial risks of building, maintaining, and operating infrastructure to private investors. These risks include construction delays, unexpectedly high maintenance costs, and the possibility that demand will be less than forecast. There is a danger, however, this transfer of risk may prove illusory if major miscalculations force the public agency to renegotiate contracts or provide financial guarantees.[68] Moreover, as GAO points out, not all the risks can or should be shifted to the private sector. For instance, private investors are unlikely to accept the risk of higher construction costs due to delays in the environmental review process.[69]

TIFIA Financing

An existing federal mechanism for providing credit assistance to relatively large transportation infrastructure projects is TIFIA financing. TIFIA stands for the Transportation Infrastructure Finance and Innovation Act, legislation that was enacted in 1998 as part of TEA-21. TIFIA provides federal credit assistance up to a maximum of 33% of project costs in the form of secured loans, loan guarantees, and lines of credit.

Federal credit assistance provides funds at a relatively low rate and lowers project risk, thereby helping to secure other financing at rates lower than would otherwise be possible. Another purpose of TIFIA funding is to leverage non-federal funding, including investment from the private sector. Loans must be repaid with a dedicated revenue stream, typically a project-related user fee but sometimes also including dedicated tax revenue. Transportation projects costing at least $50 million (or at least $15 million in the case of Intelligent Transportation Systems (ITS) projects) are eligible for TIFIA financing. As of July 29, 2010, according to the Federal Highway Administration (FHWA), TIFIA had provided assistance of $7.9 billion to 22 projects. The overall cost of the projects supported is estimated to be $29 billion.[70]

SAFETEA made a number of changes to the TIFIA program as enacted under TEA-21. These modifications included permitting public-private partnerships to apply directly instead of having to go through a government entity, expanding eligibility to freight rail and intermodal facilities, and lowering the eligibility threshold.[71] SAFETEA also broadened project eligibility by including some private rail projects. Eligibility now includes rail facilities providing benefits to highway users, intermodal freight transfer facilities, access to freight facilities, and port projects involving improved surface transportation access.

SAFETEA provided $122 million in contract authority from the highway trust fund for TIFIA in each fiscal year from FY2005 through FY2009. Extension legislation provided another $122 million for FY2010. In its notice of funding availability for FY2010, DOT noted that after administrative costs and other deductions it can apply approximately $110 million annually to covering loan subsidy costs.[72]

The subsidy cost is calculated for each loan based on an estimate of expected loss across a portfolio of loans. Historically, the subsidy cost of a loan has averaged 8%. The subsidy cost largely determines the amount of money that can be made available to project sponsors. For instance, with a subsidy cost of 8%, $110 million in contract authority represents about $1.375 billion in potential credit assistance ($110 million divided by 8% equals $1.375 billion). According to DOT, the subsidy cost has been higher in recent years, therefore lowering the amount of credit assistance available. For example, DOT estimated that the $110 million made available in FY2010 would support about $1.1 billion in TIFIA credit assistance, a subsidy cost of 10%.[73]

The demand for TIFIA credit assistance appears to be higher than program funding can support. In September 2008, DOT estimated that in FY2009 "the gap between resources and demand could be as large as $450 million, representing approximately $3.75 billion in credit assistance."[74] In FY2010, according to DOT, there were requests for almost $13 billion in TIFIA credit assistance, much more than the approximately $1.1 billion available.[75] Because of the strong loan demand, some transport interests have argued for a larger TIFIA program, while others urge the creation of a special-purpose entity, such as a national infrastructure bank.

National Infrastructure Bank

A number of proposals have been introduced in Congress over the years to create a special-purpose entity to help finance infrastructure projects. One such proposal, introduced in the 111th Congress, is the National Infrastructure Development Bank Act of 2009 (H.R. 2521). H.R. 2521 would establish an infrastructure bank as a wholly owned government corporation controlled by a five-member board of directors appointed by the President and confirmed by the Senate. The bank would have the ability to issue bonds with maturities of 30 years or more and to use the proceeds to provide loans and loan guarantees. The bank would be capitalized by appropriations of $25 billion, and another $225 billion would be callable capital, available from the Treasury only if needed by the bank to meet its obligations.

The bank would be permitted to leverage these amounts by 2.5 to 1, representing issuance of $625 billion of bonds. The bonds would be backed by the full faith and credit of the U.S. Treasury. Projects would not be limited to transportation infrastructure, but could include environmental, energy, and telecommunications infrastructure. Projects for assistance would be chosen on their merits by the board, although within the confines of the enabling law. H.R. 2521 lists a host of factors, including workforce development, reducing inequality, and public health benefits, that the board must take into account when deciding which projects to fund.[76]

One purported advantage of a national infrastructure bank is that, by issuing non-tax-exempt securities, it could tap pools of private capital that do not invest in tax-exempt bonds, the traditional source of much project finance. Tax-exempt municipal securities are unattractive to some investors, either because individual issues are too small to interest them or because the investors do not benefit from the tax preference. Taxable bonds with long maturities might be attractive to such investors, such as pension funds and foreign citizens.[77] An infrastructure bank also might reduce the federal government's share of project costs with greater reliance on nonfederal capital and user fees.

Most infrastructure bank proposals assume the bank would improve the allocation of public resources by funding projects with the highest economic returns regardless of infrastructure system or type. Selection of the projects with the highest returns, however, might conflict with the traditional desire of Congress to assure funding for various purposes. In the extreme case, many transportation projects might not be funded if the bank were to exhaust its lending authority on water or energy projects offering higher returns.

An infrastructure bank may not be the lowest-cost means of increasing infrastructure spending. The Congressional Budget Office (CBO) has pointed out that a special entity that issues its own debt would not be able to match the lower interest and issuance costs of the U.S. Treasury.[78] Moreover, in some formulations, including H.R. 2521, a national infrastructure bank exposes the federal government to the risk of default. If Congress were to direct the bank to consider factors, such as job creation and poverty reduction, as H.R. 2521 does, those obligations might constrain its ability to assist the most economically viable projects.[79]

National Infrastructure Innovation and Finance Fund

After including a $5 billion request for a national infrastructure bank in its FY2010 budget request,[80] contingent on its subsequent creation, the Obama Administration dropped this idea from its FY2011 budget in favor of $4 billion for a National Infrastructure Innovation and Finance Fund. The Obama Administration envisions this $4 billion as the first installment of five to capitalize the fund with $25 billion.[81] The fund would be set up as an operational unit of DOT and would provide loans and grants to leverage non-federal funding, including private-sector capital. Projects of national and regional significance would be chosen through some sort of merit-based analysis. The appropriations committees have stated that they do not support the idea in its current form.[82]

End Notes

[1] In 2006 the federal highway program provided $34 billion in capital assistance for highway and road programs. By comparison, state and local governments spent $40.6 billion on capital projects and another $58.5 billion on operations and maintenance for highways and roads in 2004. Source: U.S. Congressional Budget Office, *Trends in Public Spending on Transportation and Water Infrastructure, 1956 to 2004*, Pub. No. 2880, Washington, DC, August 2007, pp. 9-14, http://www.cbo.gov/ftpdocs/85xx/doc8517/08-08-Infrastructure .pdf.

[2] Mark Muro and Robert Puentes, "Helping Those Who Help Themselves," *The New Republic*, May 27, 2010.

[3] Information supplied by CBO as part of its Summer FY2010 Baseline. August 5, 2010.

[4] Ibid.

[5] CRS Report R40166, *Automobile and Light Truck Fuel Economy: The CAFE Standards*, by Brent D. Yacobucci and Robert Bamberger.

[6] http://www.transportationfortomorrow.com/final_report/index.htm.

[7] http://financecommission.dot.gov/.

[8] http://financecommission.dot.gov/Documents/NSTIF_Commission_Final_Report_Mar09FNL.pdf.

[9] http://fastlane.dot.gov/2008/07/a-new-plan-for.html.

[10] *Financing Transportation in the 21st Century: a Report of the Intergovernmental Forum on Transportation Finance*, the National Academy of Public Administration (Washington, 2008), 95 p. *The Transportation Challenge: Moving the U.S. Economy*, (Washington, National Chamber Foundation, 2008), 116 p. *ARTBA Recommendations for SAFETEALU Reauthorization* (Washington, American Road & Transportation Builders Association, 2007), 72 p. *Performance Driven: A New Vision for U.S. Transportation Policy* (Bipartisan Policy Center, 2009). *A Bridge to Somewhere* (Brookings Institution, 2008). *The Route to Reform*, Transportation for America. *AASHTO Authorization Policy* (produced as a series of topic papers) (October 2008). 230 p.

[11] http://www.fhwa.dot.gov/ohim/hwytaxes/2008/s106.cfm.

[12] Josh Mitchell, "Gas-Tax Revamp Pushed to Fund Transportation Projects," *The Wall Street Journal*, October 14, 2010.

[13] Jeffrey Ang-Olson, Martin Wachs, and Brian D. Taylor, *Variable-Rate State Gasoline Taxes*, Institute of Transportation Studies, University of California, Berkeley, Working Paper, UCB-ITS-WP-99-3, Berkeley, CA, July 1999.

[14] Finance Commission. p. 5. http://financecommission.dot.gov/Documents/NSTIF_Commission_ Final_Report_ Exec_Summary_Feb09.pdf.

[15] National Research Council. Transportation Research Board. National Cooperative Highway Research Program (NCHRP). "Implementable Strategies for Shifting to Direct Usage-Based Charges for Transportation Funding" NCHRP Project 20-24(69). Web-Only Document 143. October 2009. http://onlinepubs.trb.org /onlinepubs/nchrp/nchrp_w143.pdf.

[16] Editorial, "Kick mileage tax to the curb before it gets any further," *Sun-Sentinel, Fort Lauderdale*, September 18, 2009.

[17] Martin Wachs, "After the Motor Fuel Tax: Reshaping Transportation Financing," *Issues in Science and Technology*, Summer 2009, pp. 85-89;. Paul Sorensen, Liisa Ecola, and Martin Wachs, et al., *Implementable Strategies for Shifting to Direct Usage-Based Charges for Transportation Funding*, National Cooperative Highway Research Program, Transportation Research Board, NCHRP Web-Only Document 143, Washington, DC, June 2009, http://onlinepubs.trb.org/onlinepubs/nchrp/nchrp_w143.pdf.

[18] Miller Center of Public Affairs, University of Virginia, "Well Within Reach: America's New Transportation Agenda," Conference Report, Charlottesville , VA, October 10, 2010, http://web1.millercenter.org /conferences/report/conf_2009_transportation.pdf.

[19] Estimates of the administrative costs that could be associated with a national VMT fee collection system vary dramatically. In part this is due to the lack of experience with VMT charge collection. A tax imposed on trucks using the German autobahn system is perhaps the closest example of a currently operating system VMT system. In scale and scope, however, it is much different from the national system under discussion in this report: http://utcm.tamu.edu/mbuf/2010/proceedings/US-deployment-panel.stm.

[20] http://www.fhwa.dot.gov/policyinformation/statistics/2008/mv1.cfm.

[21] William B. Cassidy, "Trucking Group Opposes Vehicle Miles Tax," *The Journal of Commerce*, April 21, 2010.

[22] Edward Huang, Henry Lee, and Grant Lovellette, et al., "Transportation Revenue Options: Infrastructure, Emissions, and Congestion," Harvard Kennedy School, Belfer Center, Cambridge, MA, September 2010.

[23] The Transportation Research Board, through its research programs, has prepared several reports on future surface transportation finance that discuss VMT and other options, including National Cooperative Highway Research Program (NCHRP), "Future Financing Options to Meet Highway and Transit Needs," NCHRP Project 20-24, Web-Only Document 102, December 2006, available at http://onlinepubs.trb.org /onlinepubs/nchrp/nchrp _w102.pdf; and Transportation Research Board, "The Fuel Tax and Alternatives for Transportation Funding," Special Report 285, January 2006, available at http://onlinepubs.trb.org/ onlinepubs/sr/sr285.pdf.

[24] Ken Orski, *Innovation News Briefs*, Vol. 21, No. 21 2010.

[25] Robert W. Poole and Adrian T. Moore, *Restoring Trust in the Highway Trust Fund*, Reason Foundation, Policy Study, August 2010.

[26] CRS Report 98-749, *The Transportation Equity Act for the 21st Century (TEA-21) and the Federal Budget*, by John W. Fischer.

[27] *Performance Driven: A New Vision for U.S. Transportation Policy*, p. XX.

[28] The post–World War II toll road construction, most of which was "grandfathered" in to the Interstate System, was done on the initiative of the states. Prior to the passage of the 1956 Act, the states were far more active in road construction and spending on roads, spending nearly six times what the federal government did in 1955.

[29] Federal Highway Administration, *Toll Facilities of the United States 2009*, "FHWA-PL-09-00021," Washington, DC, August 2009, http://www.fhwa.dot.gov/ohim/tollpage.htm.

[30] Federal Highway Administration, *Toll Facilities in the United States: Bridges-Roads-Tunnels-Ferries*, "Publication No: FHWA-PL-91-009," Washington, DC, 1991, p. v.

[31] "Figure 6-6: Toll Facility Revenue: 1993-2008," *Our Nation's Highways: 2010*, http://www.fhwa.dot.gov/policyinformation/pubs/pl10023/fig6_6.cfm.

[32] Federal Highway Administration, *Highway Statistics: Summary to 1975*, Table HF-211, Washington, DC, 1977, pp. 107-136. Also *Highway Statistics: Summary to 1995*, Table SF-210 and *Highway Statistics*, various years, Tables SF-21, HF-10 and HF-10a. Also "Figure 6-6: Toll Facility Revenue: 1993-2008," *Our Nation's Highways: 2010*, http://www.fhwa.dot.gov/policyinformation/pubs/pl10023/fig6_6.cfm. Toll revenues grew during FY1993-FY2008 at an average annual rate approaching 8%.

[33] Federal Highway Administration, Office of Innovative Program Delivery, *Tolling and Pricing Program*, Washington, DC, http://ops.fhwa.dot.gov/tolling_pricing/index.htm.

[34] According to FHWA, 60% to 70% of toll project revenues are used to pay for new highway, bridge, and tunnel capacity, compared with 20% of total highway revenues. See *Current Toll Road Activity in the U.S.: a Survey and Analysis*, by Benjamin Perez and Steve Lockwood, Washington, DC, Federal Highway Administration, January 2009, p. 21.

[35] National Surface Transportation Policy and Revenue Study Commission, *Transportation for Tomorrow: Final Report*, Chapter 5, http://mtcfilehost.net/transportationfortomorrow/final_report/pdf/volume_2_chapter_5.pdf. The study estimated that aggressive use of tolling opportunities in SAFETEA could generate $8.9 billion in additional revenue between FY2007 and FY2017. See also National Surface Transportation Infrastructure Financing Commission, *Paying Our Way: a New Framework for Transportation Finance, Final Report*, Washington, DC, February 26, 2009, pp. 28, 25-36, 207, http://financecommission.dot.gov/Documents /NSTIF_ Commission_Final_Report_Mar09FNL.pdf.

[36] Benjamin Perez and Steve Lockwood, *Current Toll Road Activity in the U.S.: a Survey and Analysis*, Federal Highway Administration, Washington, DC, January 2009, pp. 2-3, http://www.fhwa.dot.gov /ipd/pdfs/2008_toll_ activity_white_paper.pdf.

[37] U.S. Government Accountability Office, *Highway Finance: States' Expanding use of Tolling Illustrates Diverse Challenges and Strategies*, GAO-06-554, June 2006, pp. 32-42, http://www.gao.gov/new.items/d06554.pdf. See also GAO, *Highways and Transit: Private Sector Sponsorship of and Investment in Major Projects Has Been Limited*, GAO-04-419, Washington, DC, March 2004, pp. 20-24, http://www.gao. gov/new.items /d04419.pdf.

[38] Alan E. Pisarski and Martin Wachs, *Future Financing Options to Meet Highway and Transit Needs*, National Cooperative Highway Research Program, Transportation Research Board, NCHRP Web-Only Document 102, Washington, DC, December 2006, pp. ES-8, F-9, http://onlinepubs.trb.org/onlinepubs/nchrp/nchrp_ w102.pdf. The National Surface Transportation Policy and Revenue Study Commission, *Final Report*, used the NCHRP estimates.

[39] Transportation Research Board, *Fuel Tax and Alternatives for Transportation Funding*, Special Report 285, Washington, DC, 2006, p. 154, http://onlinepubs.trb.org/onlinepubs/sr/sr285.pdf. "Fast Lanes" are electronically tolled express lanes with tolls set to limit traffic to the free-flowing maximum; the regular adjoining lanes would be free. The Express Lanes Demonstration Program enacted in SAFETEA is a version of the Fast Lanes proposal.

[40] Ginger Goodin and Chuck Fuhs, "Tolled Managed Lanes: Lessons Learned and Challenges to Meet," *TR News*, no. 263 (July-August 2009), pp. 20-21.

[41] Derek Toups, "What's in Store for Second-Generation Express Lanes in San Diego?," *TR News*, no. 263 (July-August 2009), p. 24.

[42] U.S. Congress, House Committee on Transportation and Infrastructure, Hearing on State Perspectives on Transportation for Tomorrow, Recommendations of the National Surface Transportation Policy and Revenue Study Commission, Testimony by Pete Rahn, 110th Cong., 2nd sess., February 13, 2008, http://transportation.house.gov/Media/File/Highways/20080213/Pete%20Rahn%20Testimony.pdf.

[43] Growth in nationwide toll revenues alone is not an ideal metric for the provision of increased mobility or new infrastructure because the revenue growth can, in some years, be a reflection of rate increases at existing toll facilities.

[44] Adeel Lari, David Levinson, and Zhirong Zhao, et al., *Value Capture for Transportation Finance: Technical Research Report*, Center for Transportation Studies, University of Minnesota, June 2009, http://www.cts.umn.edu/Research/Featured/ValueCapture/index.html.

[45] Government Accountability Office, *Public Transportation: Federal Role in Value Capture Strategies for Transit Is Limited, but Additional Guidance Could Help Clarify Policies*, GAO-10-781 (Washington, DC, July 2010), http://www.gao.gov/new.items/d10781.pdf.

[46] Ibid., p. 16.

[47] Ibid., p. 20.

[48] For more information, see http://www.28freeway.com/index.html.

[49] Florida Department of Transportation, I-595 Improvements, District 4, Project Overview, June 3, 2010, http://www.i-595.com/Public_Documents/I-595%20Project%20Overview_2010-06-03.pdf.

[50] Peter Samuel, "The Role of Tolls in Financing 21st Century Highways," *Reason Foundation Policy Study 359*, May 2007, http://reason.org/files/7227d934ecfa04d5db576c126f0385a6.pdf.

[51] Ibid., p. 29.

[52] Robert W. Poole, "Tolling and Public-Private Partnerships in Texas: Separating Myth from Fact," Reason Foundation Working Paper, May 2007, http://reason.org/files/f4b3060c451c35f004519f3971d05fb3.pdf.

[53] Ibid., p. 5. An exception to the difference between the public and private sector in setting toll rates is the use of dynamic tolling in congestion pricing schemes in which the toll is adjusted up and down to maintain "free-flowing" traffic. In such cases, traffic demand determines the price. An exception to the difference between the public and private sector in setting toll rates is the use of dynamic tolling in congestion pricing schemes in which the toll is adjusted up and down to maintain "free-flowing" traffic. In such cases, traffic demand determines the price.

[54] U.S. Department of Transportation, "Over $400 Billion Available Today for Road, Bridge and Transit Projects U.S. Secretary of Transportation Mary E. Peters Announces," Press Release, DOT 43-08, Wednesday, March 26, 2008.

[55] Orski, K., "A $400 Billion Solution," *Innovation Briefs*, Vol. 19, No. 8, March 10, 2008.

[56] Ibid.

[57] See McNally, Sean, "Investors Look to Banks for Help With Infrastructure Deals," *Transport Topics*, April 21, 2008, p. 14.

[58] Ianthe Jeanne Dugan, "Private Investors Push Public Projects," *Wall Street Journal*, October 14, 2010.

[59] Transportation Research Board, National Cooperative Highway Research Program, *Future Financing Options to Meet Highway and Transit Needs*, NCHRP Web-Only Document 102 (Washington, DC, 2006), p. 4-1, http://onlinepubs.trb.org/onlinepubs/nchrp/nchrp_w102.pdf; see also Organisation for Economic Cooperation and Development (OECD) and International Transport Forum, *Transport Infrastructure Investment: Options for Efficiency* (Paris, 2008); and General Accounting Office (now the Government Accountability Office), March 2004.

[60] Steve A. Steckler, "Squeezing Cash from Concrete: Navigating the Perils of Turnpike Privatization," Infrastructure Management Group, http://www.imggroup.com/transportation/documents/ Pennsylvania TollwayLeasing.pdf.

[61] John Schmidt, "The Pros and Cons of Toll Road Leasing," *Public Works Financing*, Vol. 2005, May 2006, p. 9.

[62] Government Accountability Office, *Highway Public-Private Partnerships: More Rigorous Up-front Analysis Could Better Secure Potential Benefits and Protect the Public Interest*, GAO-08-44 (Washington, DC, February 2008), p. 21, http://www.gao.gov/new.items/d0844.pdf.

[63] Ibid., p. 34.

[64] Government Accountability Office, *Federal-Aid Highways: Trends, Effect on State Spending, and Options for Future Program Design*, GAO-04-802 (Washington, DC, 2004), http://www.gao.gov/new.items/d04802.pdf.

65 U.S. Department of Transportation, *Report to Congress on Public-Private Partnerships* (Washington, DC, 004), pp. 38-39, http://www.fhwa.dot.gov/reports/pppdec2004/pppdec2004.pdf.

66 Testimony of Alan Lowenthal, Chair, California Senate Transportation and Housing Committee, in U.S. Congress, House Committee on Transportation and Infrastructure, Subcommittee on Highways and Transit, *Hearing on Public-Private Partnerships: State and User Perspectives*, May 24, 2007, http://transportation .house.gov/Media/File/Highways/20070524/Cal%20State%20Senate%20Lowenthal%20testimony.pdf.

67 Government Accountability Office, *Federal-Aid Highways: Increased Reliance on Contractors Can Pose Oversight Challenges for Federal and State Officials*, GAO-08-198 (Washington, DC, 2008), http://www.gao.gov/new.items/d08198.pdf.

68 Engel, E., R. Fischer, and A. Galetovic, "Privatizing Highways in the United States," *Review of Industrial Organization*, 2006, Vol. 29, pp. 27-53.

69 Government Accountability Office, *Highway Public-Private Partnerships*, February 2008.

70 U.S. Department of Transportation, Federal Highway Administration, "TIFIA Portfolio," http://www.fhwa .dot.gov/ipd/tifia/projects_case_studies/tifia_portfolio.htm.

71 Hedlund, K.J. and N.C. Smith, "SAFETEA-LU Promotes Private Investment in Transportation," report prepared for Nossaman, Guther, Knox, & Elliott, LLP, August 1, 2005, http://www.fhwa.dot.gov/PPP /pdf/safetea_ lu_hedlund.pdf.

72 Department of Transportation, "Notice of Funding Availability for Applications for Credit Assistance Under the Transportation Infrastructure Finance and Innovation Act (TIFIA) Program; Clarification of TIFIA Selection Criteria; and Request for Comments on Potential Implementation of Pilot Program To Accept Upfront Payments for the Entire Subsidy Cost of TIFIA Credit Assistance," 74 *Federal Register* 63497-63501, December 3, 2009, http://www.fhwa.dot.gov/ipd/pdfs/tifia/fy2010_tifia_nofa.pdf.

73 Ibid.

74 U.S. Department of Transportation, Federal Highway Administration, *Transportation Infrastructure Finance and Innovation Act: Report to Congress 2008*, Washington, DC, September 2008, p. 2, http://tifia.fhwa .dot.gov/about/rtc/tifia_2008_rtc.pdf.

75 U.S. Congress, House Committee on Transportation and Infrastructure, Subcommittee on Highways and Transit, Testimony of Christopher Bertram, Assistant Secretary for Budget and Programs and Chief Financial Officer, U.S. Department of Transportation, *Hearing on Using Innovative Finance to Deliver Highway and Transit Projects*, 111th Cong., 2nd sess., April 14, 2010, http://transportation.house.gov/Media/file/ Highways /20100414/Bertram.pdf.

76 U.S. Congress, House Committee on Ways and Means, Subcommittee on Select Revenue Measures, Testimony of Rosa L. DeLauro, *Hearing on the National Infrastructure Banks*, 111th Cong., 2nd sess., May 13, 2010, http://waysandmeans.house.gov/media/pdf/111/2010May13_DeLauro_Testimony.pdf; see also U.S. Congress, House Committee on Transportation and Infrastructure, Hearing on Financing Infrastructure Investments, "Summary of Subject Matter," 110th Cong., 2nd sess., June 10, 2008, http://transportation.house.gov /Media/File/Full%20Committee/20080610/SSM_FC_6-10-08.pdf.

77 U.S. Congress, Senate Committee on Banking, Housing, and Urban Affairs, Testimony of Felix Rohatyn, Co-Chair of the Commission on Public Infrastructure, *Hearing on Condition of Our Nation's Infrastructure and Proposals for Needed Improvement*, 110th Cong., 2nd Sess., March 11, 2008, http://banking.senate.gov/public /index.cfm?FuseAction=Hearings.Hearing&Hearing_ID=9ddc8203-a3d1-448d-946e-3b1f671fda8a; U.S. Congress, House Committee on Transportation and Infrastructure, Testimony of Bernard Schwartz, President and CEO, BLS Investments, *Hearing on Financing Infrastructure Investments*, 110th Cong., 2nd Sess., June 10, 2008, http://transportation.house.gov/Media/File/Full% 20Committee/20080610/Schwartz%20Testimony _6-10-08.pdf. The Public Infrastructure Commission, Center for Strategic and International Studies, co-chaired by Felix Rohatyn, has proposed the creation of a national infrastructure financing agency; see Ehrlich, Everett and Benjamin Landy, *Public Works, Public Wealth: New Directions for America's Infrastructure*, Center for Strategic and International Studies, November 2005.

78 U.S. Congress, House Committee of the Budget and the Committee on Transportation and Infrastructure, Testimony of Peter R. Orszag, Director, Congressional Budget Office, *Hearing on Financing Infrastructure Investment*, 110th Cong., 2nd Sess., May 8, 2008, http://transportation.house.gov/Media /File/Full%20 Committee/20080508/05-08-Infrastructure_Testimony.pdf.

[79] U.S. Congress, House Committee on Ways and Means, Subcommittee on Select Revenue Measures, Testimony of Samuel Staley, *Hearing on the National Infrastructure Banks*, 111th Cong., 2nd sess., May 13, 2010, http://waysandmeans.house.gov/media/pdf/111/2010May13_Staley_Testimony.pdf.

[80] Office of Management and Budget, *Budget of the U.S. Government, FY2010: Analytical Perspectives*, Washington, DC, 2009, table 6-2, http://www.gpoaccess.gov/usbudget/fy10/pdf/spec.pdf.

[81] Testimony of Christopher Bertram, Assistant Secretary for Budget and Programs and Chief Financial Officer, U.S. Department of Transportation, April 14, 2010.

[82] H.Rept. 111-564, p. 20; S.Rept. 111-230, pp. 16-17.

In: Surface Transportation
Editor: David M. Boche

ISBN: 978-1-61470-855-1

Chapter 3

THE DONOR-DONEE STATE ISSUE: FUNDING EQUITY IN SURFACE TRANSPORTATION REAUTHORIZATION*

Robert S. Kirk

SUMMARY

Few issues in the history of the Federal-Aid Highway Program have raised such heated debate as the argument over how closely the program's payments to the individual states should match the amount of federal highway taxes each state's highway users pay to the highway account of the Highway Trust Fund (HTF). Referred to as the donor-donee state issue, it is expected to reemerge during the debate over the reauthorization of federal surface transportation programs. The current authorization, under the Safe, Accountable, Flexible, Efficient Transportation Equity Act: a Legacy for Users (SAFETEA; P.L. 109-59), expires on September 30, 2009.

"Donor states" are states whose highway users are estimated to pay more to the highway account of the HTF than they receive. "Donee states" receive more than they pay. The basic donor state argument is a relatively straightforward call for what they view as equity or fairness. Donor state advocates generally contend that for too many years they have been subsidizing the repair and improvement of donee state infrastructure, especially the older highway infrastructure in the Northeast.

Donee state advocates argue that fairness is in the eye of the beholder and should not be separated from needs. They assert that the age of their highway infrastructure, especially in the Northeast, the high cost of working on heavily congested urban roads, and also the limited financial resources of large sparsely populated Western States justify their donee status. They further argue that there are needs that are inherently federal rather than state, and that a national highway network cannot be based solely on state or regional boundaries.

A number of interest groups and State Departments of Transportation (state DOTs) are expected to propose that reauthorization increase the rate-of-return guarantee

* This is an edited, reformatted and augmented version of a Congressional Research Service 7-5700 publication R40451 , dated March 19, 2009.

(currently 92%) and expand the scope of the statutory guarantee to cover more Federal-Aid Highway Program funding. This may be difficult to achieve in a tight budget environment. The Equity Bonus (EB) program, which is the principal means by which the rate-of-return adjustment is facilitated, is already the largest federal highway program. Others would restructure, modify or eliminate the EB altogether.

The Federal Highway Administration's (FHWA) donor-donee figures indicate that for FY2007 all 50 states were donee states. For FY2006 there were 41 donee states and no donor states fell below a 91% rate-of-return (based on a dollar in-dollar out calculation method). Some donor state advocates argue that this situation is anomalous and have argued for a method of calculation that relies on share percentages, rather than dollars, because this would eliminate the modifying effect of the recent drawing down of the unexpended balances of the HTF.

Near the end of FY2008, the balance in the highway account of the HTF had fallen to the point that Congress provided for a transfer of roughly $8 billion from the Treasury's general fund to the highway account of the HTF in the hope that the transfer would be sufficient to support the guaranteed funding authorized in SAFETEA for FY2009. This transfer of general fund monies has no connection to the transportation taxes paid by highway users to the HTF and raises questions about basing an equity guarantee primarily on the states' shares of payments to the HTF.

Background and Issue Overview

Historically, transportation policy battle lines have often formed along regional rather than partisan alignments. The regional character of transportation policy is evident in the debate over the need for an equitable distribution of federal highway aid among the states. Since 1982, Congress has included legislative provisions in every surface transportation reauthorization act to address these perceived funding distribution concerns through a variety of rate-of-return guarantee provisions. For many years, some states (mostly Southern as well as some Mid-Western and certain fast growing Western states) have complained that they receive significantly less federal highway aid than their highway users pay in federal highway taxes to the highway account of the highway trust fund (HTF).[1] These states, referred to as donor states, argue that they are not getting their perceived fair share of federal-aid highway spending and have pressed for legislative remedies that would assure them a higher rate-of-return on their tax payments. Donee states, states that receive more federal highway aid than they pay in federal highway taxes, have not opposed equity provisions per se in recent years but have opposed any reduction in their own existing percent shares of total federal highway aid.

Since the 1970s much of the debate has been data driven. The data used to designate states as either donor or donee have been drawn from Table FE-221 of the Federal Highway Administration's (FHWA) annual *Highway Statistics* publication, which estimates states' ratios of contributions to the HTF to the federal highway funding that is made available to them each fiscal year.[2] Data from the most recent (FY2007) Table FE-221 is reproduced in *Table 1* of this report.

The current authorization, under the Safe, Accountable, Flexible, Efficient Transportation Equity Act: a Legacy for Users (SAFETEA; P.L. 109-59), expires September 30, 2009. Proposals for reauthorization are expected during the first session of the 111th Congress. For an overview of reauthorization issues see CRS Report R40053, *Surface Transportation Program Reauthorization Issues for the 111th Congress.*[3]

Following a background and overview discussion, this report provides a brief history of the donor-donee issue and its origins. It also describes the existing programmatic rate-of-return guarantee mechanism, the Equity Bonus (EB) Program. The report then discusses issues related to the EB program and possible modifications that may be considered as part of the reauthorization debate. Finally, the report reviews a number of overarching issues related to the donor-donee state debate that could be of interest to Congress during the upcoming reauthorization of SAFETEA.

A number of characteristics of the Federal-Aid Highway Program (FAHP) need to be kept in mind in a discussion of the donor-donee question. First, the federal monies for highway project spending are not provided to states up front. Rather, when amounts are "distributed" to the states, it is only a notification of the availability of federal funds. Once a project is approved and the work is started, the states may submit vouchers to the FHWA for reimbursement for the project's costs as, or after, they are incurred. Second, the FAHP is an umbrella term for nearly all the highway programs administered by the Federal Highway Administration (FHWA). Most of these programs can be described as being either formula (apportioned) programs,[4] which constitute the vast majority of program funding, or discretionary (allocated) programs. The formula programs apportion funds to the State Departments of Transportation (state DOTs) based on formulas set forth in legislation. The discretionary programs are programs nominally under the control of the FHWA that were designed to provide funds to projects chosen through competition with other projects. In recent years, however, most of the discretionary program funding has been earmarked by Congress.

The distinction between formula and discretionary programs becomes especially significant in the process of creating equity programs, such as the current Equity Bonus Program (EB), that could make states' federal spending rates-of-return on their federal highway taxes more uniform. It is difficult to conceive of how discretionary programs could be constructed to guarantee a designated percent return to states on their payments to the HTF and still remain discretionary. The formula programs were originally created, at least in part, to fulfill perceived policy needs.

Some highway needs, such as roads on federal lands, border crossing infrastructure, trade corridors, and interstate system maintenance, have inherently federal aspects that would likely not be fully addressed if the Federal-Aid Highway Programs were predicated on a return to all states. Even advocates of devolving the FAHP to the states have acknowledged some federal needs.[5] In addition, donor states themselves have in the past recognized the need for some states to get a larger than normal share of federal-aid funds. During the debate that preceded passage of the Intermodal Surface Transportation Act of 1991 (ISTEA; P.L. 102-240), for example, donor states agreed that large sparsely populated states and some small states (such as Rhode Island, Vermont, and Delaware) should receive larger shares. Authorizers also thought that the sparsely populated "pass-though" states had insufficient state resources to build and maintain their parts of the national highway network, so they were given larger shares.

To deal with these problems in a way that retains these programmatic policy goals and at the same time achieves improvement in the uniformity of states' rates-of-return, Congress has decided to include some programs in the equity programs (such as the current EB) and exclude others. Often referred to as the "scope," the list of programs (as well as how large a percentage of the overall federal highway aid budget they total) that are subject to the equity adjustments, has varied since the first equity program was introduced in 1982. The major formula programs were always within the scope of the equity guarantee. Which other programs were included changed under the various surface transportation authorization acts. The scope of the equity program is important for a number of reasons. First, under a guaranteed share mechanism, the more program dollars left outside the equity program's scope, the more likely that at least some donor states will not reach their minimum percentage return relative to the entire Federal-aid highway program. Second, in general, the more inclusive the equity program's scope, the more costly the program.[6]

Third, earmarking of programs within the scope generally provides no new dollars to the state receiving the earmarks. These earmarks simply allow Members of Congress to set project priorities. Earmarks of programs outside the scope actually provide more money to the state getting the earmark. Scope issues are discussed in detail in the "Overarching Issues for Congress" section, later in this report.

The highway account of the HTF is supported by revenue from a combination of a variety of fuel taxes (15.44 cents per gallon for gasoline, 21.44 cents per gallon for diesel and kerosene, and a variety of special fuels taxes, at differing rates) as well as a number of truck taxes including, a heavy tire tax, a truck and trailer sales tax, and a heavy vehicle use tax.[7] Revenues from the fuel taxes are also distributed to the Mass Transit Account (2.86 cents per gallon) and the unrelated Leaking Underground Storage Tank Trust Fund (0.1 cents per gallon). All tire, truck and trailer, and heavy vehicle use tax revenues go solely to the highway account.

Because the federal taxes on fuel are collected at the first point of distribution (at the terminal "rack," usually at a refinery or a fuel tank farm) rather than at the retail level, most of the revenue is collected from a small number of corporations (often large oil companies or distributors that own fuel farms) located in a relatively small number of places. This means that the Treasury has no way of knowing how much fuel tax should be attributed to each state. FHWA has a process to estimate each states share of payments to the highway account. [8]

In simplified form, the process of attributing each state's shares to the highway account is as follows:

- The Treasury Department provides the basic national revenue estimates for each kind of tax (gasoline, diesel, special fuels, and truck-related sales, etc.).
- The FHWA then examines state fuel tax data to produce estimates of on-highway gallons of fuel taxed in each state (use is difficult to track as vehicles can gas up in one state and then travel in another).
- Each state's on-highway gallons are divided by national total gallons. The resulting distribution is a representation of each state's share of national consumption, measured in gallons.
- The Treasury's estimates of total revenues received from highway users are then multiplied by the derived state shares of gallons to produce each state's estimated payments to the highway account of the HTF.
- The share of the various truck-related taxes are extrapolated from diesel fuel use in the states.

- Gathering and compiling the data takes time, usually over a year. This means that the data underlying the state-by-state federal tax payments data is normally two years old when used to determine attribution.

A number of statistical issues have an impact on the rate-of-return guarantees. The use of noncurrent data (i.e., revenue estimates from two years prior) may skew the state donor-donee ratios and lead to conclusions about donor or donee status that are questionable. Also, state-by-state data may not always be completely accurate or up to date. The economic cycle can also have an impact on revenues and the budgetary process that can lead to years when revenues and spending levels differ significantly from each other: this can have an impact on relative rates-of-return. As mentioned above, the Equity Bonus and other equity adjustment proposals attempt to achieve a specified "share" return based on two year old payments data. Distribution equity, however, is almost always judged by Table FE-221 in the annual FHWA *Highway Statistics Report*, which compares estimated dollars paid and apportionments and allocations received for the same fiscal year.[9] This statistical disconnect means that even an effective equity program will face criticism when the same year dollar-for-dollar return data are released. In addition, the impact of proposed revenue changes on states' relative shares of payments to the HTF are hard to predict over the life of the reauthorization. These changes can shift some donor states to donee states, or vice versa, over the years. The statistical shifts could also influence the calculation of program size under an equity guarantee.

A Brief History of the Donor-Donee Issue

The concern by states that federal spending might benefit other states' infrastructure more than theirs has a long history. It was one of the formative forces that led to a federal policy of nonparticipation in road building during the century preceding passage of the Federal Aid Road Act of 1916. In 1808, Secretary of the Treasury Albert Gallatin recommended that the federal government provide $20 million over a ten-year period for a national network of canals and roads. The plan, however, was never funded.[10] Among the factors that mitigated against the plan was the view by Southern states, who generally opposed federal grants for roads and canals, that spending would benefit other regions more than the South. The New England states, which had relatively good roads, opposed federal funding for roads, because they expected the money would be spent for roads outside New England. Anticipating these regional concerns, of the $20 million recommended in the report, Gallatin proposed that only $16.6 million be designated for the network of roads and canals. The remaining $3.4 million was to provide benefits to those "eastern and perhaps southern states," which are part of the Union, but "are less immediately interested in those inland communications," provided for in the plan. Even with this incentive, the plan failed to gain sufficient support to be passed. This could, however, be thought of as forerunner of the modern minimum guarantees within the context of the donor-donee debate. [11] The federal government's involvement in road building ebbed to nonparticipation until the 1890s and even then its participation was primarily technical and advisory. Consequently, since there was no federal program, there were no road issues similar to donor-donee issue until after the turn of the Twentieth Century when the "good roads" movement gained traction and interest groups began to encourage legislation for federal spending on roads.

A forerunner of the modern donor-donee argument emerged during the debate on the Federal Aid Road Act of 1916 (39 Stat. 355; hereafter referred to as the 1916 Act). The 1916 Act established the first federal aid to roads on a programmatic basis. An opponent of the Act, Senator Lippitt of Rhode Island, presented a table to his Senate colleagues showing the share of highway spending each state would receive out of each $25 million of road aid provided, in comparison to the share of every $25 million in federal income and corporate tax revenues each states citizens paid. His table indicated that 12 states (except for California, all in the Northeast and upper Midwest), would receive shares of the road aid that were less than the share that they contributed in taxes. According to his table, three states: Massachusetts, New York, and Pennsylvania would together contribute more than 50% of the tax revenue but receive only between 11% and 12% of the road spending. Senator Lippitt's table, however, did not forestall passage of the bill.[12]

The Highway Revenue Act of 1956 (70 Stat. 387) established the HTF. The impetus was the construction of the Interstate System (IS). Because the rate and timing of construction would vary greatly from state-to-state, the construction of the Interstate System did not lend itself well to arguments in support of an equal rate of return on highway tax payments. Nothing equivalent to the modern donor-donee debate emerged as a major point of contention during the discussions that preceded the passage of the 1956 Act. The federal-state intergovernmental relations conflicts focused more on issues of state or federal preeminence in highway policy, as well as, state concerns that increases in the federal fuel taxes would have a crowding-out effect on states' ability to raise revenues through their own fuel taxes.[13] The passage of the 1956 Act did, however, eventually have an impact on the evolution of the donor-donee issue, because the HTF made it possible to eventually attribute the flows of revenues from states' highway users to the fund.

For the most part, however, although the argument regarding a fair return on tax payments did not disappear entirely after the passage of the 1916 Act, it did not surface as a major issue until after the first publication of Table FE-221 in the 1972 edition of the FHWA's annual *Highway Statistics.*[14] The table's publication provided a statistical source that supported concerns about the state "fair share" issue that persist to this day. Table FE-221, "Comparison of Estimated State Payments into and Receipts from the Highway Trust Fund, and Federal-Aid Apportionments," published for each state, presented in side-by-side format not only the state payments to and receipts from the HTF, but also the ratio of aggregate payments to receipts for fiscal year 1957 through June 30, 1973. The receipt of federal aid for each dollar paid to the highway trust fund varied greatly from state to state. Alaska appeared to fare best and North Carolina worst at $8.34 and $0.52, respectively. During the 1970s, significant construction was still underway on the Interstate Highway System, and the degree of effort required continued to vary significantly from state to state. This may have, in the minds of some, provided a reasonable justification for the disparity among state rates-of-return. By the early 1980s, however, the interstate system was nearing completion. At the same time, a general perception that U.S. roads and bridges had deteriorated coincided with growing support for increased spending on transportation infrastructure, in part, as an economic stimulus measure.

The Surface Transportation Assistance Act of 1982 (STAA; P.L. 97-424) included the first attempt to mitigate the dissatisfaction of donor states by providing that each state would receive a minimum core program allocation of 85% of its estimated highway tax payments to the highway account of the HTF (STAA established the mass transit account). Between STAA and SAFETEA all surface transportation reauthorization bills included equity provision modifications changing the rate-of-return guarantee percentages and scope of the various equity programs. For a detailed legislative history of these changes, see *Appendix A*.

The Donor-Donee State Arguments

The donor state argument is that for the sake of equity each state should receive federal highway funding roughly equal to the fees and taxes that their state's highway users pay into the HTF. Donor state advocates generally contend that they have been subsidizing the repair and improvement of donee state infrastructure, especially of the older highway infrastructure in the Northeast. Most also argue that they are more road dependent and do not benefit from federal transit spending to the same degree as some donee states. Southern and certain Western donor states also argue that they are fast growth areas, relative to most donee states, and that consequently their needs are as great or greater. Finally, they argue that with the completion of the Interstate Highway System there is no valid rationale for any donor-donee disparity.

Donee states argue that fairness should not be separated from needs. They assert that the age of their highway infrastructures (especially those in the Northeast), the high cost of working on heavily congested urban roads, as well as the limited financial resources of large, sparsely populated western states justify their donee status. They also argue that some needs exist that are inherently federal, such as a national highway network, that cannot be based solely on state or regional boundaries. Furthermore, donee states argue that Mid-Western and Southern donor states often spend less local and state money on highways than donee states, and chide these donor states for pleading for federal funds when they are unwilling to ante up their own state and local resources.

Historically there has also been a third view that has challenged the basic concept that states should be entitled to a balance between the federal taxes collected from their citizens, businesses, or highway users versus the federal spending that eventually occurs in the state. The Federal-Aid Highway Program is the only federal program that considers rate-of-return criteria. Those who challenge the basic donor-donee conceptual framework generally refer to studies showing that some highway program donor states are overall donee states in terms of federal tax and spending flows in general, or in other kinds of federal spending such as defense or human service programs.[15] They also argue that rate-of-return mechanisms inherently constrain the federal government's ability to address changing national needs, creating a framework where state and local priorities trump federal priorities. They also point out that, especially in regard to freight, road improvement in some states (such as for ports or freight bottleneck areas) benefit the surrounding states, the region, and the nation as a whole. They argue that such projects' funding decisions should be based on efficiency not equity. In addition, some cast doubt on the mind-set that construction spending, including wages, remains in the state where a project is built by pointing out that construction companies from all over the nation bid for federally funded projects and that construction labor is mobile.

Policy Dilemmas

The 111th Congress faces difficult policy choices in resolving the seemingly contradictory goals of meeting donor state demands for a higher rate-of-return and donee state demands to be held harmless at a time when the revenue base of the Highway Trust Fund's (HTF) highway account is insufficient (at least in real terms) and is expected by most observers to be insufficient to fund both goals. Part of the problem is that a bill that simply reduces the shares of donee states to increase the shares of donor states would have difficulty overcoming a filibuster by donee states in the Senate. To provide an equitable rate-of-return structure to overcome this obstacle, reauthorization bills have, in past practice, included "hold harmless" provisions that maintained certain base shares. This process of bringing donor state shares up to the guaranteed percentage return has required increasing the overall federal highway program size, usually by a large amount (since donee state funding could not be reduced). In other words, providing equity remedies that keep both donor and donee states reasonably content has been accomplished by giving more money to all states, but even more to donor states to meet their guaranteed share requirement, currently 92%. Providing equity in this way is very expensive. The Equity Bonus program (EB) under SAFETEA, in fact, is the largest highway program ($41 billion over the five year life of the bill). Finding sufficient funds to support an equity distribution mechanism is likely to be a major difficulty in reauthorization.

In a broader sense, the debate over equity remedies has implications for a number of issues. As was referred to earlier, a guaranteed rate-of-return that approaches roughly 95% or higher could leave little room for addressing additional transportation needs that are viewed as uniquely federal, such as the Federal Lands Highway Program or the Interstate Maintenance Program. Further, the role of the federal government vis-a-vis the states comes into question as the minimum guarantee approaches 100%. If the federal government is essentially collecting HTF revenues only to return them to the states with no redistribution, some would argue the need for a federal role is questionable.

In addition, not all highway funding has originated from the highway user taxes that provide revenue to the highway account of the HTF. Spending originating from the Treasury's general fund has been significant since passage of the Federal-Aid Highway Act of 1956.[16] This is the primary reason that (in *Table 1)* the cumulative ratio of apportionments and allocations to payments to the HTF for FY1957-FY2007 exceeds the 1.0 break-even point by 0.12. This inclusion of general fund monies muddles the rationale for a 1.0 ratio return that underlies the donor-donee debate. The highway user taxes have nothing to do with the revenues that support the Treasury's general fund, which is supported mostly by individual income, corporate income and payroll taxes.[17] This issue is discussed in more detail in the "Overarching Issues for Congress" section of this report.

The Statistics Underlying the Debate

Table 1, below, reproduces Table FE-221 from the 2007 edition of *Highway Statistics,* which is published annually by the Federal Highway Administration.[18] Since 1972, Table FE-221 has provided the statistical underpinnings of the donor-donee state debate. Following the state column, the first group of four columns sets forth the dollar amount of and percentage of the total payments into the fund for both FY2007 and for the aggregate payments from the beginning of FY1957 through FY2007. The second group of four columns sets forth the dollar amounts and percentages of the national total for the flow of funds (apportionments and allocations) from the HTF for the same time periods, respectively. The last two groups of dual columns calculate the ratios that are used to determine donor or donee status via two calculation methods used by various parties to the debate: dollar-in/dollar-out and percentage-in/percentage-out.[19]

Ratio of Apportionment and Allocations to Payments (Dollar-in/Dollar-Out Method)

To calculate the dollar-in/dollar-out ratio, each state's total apportionments and allocations from the fund for the year are divided by the estimated payments made by each state's highway users to the highway account of the HTF for the same year (based on the most recent data available, generally two years prior). The same is done for the cumulated amounts since FY1957. Assuming that the total national amounts flowing into and from the HTF are equal, if a state receives as much as it pays in, its dollar-in/dollar-out ratio is 1.0. If a state receives less than it pays in, its ratio will be below 1.0 and it may be considered a donor state. If a state receives more than it pays in, its ratio is above 1.0 and it may be considered a donee state. For example, for FY2007 Alabama is estimated to have paid into the HTF $680,178,000 and had apportionments and allocations from the HTF made available to the state totaling $817,468,000. Since Alabama, according to Table FE-221, received more than it paid in, its ratio of 1.20 and for the year it can be considered a donee state (i.e. it received $1.20 for each $1 it paid into the HTF). With a cumulative ratio of 1.12 for the period FY1957 through FY2007, Alabama is also historically a donee state. Using the percentage-in/percentage out calculation method, discussed below, Alabama's ratio for FY2007 is 1.0: Alabama is neither a donor state nor a donee state.

In recent years, the authorization legislation has been intentionally drawing down what was the unexpended balance of the highway account. Because the HTF was paying out more than was flowing into the highway account for these years, most states' ratios have exceeded 1.0 and for FY2007 all 50 states received more than they were estimated to have paid in and there were, on a dollar-in/dollar-out basis, no donor states. All states had a ratio above 1.0. The excess of spending over payments at the national level is reflected in the grand total for FY2007, which was 1.20. The cumulative grand total (FY1957-2007), however, is not significantly affected by the draw down of the HTF's unexpended balance, yet at 1.12, it is also over the 1.0 level. This is mostly because of general fund monies spent over the life of the HTF.

Table 1. Comparison of Federal Highway Trust Fund Highway Account Receipts Attributable to the States and Federal-Aid Apportionments and Allocations from the Highway Account: FY1957-FY2007 (FHWA Table FE-221A) (Thousands of Dollars)

State	Payments Into The Fund [a]				Apportionments And Allocations From The Fund[b]				Dollar-in—Dollar-out Ratio[c]		Percentage-in—Percentage-out Ratio[d]	
	Fiscal Year 2007	Percent of Total	Cumulated Since 7-1-56	Percent of Total	Fiscal Year 2007	Percent of Total	Cumulated Since 7-1-56	Percent of Total	Fiscal Year 2007	Cumulated Since 7-1-56	Fiscal Year 2007	Cumulated Since 7-1-56
Alabama	680,178	1.949	12,717,931	1.976	817,468	1.955	14,197,192	1.974	1.20	1.12	1.00	1.12
Alaska	124,331	0.356	1,423,821	0.221	541,251	1.295	8,901,517	1.237	4.35	6.25	3.63	6.25
Arizona	742,254	2.127	10,879,146	1.690	762,180	1.823	11,375,455	1.581	1.03	1.05	0.86	1.05
Arkansas	441,239	1.264	8,476,116	1.317	541,826	1.296	8,950,473	1.244	1.23	1.06	1.03	1.06
California	3,466,984	9.934	65,434,541	10.166	4,232,975	10.124	64,807,093	9.009	1.22	0.99	1.02	0.99
Colorado	525,442	1.506	8,615,996	1.339	554,380	1.326	9,913,796	1.378	1.06	1.15	0.88	1.15
Connecticut	340,150	0.975	7,031,575	1.092	530,357	1.269	11,750,058	1.633	1.56	1.67	1.30	1.67
Delaware	91,167	0.261	1,810,797	0.281	176,331	0.422	2,954,030	0.411	1.93	1.63	1.61	1.63
Dist. of Col.	26,904	0.077	895,527	0.139	159,815	0.382	3,763,660	0.523	5.94	4.20	4.96	4.20

State	Payments Into The Fund [a]				Apportionments And Allocations From The Fund[b]				Dollar-in—Dollar-out Ratio[c]		Percentage-in—Percentage-out Ratio[d]	
	Fiscal Year 2007	Percent of Total	Cumulated Since 7-1-56	Percent of Total	Fiscal Year 2007	Percent of Total	Cumulated Since 7-1-56	Percent of Total	Fiscal Year 2007	Cumulated Since 7-1-56	Fiscal Year 2007	Cumulated Since 7-1-56
Florida	1,915,336	5.488	31,411,215	4.880	2,003,500	4.792	30,378,489	4.223	1.05	0.97	0.87	0.97
Georgia	1,293,316	3.706	22,815,506	3.545	1,343,422	3.213	21,365,242	2.970	1.04	0.94	0.87	0.94
Hawaii	91,252	0.261	1,629,457	0.253	216,929	0.519	5,009,549	0.696	2.38	3.07	1.98	3.07
Idaho	187,619	0.538	3,330,993	0.518	295,283	0.706	5,452,926	0.758	1.57	1.64	1.31	1.64
Illinois	1,310,293	3.755	24,748,815	3.845	1,579,222	3.777	26,497,537	3.683	1.21	1.07	1.01	1.07
Indiana	962,021	2.757	17,266,009	2.683	988,156	2.363	15,587,311	2.167	1.03	0.90	0.86	0.90
Iowa	456,043	1.307	8,182,632	1.271	475,913	1.138	9,064,692	1.260	1.04	1.11	0.87	1.11
Kansas	345,899	0.991	7,472,028	1.161	407,799	0.975	8,299,086	1.154	1.18	1.11	0.98	1.11
Kentucky	637,626	1.827	11,543,571	1.793	700,301	1.675	11,985,559	1.666	1.10	1.04	0.92	1.04
Louisiana	664,405	1.904	11,474,919	1.783	756,201	1.809	14,095,804	1.959	1.14	1.23	0.95	1.23
Maine	176,566	0.506	3,429,345	0.533	202,084	0.483	3,820,442	0.531	1.14	1.11	0.96	1.11

Table 1. (Continued)

State	Payments Into The Fund [a]				Apportionments And Allocations From The Fund[b]				Dollar-in—Dollar-out Ratio[c]		Percentage-in—Percentage-out Ratio[d]	
	Fiscal Year 2007	Percent of Total	Cumulated Since 7-1-56	Percent of Total	Fiscal Year 2007	Percent of Total	Cumulated Since 7-1-56	Percent of Total	Fiscal Year 2007	Cumulated Since 7-1-56	Fiscal Year 2007	Cumulated Since 7-1-56
Maryland	603,323	1.729	11,285,823	1.753	661,588	1.582	14,161,022	1.969	1.10	1.25	0.92	1.25
Massachusetts	562,678	1.612	12,215,087	1.898	654,592	1.566	17,476,471	2.429	1.16	1.43	0.97	1.43
Michigan	1,044,882	2.994	22,566,088	3.506	1,171,364	2.802	21,114,145	2.935	1.12	0.94	0.94	0.94
Minnesota	632,337	1.812	10,657,059	1.656	733,286	1.754	12,494,444	1.737	1.16	1.17	0.97	1.17
Mississippi	471,171	1.350	8,420,525	1.308	537,044	1.285	9,587,769	1.333	1.14	1.14	0.95	1.14
Missouri	854,175	2.448	16,398,573	2.548	979,126	2.342	16,115,967	2.240	1.15	0.98	0.96	0.98
Montana	163,460	0.468	3,017,367	0.469	415,349	0.993	7,212,037	1.003	2.54	2.39	2.12	2.39
Nebraska	261,446	0.749	5,086,071	0.790	299,915	0.717	5,629,245	0.783	1.15	1.11	0.96	1.11
Nevada	314,866	0.902	4,096,365	0.636	321,892	0.770	5,165,628	0.718	1.02	1.26	0.85	1.26

State	Payments Into The Fund [a]				Apportionments And Allocations From The Fund[b]				Dollar-in—Dollar-out Ratio[c]		Percentage-in—Percentage-out Ratio[d]	
	Fiscal Year 2007	Percent of Total	Cumulated Since 7-1-56	Percent of Total	Fiscal Year 2007	Percent of Total	Cumulated Since 7-1-56	Percent of Total	Fiscal Year 2007	Cumulated Since 7-1-56	Fiscal Year 2007	Cumulated Since 7-1-56
New Hamp.	141,331	0.405	2,676,622	0.416	178,129	0.426	3,473,838	0.483	1.26	1.30	1.05	1.30
New Jersey	982,550	2.815	18,636,580	2.895	1,044,152	2.497	18,479,217	2.569	1.06	0.99	0.89	0.99
New Mexico	326,560	0.936	5,416,536	0.842	389,821	0.932	6,866,989	0.955	1.19	1.27	1.00	1.27
New York	1,341,636	3.844	28,979,180	4.502	1,786,606	4.273	36,582,638	5.085	1.33	1.26	1.11	1.26
North Carol.	1,051,100	3.012	19,184,186	2.981	1,111,941	2.660	17,584,954	2.445	1.06	0.92	0.88	0.92
North Dakota	109,008	0.312	2,210,368	0.343	252,257	0.603	4,697,786	0.653	2.31	2.13	1.93	2.13
Ohio	1,335,416	3.826	26,606,692	4.134	1,536,682	3.675	25,253,242	3.510	1.15	0.95	0.96	0.95
Oklahoma	538,021	1.542	10,743,580	1.669	677,902	1.621	10,154,988	1.412	1.26	0.95	1.05	0.95
Oregon	424,654	1.217	8,172,896	1.270	544,644	1.303	9,589,285	1.333	1.28	1.17	1.07	1.17
Pennsylvania	1,328,157	3.806	27,393,966	4.256	1,723,126	4.121	33,006,412	4.588	1.30	1.20	1.08	1.20
Rhode Island	81,057	0.232	1,854,723	0.288	241,579	0.578	4,350,079	0.605	2.98	2.35	2.49	2.35

Table 1. (Continued)

	Payments Into The Fund [a]				Apportionments And Allocations From The Fund[b]				Dollar-in—Dollar-out Ratio[c]		Percentage-in—Percentage-out Ratio[d]	
State	Fiscal Year 2007	Percent of Total	Cumulated Since 7-1-56	Percent of Total	Fiscal Year 2007	Percent of Total	Cumulated Since 7-1-56	Percent of Total	Fiscal Year 2007	Cumulated Since 7-1-56	Fiscal Year 2007	Cumulated Since 7-1-56
South Carolina	627,649	1.798	10,819,751	1.681	650,292	1.555	10,011,545	1.392	1.04	0.93	0.86	0.93
South Dakota	127,134	0.364	2,358,628	0.366	297,765	0.712	5,033,883	0.700	2.34	2.13	1.96	2.13
Tennessee	833,578	2.389	15,365,666	2.387	924,124	2.210	15,089,575	2.098	1.11	0.98	0.93	0.98
Texas	3,202,376	9.176	52,853,228	8.211	3,216,831	7.694	47,224,339	6.565	1.00	0.89	0.84	0.89
Utah	317,353	0.909	5,005,603	0.778	319,569	0.764	6,601,323	0.918	1.01	1.32	0.84	1.32
Vermont	74,545	0.214	1,567,298	0.244	221,461	0.530	3,406,527	0.474	2.97	2.17	2.48	2.17
Virginia	987,250	2.829	17,355,562	2.696	1,102,630	2.637	18,787,471	2.612	1.12	1.08	0.93	1.08
Washington	640,626	1.836	11,884,286	1.846	759,593	1.817	15,780,240	2.194	1.19	1.33	0.99	1.33
West Virginia	229,209	0.657	4,863,548	0.756	449,142	1.074	9,472,901	1.317	1.96	1.95	1.64	1.95
Wisconsin	637,934	1.828	12,446,497	1.934	765,287	1.830	12,590,891	1.750	1.20	1.01	1.00	1.01

State	Payments Into The Fund [a]				Apportionments And Allocations From The Fund[b]				Dollar-in—Dollar-out Ratio[c]		Percentage-in—Percentage-out Ratio[d]	
	Fiscal Year 2007	Percent of Total	Cumulated Since 7-1-56	Percent of Total	Fiscal Year 2007	Percent of Total	Cumulated Since 7-1-56	Percent of Total	Fiscal Year 2007	Cumulated Since 7-1-56	Fiscal Year 2007	Cumulated Since 7-1-56
Wyoming	174,748	0.501	2,924,614	0.454	272,733	0.652	5,025,477	0.699	1.56	1.72	1.30	1.72
Total	34,899,255	100.000	643,652,908	100.000	41,525,815	99.322	716,190,239	99.559	1.19	1.11	0.99	1.11
Amer. Samoa	-	-	-	-	15,180	0.036	131,260	0.018	-	-	-	-
Guam	-	-	-	-	24,387	0.058	328,147	0.046	-	-	-	-
N. Marianas	-	-	-	-	11,672	0.028	88,370	0.012	-	-	-	-
Puerto Rico	-	-	-	-	201,031	0.481	2,303,629	0.320	-	-	-	-
Virgin Islands	-	-	-	-	31,196	0.075	323,647	0.045	-	-	-	-
Grand Total	34,899,255	100.000	643,652,908	100.000	41,809,281	100.000	719,365,292	100.000	1.20	1.12	1.00	1.12

Source: Federal Highway Administration. Office of Highway Policy Information. Dollar-in—dollar-out ratio and Percentage-in—percentage-out headings added by CRS.

[a] Payments into the Fund include only the net highway user tax receipts and fines and penalties deposited in the highway account of the Federal Highway Trust Fund (HTF). Excluded are motor fuel tax amounts transferred to: the Mass Transit Account of the HTF; the Leaking Underground Storage Tank Trust Fund; and amounts representing motor-boat use of gasoline, which are transferred to the Aquatic Resources Trust Fund and the Land and Water Conservation Fund. Total HTF receipts (for apportionment purposes only) are reported by the U.S. Dept. of the Treasury. Payments into the HTF attributable to highway users in each state are estimated by the FHWA.

[b] Includes all funds apportioned or allocated from the HTF except where FHWA does not directly allocate the funds to the states, e.g., portions of Indian Reservation Roads and safety programs.

[c] Ratio of apportionments and allocations to payments.

[d] The ratio of each state's apportionments and allocations to total apportionments and allocations relative to the ratio of each state's payments to total payments.

Relative Ratio of Apportionments and Allocations to Payments (Percentage-in/Percentage-out Method)

Some participants in the donor-donee debate, usually donor state advocates, have argued that the dollar-in/dollar-out method of calculating the ratio is misleading because in years when the trust fund balance is drawn down, it makes many states that historically have been donor states look like donee states. They argue that the years when spending exceeds revenues are anomalous and mask the true status of donor states shares of the total relative to those of donee states. To remedy this a second method of calculation has been devised. This method is set forth in the last two columns of *Table 1.* The "relative ratio of apportionment and allocations to payments" (percentage-in/percentage-out method) is calculated by dividing a state's percentage of total nationwide apportionments and allocations from the HTF by the state's percentage of the total nationwide payments into the HTF to generate a third ratio. Using Arizona[20] in FY2007 as an example, Arizona's payments to the fund were 2.127% of the national total and its apportionments and allocations received from the fund were 1.823% of the national total.

Dividing Arizona's percent of total nationwide apportionments and allocations from the fund (1.823) by Arizona's percent of nationwide payments into the fund (2.127) results in a ratio of 0.86. By contrast, Arizona's dollar-in/dollar-out ratio for FY 2007 is 1.03. This percentagein/percentage-out method eliminates the impact of the spending down of the fund's unexpended balances on the determination of donor-donee status.[21] It also allows donor states to argue that, even in years when in dollar terms they get more than they pay into the fund, they are not getting the share of the total distribution of funds they should be getting because their relative ratio of what they receive to their payments is below 1.0.

It is important to note that even using the percentage-in/percentage-out method, the cumulative grand total (the extreme right hand column in Table 1) is 1.12, as it is using dollar-in/dollar-out method. This indicates that, even accounting for the recent drawdown of the fund's balances, the federal government has spent more on highways than has been paid into the fund, via highway user taxes and fees, during its existence.

The outcomes from these differences in the calculation methods are significant, as indicated in *Table 2.* For FY2007, using the dollar-in/dollar-out method there were no states that did not have more money made available to them than their highway users paid to the HTF. Using the percentage-in/percentage-out method, however, produces 27 states below the 1.0 ratio. Using the historical data for FY1957-2007, results in 13 states below the 1.0 threshold.

It is important to keep in mind that a 100% return on payments to all states is considered by most observers to be unrealistic. There are administrative FHWA and other costs to cover and also some programs and activities, for example the Federal Lands Highways Program, that do not lend themselves to effective distribution if based on rate-of-return on state payments to the HTF. During the last two reauthorizations, donor state advocates have pressed for a rate-of-return of 95%. The case can be made by some that a 0.95 ratio is a more realistic benchmark for determining donor state status. Using below a 0.95 ratio as the measure, the number of historical donor states (i.e. FY1957-FY2007 cumulative) drops to 6 using either dollar-in/dollar-out or percentage-in/percentage-out methods. For FY2007, using the dollar-in/dollar-out method, the number of states under 0.95 is 0, while under the percentage-in/percentage-out method, the number of states under 0.95 is 17.

Table 2. Number of Donor States Under Dollar-in—Dollar-out and Percentage-in—Percentage-out Methods (Calculated for donor states defined as under 1.0 and 0.95 rate-of-return ratios)

Year(s)	Dollar-in/Dollar-out (under 1.0 ratio)	Percentage-in/Percentage-out (under 1.0 ratio)	Dollar-in/Dollar- out (under 0.95 ratio)	Percentage-in/Percentage-out (under 0.95 ratio)
FY2007	0	27	0	17
FY1957-FY2007	13	13	6	6

Source: Data compiled by CRS from Federal Highway Administration, Highway Statistics, 2007: Table FE-221.

Some states move back and forth across the donor-donee divide from year to year. HTF revenues are sensitive to the condition of the economy and can have a significant impact in the pattern of payments to the HTF across the states. Some of the results can seem counterintuitive. For example, a donor state may become a donee state because an economic downturn reduces the expenditures on fuel and sales of trucks and heavy tires. Thus, a state may become a donee state not because it is getting more money but because its economy is generating fewer transportation tax revenues for the HTF. This reduces the amount of federal funding needed to bring the state's ratio up to 1.0 (or 0.95 depending on your definition of donor status). Another example that can influence donor-donee status is shifts in fuel use. Gasoline, and diesel fuel have different tax rates and, because of this, shifts in use can influence the amount of revenue produced in a state. A shift from gasoline special fuels, for example, could lead to a drop in overall revenues because some special fuels are taxed at a lower rate.

Existing Law: SAFETEA's Equity Bonus Program (EB)

The current equity mechanism is the Equity Bonus Program (P.L. 109-59, section 1104; U.S. Code, Title 23, section 105). Simply put, the way it works is that the individual program formulas determine the initial apportionment amounts provided to each state, and then the equity bonus funding is added to these levels to bring donor states up to their guaranteed rate-of-return. The EB is funded on a such sums as necessary basis. The EB program contains a number of complex requirements of implementation. This section briefly explains these complexities.

The State Percentage Guarantee

Under the SAFETEA EB program, FHWA is directed to allocate sufficient funds to ensure that each state receives a minimum return of 90.5% for FY2005-2006, 91.5% for FY2007, and 92% for FY2008-2009, on their estimated payments to the highway account of the HTF. This percentage calculation is based on a subset of all the FAHP. The programs subject to the EB program are the Interstate Maintenance Program (IM), the National Highway System (NHS), the Surface Transportation Program (STP), the Congestion Mitigation and Air Quality Improvement Program (CMAQ), the Highway Bridge Program (HBP), Recreational Trails, Appalachian Development Highway System, High Priority

Projects (HPP), metropolitan planning, the Coordinated Border Infrastructure Program, the Safe Routes to School Program, the Highway Safety Improvement Program (HSIP), and Rail-Highway Grade Crossing Program.

Together these programs and the money apportioned to them are referred to as the "scope" of the EB. As mentioned earlier, these programs are also sometimes referred to as being "below-the- line" (programs and spending outside the scope are referred to as "above-the-line). Since the EB percentage guarantee is only applied to funding within the scope of the EB program, some view the guarantee as a partial one. For example, the 92% guarantee for FY2008 and FY2009 is only to be applied against just over 90% of the total SAFETEA authorization.

Hold Harmless

The EB program also includes a number of "hold harmless" provisions that provide that certain states will either receive the greater of the annual percent return described above, or otherwise receive their percentage share of total apportionments and High Priority Projects over the six-year life of the previous surface transportation reauthorization act, the Transportation Equity Act for the 21st Century (TEA-21; P.L. 105-178). These provisions include certain eligibility thresholds based on state population, population density, highway fatality rates, median household income, and state fuel tax rates. In SAFETEA as passed, the District of Columbia and the following 26 states qualify for funding as hold harmless states under these criteria: Alabama, Alaska, Arizona, Arkansas, Colorado, Delaware, Florida, Idaho, Kentucky, Louisiana, Mississippi, Missouri, Montana, Nebraska, Nevada, New Mexico, North Dakota, Oklahoma, Oregon, South Dakota, Texas, Vermont, Utah, West Virginia, Wisconsin, and Wyoming.

The Minimum Combined Allocation

The EB program sets an annual percentage funding floor, relative to a state's TEA-21 average apportionments and High Priority Projects, beneath which no state can fall. The annual percentage floors are as follows: 117% for FY2005, 118% for FY2006, 119% for FY2007, 120% for FY2008, and 121% for FY2009.

Calculation of the FY2008 Equity Bonus Apportionment

Based on these provisions, a series of calculations is used to determine the EB apportionments needed to bring each state's total apportionment into compliance with the provisions of the EB program. The EB calculation process (using FY2008) is a ten step process. For a detailed explanation, and to get an idea of the complexity of the process, see the FHWA explanatory tables, reproduced in *Appendix B* of this report.

Step 1: Each state's guaranteed minimum program share of the amounts within the scope of the EB program is determined by calculating each state's percent share of total FY2006 payments to the highway account and then multiplying these percentages by the guaranteed 92%. In other words the estimated dollar amounts contributed by each state to the highway account is divided by the estimated national total of highway account contributions received. This creates a percentage share of the total for each state. Since each state is guaranteed a 92% share of its contributions, each state's contribution share percentage is multiplied by 92%.

Step 2: The dollar floor is determined by multiplying each state's average annual TEA-21 apportionments and High Priority Project amounts by 120%. This establishes a dollar amount for each state below which its apportionments and High Priority Projects funding for FY2008 may not fall.

Step 3: The amounts needed to raise each of the 50 states and the District of Columbia to their required dollar floor levels (calculated in step 2) are determined.

Steps 4-8: The total amount of funding needed to bring all states' apportionments plus High Priority Projects into compliance with the EB are estimated and tested until the amount is reached that brings all states up to their minimum share. In FY2008 there were five iterations before the total was identified. For FY2008 the total program size needed to bring all states up to their required share was $37,998,923,126.

Step 9: The EB distribution is determined by calculating the difference for each state's share of the overall program level required and the initial apportionments and High Priority Projects from step 3. The overall difference for FY2008 was $9,235,351,320 which represents the size of the total EB distribution (keep in mind the EB program is authorized on a such sums as necessary basis).

Step 10: The EB distribution is broken down into three categories: the $639 million that is exempt from the obligation limitation; the $2 billion subject to special no-year limitation; and the remainder that is subject to formula limitation (i.e. are distributed to the six core formula programs).

As mentioned earlier, the EB is the largest federal-aid highway program. For FY2008 the EB distribution was almost 25% of total apportionments.

Programmatic Distribution of EB Funding

The programmatic distribution of Equity Bonus Program funds to the states is accomplished by increasing the amounts apportioned to the core formula programs. Each year, the first $2.639 billion is apportioned to the Surface Transportation Program (STP). The rest of the distribution is to each of the core formula programs based on the ratio of each program's apportionment to the total apportionment of all six programs for each state.

Unexpected Consequences

The structure of the EB program and its method of distribution had consequences that were a surprise to some state DOTs as well as some Members of Congress. Some Members were surprised to find that the High Priority Project program earmarks that they had secured did not bring any new funds to their states. Affected Members of Congress and state officials were surprised at how significantly the HPP earmarking reduced the funding they received under the core federal formula programs. In addition, the distribution of EB funds to the core formula programs negated some of the penalties that were designed to discourage certain activities by the states. Most of the unexpected consequences are discussed in more detail in the discussion of "scope" issues in the "Overarching Issues for Congress" section of this report.

Equity Bonus Reauthorization Issues

The persistence of the donor-donee debate in the reauthorization of federal surface transportation programs is a reflection of the differing views and expressed needs of the many stakeholders in federal highway spending policy and the difficulty in addressing these differences. Since 1982, all reauthorization bills have had some form of equity adjustment designed to even out distribution of funds to the states. As mentioned earlier, historically this was achieved by providing large amounts of money to all states but relatively more to the donor states. The current problem of the sufficiency of the HTF could make this historical solution less feasible. A recent forecast by the Congressional Budget Office projected that if spending on highways and highway safety were held at SAFETEA levels, over the next seven years (FY2010-FY2016), adjusted for inflation, the highway account of the HTF would need an additional $64.7 billion (or about $9 billion per year) in new tax revenues or general fund transfers to remain solvent.[22]

Given the condition of the highway account, as well as the constrained overall budgetary environment, there are two major underlying issues regarding the EB program: whether an equity program the size of the EB can be funded and, if so, where will the funding come from. If highway user tax revenues are insufficient and trust fund tax increases are considered out of the question, the expected source would be the Treasury general fund. However, injecting significant amounts of general fund monies into the federal-aid highway programs undercuts the basic rationale for a federal highway spending rate-of-return guarantee based on attribution of highway user tax payments by state.

President Barack Obama's fiscal year 2010 budget outline proposes to make the entire DOT budget discretionary for scorekeeping purposes.[23] The impact of the proposal is uncertain.[24] In any case, equity guarantees operated prior to passage of TEA-21 which created the so-called firewall protections and funding guarantees, and could continue to do so.

Some observers, have expressed concern that that the scorekeeping change would allow appropriators to lower the obligation limitation and replace contract authority with regular appropriations, which could lead to more general fund spending on highways.[25]

Modification of the Equity Provisions

Since 1982, the equity provisions have been changed several times in various reauthorization bills and changes are also likely in SAFETEA reauthorization. An increase in the guaranteed rate-ofreturn percentage of 92% could be considered. Expanding the scope of the equity provisions is also something favored by donor states. In either case, such changes would require a growth in program size or a reduction in funds going to donee states to fund a larger equity overlay unless the underlying core program formulas were rewritten to bring the initial program apportionments more in line with the goals of an increased percentage return guarantee.

Ways to Modify the Existing EB Program

If Congress wishes to change the EB program, it could consider a number of strategies such as:

Phase-in Increases in the Share Guarantee

This is perhaps the simplest cost reducing option. SAFETEA phased in the increase from 90.5% to 92% over the life of the authorization. Although this tactic may save some money, it has drawbacks. First, the annual amounts saved would be small. Second, some of the large donor states would be unhappy with the phase-in proposal, believing equity delayed is equity denied.

Eliminate or Modify the "Hold Harmless" Provisions

The "hold harmless" provisions that protect certain donee states from losing share amounts, could be retained, modified or eliminated. Again, to bring the percentage guarantee closer to 100% would probably require a weakening of some of the hold harmless provisions (under SAFETEA, 26 states and the District of Columbia were held harmless). Hold harmless provisions, however, more than any other characteristic of equity legislation, are designed to retain or attract votes, especially in the Senate.

Determine Program Size Based on Total Annual Payments to the Highway Account of the HTF

The uncertainties of projecting total program size based on share has led to some discussion of eliminating this process (see step 7 in the earlier section on the EB calculation) and simply using the total annual payments to the highway account of the HTF to determine the program size for each fiscal year. Proponents argue that this change would not only simplify the EB calculation process but would also reduce the unexpected outcomes of tax or other revenue changes. Having total annual payments to the highway account set the total highway program size, according to supporters, would also more effectively align state payments with their allocations.

There are a number of possible disadvantages to using total annual payments to the HTF to determine the total program size. As mentioned earlier, the data on contributions are not generally available until early in the second fiscal year after the contributions are made, so the program size would be set according to older data. Also, this method would, in effect, set a ceiling on each year's spending (i.e., there would be no need for the "such sums as may be necessary" authorization for the EB). This could force a reduction in core program authorizations to make room for the EB distributions. Finally, revenues to the HTF can decline (as they did in FY2001 and FY2008). This could put Congress in the uncomfortable position of having to either draw monies from the general fund, draw down the unexpended balance of the HTF (if there is anything left to draw down), or allow program spending to drop for the year.

Restrict the Program Scope of the EB

One way to reduce the cost of the EB is to reduce the number of programs covered by the guarantee (assuming that other attributes are held constant). The states' percent share return on payments to the HTF could be applied to as small a number of the federal-aid highway programs as needed to stay within budget. In the past, donor states have usually supported as broad a scope as possible. As was mentioned earlier, however, adjustments of scope during the authorization process can lead to unexpected consequences.

Integrate the Guaranteed Rate of Return into All Federal-Aid Highways Programs

If the assumption is that the ultimate goal of federal-aid highway programs is to guarantee each state a certain percentage rate-of-return, for example 95%, then one way to accomplish this would be to eliminate all other formula criteria and weight all the programs within the scope of the EB based on that rate-of-return. Congress would still authorize each program's dollar amount and the old core formula programs could still retain their program goals and requirements, but the apportionment of program funds to the states would be strictly determined by each state's percent share of contributions to the HTF. Funding for allocated (discretionary) programs within the scope of EB could also be divided among the states based on a 95% share of contributions to the HTF. The remaining 5% of revenues could be used to fund program administration, the Federal Lands Highways Program, Emergency Relief, and other small programs that do not lend themselves to a strict rate of return distribution.

This approach has advantages and disadvantages. The main advantage is that it would achieve the goal of a guaranteed percentage share return to the states without requiring an expensive equity program. There would be no separate equity program funding per se, since the rate of return minimum would be integrated into the individual programs. It would also have the advantage of simplicity over the existing EB program. Congress could set the size of the various programs without having to consider the impact on the core programs of the EB distributions.

On the other hand, such an option could limit the ability of the federal government to fund federal policy priorities. The program formulas that include such factors as lane miles, vehicle miles traveled, diesel fuel used, cost to repair or replace deficient bridges, or weighted non-attainment and maintenance area population, were originally, at least in part, an attempt to direct federal funding where it is needed to fulfill the program goals. Some would also argue that basing federal funding distribution primarily on the rate of return of payments to the HTF will lead to inefficiencies where states, for example, with relatively few deficient bridges could receive more bridge program funds than states with relatively more, or states with no air quality non-attainment areas could get more CMAQ funding than some states with non-attainment areas. Perhaps the main disadvantage of basing all programs on a guaranteed rate of return is that it would doubtless be opposed by donee states who could not only see their shares reduced, but would, in some cases, actually see a reduction in dollars received under the federal programs.

Reduce the Target Minimum Percent Return below the 95% Level

Some have begun making the case that, under the current fiscal constraints, a higher return percentage is an unrealistic goal for this reauthorization cycle. During SAFETEA reauthorization there was also a major effort to increase the minimum return to 95%. In the end, as discussed previously, only a phased-in increase to 92% was enacted. In the current fiscal environment it is doubtful that an equity program structured like the SAFETEA EB could provide a 95% return. Unless the EB framework is replaced or altered, the minimum rate of return guarantee can only be maintained or modestly increased or decreased.

Statistical Caveats

Statistical analysis of the EB and EB proposals can be problematic. As mentioned earlier, the process of calculating shares and projecting the federal highway program size can lead to results that appear counterintuitive. In addition, because most supporting statistics set forth by proponents or opponents of change in the EB are based on analysis of previous years revenue and funding data, while reauthorization legislation is for future years, the analysis is limited at the outset. Because of uncertainty in future revenue and funding allocations, there is a significant degree of uncertainty in the impact of changes in the EB. Only the FHWA has the databases and expertise to project the impact of these options on equity guarantee calculations in detail and even FHWA must base future projections on assumptions that may not come to pass.

Eliminating the Equity Bonus Program

Congress could decide to forgo an equity provision altogether and allow the program formulas to determine the distribution of highway funds to the states. This scenario, however, would probably require a consensus on programmatic changes that would mitigate the donor-donee state conflicts without requiring a large spending overlay such as is provided by the EB. One way of doing this, as mentioned above, would be to modify the core formula programs so that they are all entirely weighted at or near 100% of states' annual contributions to the highway account of the HTF. Most donee states as well as some donor states would probably oppose such a change.

OVERARCHING ISSUES FOR CONGRESS

Although much of the reauthorization debate has focused on the state-by-state estimates of funding flows under the various bills and amendments proposed, there are broad policy implications of the equity guarantee proposals, including the appropriate federal role vis-a-vis the states, program purpose, possible implications for mass transit, as well as a number of other budgetary issues.

The Role of the Federal Government Vis-a-Vis the States

The federal-state partnership in surface transportation has been a fundamental element of federal highway policy since the passage of the 1916 Act (39 Stat. 355), although the nature and extent has changed over time.[26] Under the Act, funding was apportioned by formula to the state highway departments, which were responsible for the construction and maintenance of the federal aid highways. The state and federal governments were seen as equal partners and this was, in part, the rationale for the 50% federal match for highway construction projects. With the passage of the Federal Aid-Highway and Federal-Aid Revenue Acts of 1956 (70 Stat. 374 and 70 Stat 387), authorizations for the Interstate Highway System were greatly increased over a 13 year period. It also established the federal match for Interstate construction at 90%. The revenue title of the act established the HTF and raised the gas and other transportation taxes to support it. These taxes were to revert back to their original rates in FY1973, the estimated completion date for the Interstate System.[27] However, although the obligations for the Interstate System as a percent of total obligations supported by the trust fund began to decline after 1967, increasing obligations for non-interstate highway programs more than made up for the difference. In addition, with the encouragement of the states, as well as construction and other interest groups, the federal match for the major non-interstate programs was increased from 50% to 70% in 1970, to 75% in 1978, and to 80% in 1992. Over time the relative financial commitment for the federal-aid system has shifted away from the states and toward the federal government.[28]

While the federal financial role was increasing, states were pressing for increased flexibility to move their formula apportionments among the programs, or to transit, thereby, significantly increasing state control over their spending choices under the FAHP. The case can be made that by the enactment of SAFETEA, while the federal financial role had increased significantly, through higher spending and increased federal share, state control over spending decisions was also increasing.

In addition, the EB distribution itself, which averaged roughly $8 billion per year during SAFETEA, dilutes the impact of the program apportionment formula factors, which were originally designed, at least in part, to help achieve federal program goals.

These trends, the enhanced federal financial role, increased state authority over spending decisions, as well as calls during the current reauthorization debate for an increased guaranteed rate of return on a wider scope of FAHP programs, raises important policy questions. At what point does the federal role in decision making become so limited that it might make sense to convert the FAHP to a revenue-sharing or a block grant program? Some would argue that point has already been reached, especially as federal administrative, labor, and environmental requirements do add to most states' project costs. On the other hand, some would argue that despite state complaints concerning the costs of complying with the federal highway program requirements and donor state displeasure with their rates of return, the existing federal highway programs are still seen by many as serving a national purpose and continue to be very popular with most state DOTs.

What Really is a Donor State?

For most years under the last two authorization bills (TEA-21 and SAFETEA, FY1998-FY2009) more HTF highway account funding was being spent than was flowing in through revenues. Because of this, on a dollar-in/dollar-out basis, almost all states have become donee states (i.e. the excess of spending over revenues has pulled most donor states' ratio to near or above 1.0). As was mentioned earlier, donor state advocates began to argue against the dollar-in/dollar-out method for determining donor-donee status. They argued that, instead of using dollars, each state's percentage share of tax payments to the highway account should be compared to the states percentage share of total highway funding distribution (percentage-in/percentage-out).[29] This method of calculation allows most donor states to continue to argue that they still are not getting their fair share while in dollar terms most have been getting nearly as much or more than they have been paying into the highway account each year. Among the supporters of the percentagein/percentage-out method are those who argue that inequitable distribution of highway fund is a reason to eliminate the federal highway program and devolve its responsibilities and financing to the states.[30] Some observers within the transportation community argue that the percentagein/percentage-out statistical method is questionable and are especially critical of applying percentage-in/percentage-out ratios against spending totals to project a dollar figure that a donor state should be receiving, noting that the projection has no connection to the budget process.

Also, the case can be made that the percentage-in/percentage-out calculation makes the donor-donee controversy self-perpetuating. Under this calculation here will always be donor states unless the distribution of every cent of federal spending is based on 100% rate-of-return on state payments to the highway account of the HTF.

General Fund Transfers to the HTF and the Donor-Donee Debate

Over the first 50 years of the life of the HTF significant amounts of money have been transferred from the Treasury's general fund to the HTF.[31] Although much of the transferred funding reflected federal interest payments on the HTF's unexpended balances (theses transfers ended in 1998), the interest was paid by revenues provided by the general taxpayers, and not directly by highway user fees. Some other funds have been transferred to the HTF for a variety of reasons, including the impact of compensating the HTF for lower ethanol tax rates. Given the sufficiency problems faced by the HTF, general fund support for the FAHP (similar to that which is in place for Federal Transit Administration authorization) is one of the options likely to be considered. The use of general funds are problematic for the basic donor-donee argument which is based on return of user fees and taxes paid by highway users. As was mentioned earlier, the pattern of the flow of revenue from the taxpayers in the states to the general fund is different from and has nothing to do with highway user taxes and fees. For example, some long-term HTF donee states such as New York, Massachusetts, and Connecticut are donor states when it comes to general fund expenditures.[32] The larger the general fund contribution to the HTF, the harder it is to argue that states should get a return based on their highway users payments to the highway account.

In September 2008 Congress approved the appropriation of $8.017 billion of general fund revenues to the highway account of HTF (P.L. 110-318). This transfer is equal to roughly 20% of FY2009 funding for highways. Within the context of the donor-donee debate, how general fund money is to be credited could become a significant issue. Should general fund money be treated as if it were highway taxes and credited on that basis across all states or should general fund money be treated differently, perhaps being credited according to state shares of general fund revenues?

Treatment of Stimulus Spending

The American Recovery and Investment Act of 2009 (P.L. 111-5) provided for $27.5 billion in funding from the Treasury general fund to be apportioned and distributed through existing federal-aid highway programs. The version that originally passed the House would have apportioned funds to the states based on their shares of the FY2008 obligation limitation. This method would have reflected the Equity Bonus distribution in its totals. The version that originally passed in the Senate would have simply apportioned the stimulus highway funds according to the STP formulas. As such, the Senate bill would not have reflected an Equity Bonus distribution. As was mentioned earlier, some have questioned the appropriateness of applying shares based on highway tax payments to the spending of general fund-based stimulus spending.[33] In the end, P.L. 111-5 split the difference. After funding a number of set asides, 50% of the remaining funds were to be apportioned according to the House method and 50% according to the Senate method.

The surge of general fund money as stimulus funding could also increase the likelihood of a reexamination of the donor-donee calculation methodology.

"Scope" Issues

An issue that may be seen as being a corollary to the federal role issue is whether a high rate of return percentage, such as 95%, coupled with a similarly broad program scope could constrain a federal programmatic response to federal needs as they arise. Some federal programs, such as the Federal Lands Highways programs, are accepted as being federal in nature and not lending themselves to equal distribution across 50 states. For some programs there is less of a consensus.

As was mentioned earlier, having a 95% or higher guaranteed rate of return and a similar percentage scope would leave little room for targeted federal programs outside the EB. Given the combination of the impact of the EB distribution on apportionments and program flexibility that allows states to flex much of their core program funding among these programs or to transit, the case can be made that programs that are directed toward transportation infrastructure needs that are inherently federal in nature should be outside the scope of the EB. Perhaps an option would be Congress to redefine scope in a way that only programs that serve what are clearly federal purposes could be outside the scope of the EB. These programs could be designated in law as being inherently federal. Any other programs whether formula or discretionary would be retained within the scope of the EB. The EB debate would then be focused on a more clearly defined concept of scope. Doing this would require a broad consensus among both donor and donee state Members of Congress. Donor state advocates would probably be concerned that programs defined as being federal in nature could add up over time to the detriment of donor state rates of return. The issue is whether the need for equity is greater than needs that are inherently federal.

The Impact of Scope on Earmarking

Substantial earmarking of federal-aid highway funds is a relatively recent phenomenon. Until the late 1980s, earmarks amounted to about 1% of authorized federal-aid highway spending.[34] In SAFETEA, almost $22 billion or roughly 11% of the $199.5 billion total contract authority in Title I (the highway construction title) of the bill was earmarked.

The issue of earmarking within and outside the scope of the EB surfaced quickly as an issue after the passage of SAFETEA. These SAFETEA earmarks were broadly described as being either "below" or "above the line." It is important to keep in mind that the terms above and below the line, described in this report, are not legal or official budget terms and have no formal meaning to the FHWA, but are informal terms that emerged during the surface transportation reauthorization debate. Below the line refers to earmarks in programs that are subject to provisions of the EB program. These programs are listed in SAFETEA section 1104 (a)(2). Above the line refers to funded programs and activities that are not listed in section 1104 (a)(2) and therefore not subject to the EB.

"Below the Line" Programs

The only below the line earmark program in SAFETEA is the High Priority Project program (HPP). It is, however, by far the largest of the earmarked programs in the Act. SAFETEA provided almost $15 billion under the HPP.

HPP earmarks allow Members of Congress to define their project priorities through the authorization process to their State DOTs.[35] HPP earmarks, however, do not add money to a state's total below the line funding (i.e., the total of core formula funds plus total HPP funds). This seemingly counterintuitive situation occurs because the below the line funding is subject to the EB Program. As has been mentioned earlier, under the EB, funds are distributed across the formula programs under a complex calculation that is designed to assure that all states get a certain minimum share of the below the line funding. Because the total funding under the line is fixed in the authorization bill, this leads to the situation where states that do not get many HPP earmarks tend to receive, in a relative sense, larger distributions from the EB program while states that get a high value of HPP earmarks tend to receive relatively smaller EB distributions (or no EB distribution). This means that the total amount received by a state under the line tends to be roughly the same whether or not they receive high or low dollar totals of HPP funds.

A further implication of this situation is that the more of a state's total below the line funding is derived from HPP funds the less funding is ultimately available to the state for the federal-aid highway core formula programs, upon which the state DOTs depend to fulfill their state transportation improvement plans.

"Above the Line" Programs

In SAFETEA the major earmarked programs above the line are the National Corridor Infrastructure Improvement Program ($1.9 billion), Projects of National and Regional Significance ($1.8 billion), and Transportation Improvements ($2.5 billion

In contrast to the below the line earmarks, these earmarks have no direct impact on the core formula programs' share of the below the line funding and are viewed as providing additional funding to the state DOTs.

Should policymakers decide to allow earmarking in the upcoming reauthorization legislation, what programs and how much funding should be above or below the line could be an issue.

The Impact of Scope on Penalties

Money forgone due to penalties, such as the penalty for transferring Highway Bridge Program funds, that are, at least in theory, imposed prior to distribution of the EB tend to, in effect, be replaced with EB funds. What the penalty takes away, the EB gives back.[36] Congress could also consider eliminating the counteracting impact of the EB distribution on the FAHP penalty provisions perhaps by imposing the penalties after the distribution of the EB funding. This could affect some states guaranteed percentage share, however.

Minimum Guarantee for Transit?

Although the minimum guarantee/equity remedy debate during the current surface transportation reauthorization debate in Congress has focused exclusively on a guaranteed rate of return on payments to the highway account, some have argued that a similar guarantee should be applied to payments to the mass transit account of the HTF.[37] The mass transit account is credited with the revenues from 2.86 cents of the 18.4 cents federal fuel tax (0.1 cents per gallon of this amount is also directed to the unrelated Leaking Underground Storage Trust Fund). Roughly 80% of the Federal Transit Administration's funding comes from the mass transit account, with the remaining funding provided by treasury general funds. The distribution of nearly all of these funds is, by formula and by earmark, from the federal government to the individual transit authorities (i.e., it differs from the highway programs which are funded through the state DOTs). From a state perspective, the program set-up tends to favor states that have large cities with existing fixed guideway type transit systems (heavy rail, light rail, dedicated bus lanes). Rural states and states with bus dependent transit tend to get less. The top five states receiving federal transit funding (as of FY2007), California, New York, New Jersey, Illinois, and Pennsylvania, received 53% of total transit obligations. Some transit donor states see their tax payments as subsidizing the urbanized states and argue that they have transit needs themselves that are unmet. They also argue that FTA programs unfairly underfund bus-only transit systems in general and that the need for public transportation in rural areas is, in particular, mostly ignored by the current funding distribution.

Supporters of the FTA programs can make a number of arguments in defense of the uneven geographic distribution of transit funding. The main argument is one of program national purpose. Under the statement of policies, findings, and purposes in 49 U.S.C. 1501, the focus is clearly on urban mass transportation with a goal to "efficiently maximize mobility of individuals and goods in and through urbanized areas and minimize transportation-related fuel consumption and air pollution." For transit systems to be efficient they need to serve areas of concentrated population. A mass transit 95% guaranteed rate of return would shift large amounts of funding to less densely populated areas where the number of people served would be low and the costs per passenger mile would be high (i.e. would lead to inefficiencies). Some would also argue that the support for a transit minimum guarantee is really based on the assumption by states that they could flex a significant portion of their transit funding to highway programs. Transit donee states may argue that a transit guaranteed rate of return would punish the urban areas that have taken the initiative to build, in some cases before significant federal funding was available, transit systems that are in line with federal policy goals of enhancing urban mobility, reducing fuel consumption, and improving air quality. Finally, transit interests argue that the role of cities as economic centers means that urban mobility benefits not just the cities but the nation as a whole.

The transit minimum guarantee debate has not garnered wide-spread support during the current reauthorization cycles but it would not be surprising for some form of transit equity provision to be at issue in the next reauthorization cycle. The big losers could be California and New York. Interestingly, some states that view themselves as highway donor states are major beneficiaries of the transit program. For example, should California and New Jersey support a donor state position on payments to the highway account of the HTF, they could be in the position of having to oppose a transit minimum guarantee or risk a loss of much more transit funding than they gained through the highway program guarantee. In addition, such a major shift in funding would probably require a major rewriting of the federal transit programs for the programs to make sense as a whole. It would also overturn what many see as the great compromise of 1982 under which the transit account of the HTF was created. Transit dependent states supported an expanded highway program in return.

Devolve the Highway Program to the States?

One approach to the donor-donee controversy that attracted attention during the debate prior to passage of TEA-21, but that has not yet garnered much interest in the current reauthorization debate, would be to simply devolve most of the federal highway program role to the states.[38] The Transportation Empowerment Act (H.R. 1470 and S. 667, 105th Congress), sponsored by former Senator Connie Mack of Florida and former Representative John Kasich of Ohio, would have devolved much of the federal highway program role to the states.[39] Only a program for maintaining the Interstate System, federal lands highways, National Security Highways, Emergency Relief, and a proposed Infrastructure Special Assistance Fund would have remained federal. A four year phase out of 12 cents of the federal gas tax would have corresponded with the declining federal role. States would have had the option of replacing the declining federal taxes with gas tax increases of their own. States would then have had the freedom to spend, or not spend, on their own roads and transit systems as they saw fit.

Although this proposal garnered some support from advocates of a reduced federal role in transportation, it did not obtain broad support from many governors, state legislatures, or state DOTs, many of whom were wary of the political implications of pushing large replacement gas tax increases through their state legislatures, and at the same time keeping these funds dedicated to transportation. Despite the failure of devolution proposals to be enacted, some would make the case that the closer the EB guarantee gets to 100%, the more sense devolution to the states makes.

They would argue that as the guaranteed rate of return increases, the FHWA's role becomes more like a tax collector for the states. The need for and efficiency of the federal government as middleman comes into question. At this time, however, there appears to be limited interest at the state or federal level for any radical change in the federal role in the highway program.

On the other hand, some argue that, given the nature of the practical politics required to pass surface transportation reauthorization bills, the perceived inequitable nature of the funding distribution relative to payments to the HTF is intractable. From this view, some argue that devolution is the solution to both the rate-of-return inequity in particular and the donor-donee issue as a whole.[40]

Appendix A. Legislative History

Surface Transportation Assistance Act of 1982 (STAA)

STAA (P.L. 94-424) authorized a significant increase in funding for the Federal-Aid Highway system for FY1983-FY1986 and included a provision designed to mitigate the dissatisfaction of donor states by providing that each state would receive a minimum allocation (also known as the minimum guarantee) from the core FHWA programs.[41] Specifically, the bill ordered the FHWA to allocate among the states sufficient funds to assure that each state's total apportionments from the core highway and safety programs (Interstate Highway Substitution, Primary, Secondary, Interstate, Urban, Bridge Replacement and Rehabilitation, hazard elimination, and rail-highway crossings, and section 203 of the Highway Safety Act of 1973) would not be less than 85% of the percentage of estimated tax payments each state paid into the highway account of the HTF. These "equity adjustment" allocations could be obligated to the core highway programs.

Surface Transportation and Uniform Relocation Assistance Act of 1987 (STURAA)

STURAA (P.L. 100-17) authorized the Federal-Aid Highway Program for FY1987-1991, retaining the 85% minimum allocation, but altering the basis of its calculation. The act revised the calculation to include the allocated (sometimes referred to as discretionary) programs, with the exception of federal lands programs and safety programs. For FY1987 and FY1988 emergency relief funds and interstate construction discretionary funds were not included in the calculation. The act continued the minimum allocation provision established by STAA.

With the exception of the changes in the treatment of the minimum guarantees, the formulas for allocation of funds under STAA and STURAA remained the same. Minor changes were made in the criteria for awarding discretionary program grants. Emergency Relief and Federal Lands Highways grants continued to be distributed on a project-by-project and needs basis, respectively.

Intermodal Surface Transportation Efficiency Act of 1991 (ISTEA)

ISTEA (P.L. 102-240) reauthorized surface transportation programs, including Federal-Aid Highway Programs, for FY1992-FY1997, making major changes in the overall program structure, program formulas, minimum allocation, and other provisions that could impact the state donor-donee ratios. To a great extent, the changes were an outgrowth of the fact that the remaining unfinished portions of the interstate system would be completed under ISTEA. The act also enunciated a broader vision of the mission of federal highway programs to include air quality, alternative transportation, and historic preservation. ISTEA retained the three formula programs that provided funding for the Interstate system (Interstate Construction, Interstate Maintenance, and Interstate Highway Substitution) as well as the Bridge Replacement and

Rehabilitation Program. The other formula programs, such as, the Primary System, Secondary System, Urban System, and Urban Transportation Planning, were replaced by the National Highway System Program, the Surface Transportation Program, and the Congestion Mitigation and Air Quality Program. The distribution criteria for projects under the discretionary programs remained the same except that the Interstate Construction Program (renamed the Interstate Discretionary Program) was changed to be at the discretion of the U.S. Department of Transportation (USDOT) and the Interstate 4R (for resurfacing, restoring, rehabilitation, and reconstructing lanes on the Interstate System) program funds were now a set-aside within the new National Highway System Program.

Equity Adjustment Provisions

ISTEA included five provisions, with separate funding, designed to assure a more equitable distribution of federal funds to the states.

The 90% Guarantees

The act raised the minimum allocation to 90% of estimated state contributions to the highway account of the HTF (although narrowing its calculation to the core formula programs, scenic byways, safety belt and motorcycle safety grants).

The act also included a new minimum payments guarantee (of a broader scope than the minimum allocation discussed above) that assured that each state's apportionments (for the core formula programs) for the fiscal year and allocations (to the discretionary programs) from the previous year would be at least 90% of its estimated state contributions (i.e., calculated from all programs except special projects).

Donor State Bonus

For each fiscal year, donor states were identified by comparing projected contributions to the HTF with the apportionments to be received that year by each state. Under the donor state bonus, starting with the state with the lowest return, each state was brought up to the level of the state with the next highest level of return. This was repeated successively for each state until the ISTEA authorized program amount was exhausted.

Hold Harmless

This provision set a specific percentage that each state was to receive from the core formula highway programs plus Federal Lands Highway Programs, minimum allocation, donor state bonus, and Interstate Reimbursement. Each state received an addition to its regular apportionments to raise its total to the set percentage.

Reimbursement for Interstate Segments

ISTEA authorized $2 billion for FY1996 and FY1997 to reimburse each state for the costs to them of building segments of the Interstate System without federal assistance prior to or during the early days of the Interstate Construction Program.

Despite all of the above provisions significant gaps remained among states on their share return on contributions to the HTF. As reauthorization of ISTEA approached, dissatisfaction with the effectiveness of the equity provisions led to challenges to the ISTEA program paradigm.

Transportation Equity Act for the 21st Century (TEA-21)

The reauthorization debate that preceded passage of TEA-21 (P.L. 105-178) included a wide range of views on the donor-donee state issue and is worth reviewing because all the major underlying arguments that had emerged over time, reemerged during the TEA-21 debate. Significant characteristics of the debate included a greater, primarily regional role and virtually no role for party affiliation. Also in play were different philosophies of the appropriate role of the federal government vis-a-vis the states, differing views of whether the completion of the Interstate Highway system should trigger a reduction in federal involvement in highway construction; how national highway needs criteria can fit a return-on-the-tax-dollar view, and the influence of a large increase in gas tax revenue to the HTF on program structure.

Regional Conflict over Funding

Under ISTEA, Southern and Mid-Western States made up most donor states while Northeastern, Pacific coast, and large sparsely populated Western States made up most of the donee states. In general, donee states were satisfied with the distribution under ISTEA and supported the "ISTEA works" legislation that, in general, adhered to the ISTEA funding formulas. Most of the donor states joined "STEP-21," a coalition whose centerpiece proposal was a guarantee that each state receive at least a 95% return on its estimated contribution to the highway account of the HTF. The dominance of regional differences over party affiliation was reflected on the Senate Committee on Environment and Public Works, where the Republican committee leadership supported the donee friendly "ISTEA works" bill while a Republican colleague, sponsored the Streamlined Transportation Efficiency Program for the 21st Century (STEP 21) which included the 95 cents on the dollar guarantee, as well as program formula changes supported by donor states.

Devolution

What most observers considered a more radical approach was the Transportation Empowerment Act, sponsored by Senator Connie Mack of Florida and Representative John Kasich of Ohio. This bill would have devolved much of the federal highway program role to the states. Only a program for maintaining the Interstate System and federal lands highways would have remained federal. A four year phase out of 12 cents of the federal gas tax would have corresponded with the declining federal role. States would have had the option of replacing the declining federal taxes with gas tax increases of their own. States would then have had the freedom to spend, or not spend, on their own roads as they saw fit. Although this proposal garnered some support from advocates of a reduced federal role, it did not obtain broad support from many Governors, state legislatures, or state departments of transportation, many of whom were wary of the political implications of pushing large replacement gas tax increases through their state legislatures, and at the same time keeping these funds programmed for highways.

TEA-21 Equity Provision Changes

The equity changes that followed the debate and were included in TEA-21 were more limited than most would have expected early in the reauthorization debate. The main reason for this was the large increase (roughly 40%) in overall funding levels. Still there were equity provisions that were included in the hope that they would narrow the donor-donee divide.[42]

Minimum Guarantee

The TEA-21 minimum guarantee had three components:

Guaranteed Base Share

TEA-21 guaranteed each state a percentage share (set forth in a table in 23 U.S.C. 105) of the total program, defined as all the apportioned programs: Interstate Maintenance Program (IM), National Highway System Program (NHS), Surface Transportation Program (STP), Highway Bridge Replacement and Rehabilitation Program (HBRRP), Congestion Mitigation and Air Quality Program (CMAQ), Metropolitan Planning, Recreational Trails Program, Appalachian Development Highway System Program and Minimum Guarantee, as well as High Priority Projects.

Minimum 90.5% Share on Contributions

All states were guaranteed at least 90.5% return (up just 0.5% over ISTEA) on their share of tax contributions to the highway account of the HTF (based on the most recent year for which the data are available — generally from two fiscal years before). Using Ohio as an example, of total FY2001 highway account contributions, Ohio's percentage share contributions amounted to 3.7578%. Ohio was guaranteed 90.5% of its share of estimated FY2001 contributions and was thus guaranteed a minimum share of 3.4008% of the FY2003 apportionments (i.e., the core formula programs), plus High Priority Projects and the Minimum Guarantee itself. If the above base share was less than a 90.5% return to a state then the share was adjusted upward until the 90.5% share was reached. The money to raise shares to 90.5% was provided by "squeezing" down the percentages (but not the total amounts) of those states that were above the minimum.

Minimum State Payment

Each state was guaranteed that as part of the minimum guarantee it would receive at least $1 million in Minimum Guarantee funds.

It is important to keep in mind that the TEA-21 Minimum Guarantee was a compromise provision. It was constructed in such a way as to give money to all states in the process of bringing the donor states up to the 90.5% minimum guarantee.[43] Each state received the $1 million minimum. Then, the lowest percent share of any state or the District of Columbia (generally the District) was used to extrapolate the total program funding (as defined under Minimum Guarantee) needed for the District to retain its total program percentage. For example, using FY2003, because the District's program level percent share of 0.3860% was lower than the District's percentage of total apportionments (roughly 0.5%), high priority projects, and $1 million guarantee, and because no money could be taken back, the only way to achieve the District's 0.3860 % was to raise the national total. To achieve that percentage for the District, a total FY2003 program size of $27.76 billion was needed. The total Minimum Guarantee program funding needed to achieve this total was over $6 billion. Ironically, the degree of the District's donor status meant more money for all states (in absolute, not relative terms).

Minimum Guarantee Distribution

Each year, the first $2.8 billion of Minimum Guarantee funds were administered as STP funds (see STP discussion below) except that set-asides for Transportation Enhancements, Safety Construction, and certain population-based sub-state allocations did not benefit from this distribution. Any Minimum Guarantee funds above $2.8 million were distributed to the five core programs: STP, Interstate Maintenance (IM); Highway Bridge Replacement and Rehabilitation Program (HBRRP); National Highway System (NHS); Congestion Mitigation and Air Quality Improvement (CMAQ). The distributions to the states were based on the ratio of each core program's apportionment to the total apportionment of all five programs for each state.[44]

Program Formula Changes

TEA-21 also included formula changes that were perceived as benefitting donor states.[45]

Interstate Maintenance Program

TEA-21 reduced the weight given each state's share of total Interstate Highway System lane miles and total state share of Interstate System vehicle miles traveled to 1/3 each and created a third weighed category that provided the final 1/3 be distributed based on each state's percent share of annual contributions to the HTF attributable to commercial vehicles. This final weighted third was expected to benefit donor states.

Surface Transportation Program

STP's apportionment formula under TEA-21 was weighted 35% to estimated state share of tax payments paid into the highway account of the HTF. This also was expected to benefit donor states. State share of total lane miles of Federal-aid highways (25%) and share of total vehicle miles traveled on Federal-aid highways (40%) were the other weighted attributes in the STP apportionment formula.

National Highway System Program

TEA-21's NHS apportionment formula was weighted at 30% of a state's share of diesel fuel used on highways. Some observers expected that this would also benefit donor states.

The Resolution of the TEA-21 Donor-Donee Debate

In the end, what many observers had predicted would be a major battle between donor and donee states was resolved relatively amicably.[46] This occurred despite the donor states only being able to achieve a 0.5% increase in the minimum guarantee percentage and formula changes, which some predicted would have little impact on donor state returns on the tax revenues these states paid to the highway account of the HTF. Some even argued that donor states would have been better off if TEA-21 had retained the ISTEA formulas. In the case of TEA-21, what alleviated the concerns of STEP-21 and other donor state advocates was the amount of money available during TEA-21's lifetime. By shifting, in 1997, revenues generated by the 4.3 cent deficit reduction gas tax to the HTF, Congress was able to provide large increases in highway funding for all states. The extra money made the donor-donee debate less urgent to the donor states. As the TEA-21 authorization neared its expiration (FY2003), however, the donor-donee state issue resurfaced.[47]

TEA-21 created a so-called "firewall" around the highway account to prevent highway account funds being used for non-highway purposes. It also required that spending from the highway account approximately equal the revenues flowing into the account on an annualized basis. To make sure that annual spending and revenues were roughly equal each year, the Act provided for Revenue Aligned Budget Authority (RABA) to be distributed proportionally across all states to maintain a balance of spending and revenue flows. Although these changes did not affect the operation of the TEA-21 minimum guarantee they did have an overall impact on the availability of funds to support the minimum guarantee program, which was funded on a "such sums as necessary" basis.

APPENDIX B. HOW FHWA CALCULATES THE EQUITY BONUS APPORTIONMENT[48]

Table B-1. Calculating the Equity Bonus Apportionments for FY2008

Step 1:	Determination of Minimum Program Share					Revised July 2008	
	Based on Contributions to Highway Account			Based on Special Rule (Qualified States Only)		Minimum Share	
State	FY 2006 Highway Account Contributions ($000)	Share of Contributions	Share Based on Contributions (Share of Contributions times 92%)	Does State Qualify for Special Rule?	Share of Apportionments and High Priority Projects under TEA-21	Greater of Two Shares	
	(1)	(2)	(3)	(4)	(5)	(6)	The Equity Bonus (EB) is calculated after
ALABAMA	660,130	1.9598%	1.8030%	Yes	1.99950%	1.9995%	All other apportionments.
ALASKA	119,894	0.3559%	0.3275%	Yes	1.17044%	1.1704%	
ARIZONA	707,320	2.0999%	1.9319%	Yes	1.65867%	1.9319%	The Equity Bonus provision guarantees
ARKANSAS	425,049	1.2619%	1.1609%	Yes	1.30921%	1.3092%	that each State's share of the sum of apportioned programs--IM, NHS, STP, Bridge, CMAQ, Rec. Trails, ADHS, Metro Planning, HSIP, Safe Routes to School, Rail-Highway Grade Crossing, Border, and the Equity Bonus itself--along with High Priority Projects will be at least a specified percentage (92% for FY 2008) of its share of Highway Account contributions
CALIFORNIA	3,376,775	10.0250%	9.2230%			9.2230%	
COLORADO	503,241	1.4940%	1.3745%	Yes	1.19826%	1.3745%	
CONNECTICUT	339,201	1.0070%	0.9265%			0.9265%	
DELAWARE	89,414	0.2655%	0.2442%	Yes	0.43478%	0.4348%	
DISTRICT OF COL.	28,484	0.0846%	0.0778%	Yes	0.38859%	0.3886%	
FLORIDA	1,839,725	5.4618%	5.0249%	Yes	4.66821%	5.0249%	

Step 1: Determination of Minimum Program Share — Revised July 2008

State	Based on Contributions to Highway Account			Based on Special Rule (Qualified States Only)		Minimum Share
	FY 2006 Highway Account Contributions ($000)	Share of Contributions	Share Based on Contributions (Share of Contributions times 92%)	Does State Qualify for Special Rule?	Share of Apportionments and High Priority Projects under TEA-21	Greater of Two Shares
	(1)	(2)	(3)	(4)	(5)	(6)
GEORGIA	1,324,981	3.9336%	3.6189%			3.6189%
HAWAII	83,576	0.2481%	0.2283%			0.2283%
IDAHO	174,310	0.5175%	0.4761%	Yes	0.76033%	0.7603%
ILLINOIS	1,270,327	3.7714%	3.4697%			3.4697%
INDIANA	929,679	2.7600%	2.5392%			2.5392%
IOWA	429,483	1.2751%	1.1731%			1.1731%
KANSAS	336,280	0.9984%	0.9185%			0.9185%
KENTUCKY	618,546	1.8364%	1.6894%	Yes	1.73855%	1.7385%
LOUISIANA	570,683	1.6943%	1.5587%	Yes	1.59396%	1.5940%
MAINE	169,306	0.5026%	0.4624%			0.4624%
MARYLAND	586,076	1.7400%	1.6008%			1.6008%
MASSACHUSETTS	558,798	1.6590%	1.5263%			1.5263%
MICHIGAN	1,042,640	3.0954%	2.8478%			2.8478%
MINNESOTA	615,227	1.8265%	1.6804%			1.6804%
MISSISSIPPI	444,328	1.3191%	1.2136%	Yes	1.23459%	1.2346%
MISSOURI	827,700	2.4573%	2.2607%	Yes	2.36963%	2.3696%

The Equity Bonus (EB) is calculated after

In columns (1)-(3) we (FHWA) determine the share of apportionments (including the EB) and high priority projects that a State must receive to meet the guaranteed 92% return on its share of Highway Account contributions.

This computation is based on estimated contributions for the latest fiscal for which data are available. For the FY 2008 Equity Bonus calculations, FY 2006 Highway Account contributions are used (shown in column (1)).

In column (2) we determine what share of the total Highway Account contributions came from each State by dividing each State's

Table B-1. (Continued)

Step 1:	Determination of Minimum Program Share					Revised July 2008	
	Based on Contributions to Highway Account			Based on Special Rule (Qualified States Only)		Minimum Share	
State	FY 2006 Highway Account Contributions ($000)	Share of Contributions	Share Based on Contributions (Share of Contributions times 92%)	Does State Qualify for Special Rule?	Share of Apportionments and High Priority Projects under TEA-21	Greater of Two Shares	
	(1)	(2)	(3)	(4)	(5)	(6)	The Equity Bonus (EB) is calculated after
MONTANA	153,906	0.4569%	0.4204%	Yes	0.97579%	0.9758%	
NEBRASKA	257,528	0.7646%	0.7034%	Yes	0.76357%	0.7636%	
NEBRASKA	257,528	0.7646%	0.7034%	Yes	0.76357%	0.7636%	Contributions by the national total.
NEVADA	288,552	0.8567%	0.7881%	Yes	0.71225%	0.7881%	
NEW HAMPSHIRE	139,570	0.4144%	0.3812%			0.3812%	
NEW JERSEY	950,270	2.8212%	2.5955%			2.5955%	Since the Equity Bonus promises a 92%
NEW MEXICO	304,666	0.9045%	0.8321%	Yes	0.97065%	0.9706%	return on each State's share of Highway Account contributions, we multiply the share
NEW YORK	1,323,492	3.9292%	3.6149%			3.6149%	of contributions in column (2) by 92%. The result is in column (3).
NORTH CAROLINA	1,016,722	3.0185%	2.7770%			2.7770%	
NORTH DAKOTA	107,620	0.3195%	0.2939%	Yes	0.64402%	0.6440%	
OHIO	1,317,878	3.9125%	3.5995%			3.5995%	
OKLAHOMA	525,055	1.5588%	1.4341%	Yes	1.52120%	1.5212%	
OREGON	410,792	1.2196%	1.1220%	Yes	1.21695%	1.2169%	For States that qualify, the Equity Bonus
PENNSYLVANIA	1,302,050	3.8656%	3.5563%			3.5563%	guarantees that the State's share of
RHODE ISLAND	81,237	0.2412%	0.2219%			0.2219%	apportionments (including the EB) and High
SOUTH CAROLINA	596,456	1.7708%	1.6291%			1.6291%	Priority Projects will be at least equal to its
SOUTH DAKOTA	123,133	0.3656%	0.3363%	Yes	0.71620%	0.7162%	share of apportionments and High Priority

Step 1:	Determination of Minimum Program Share					Revised July 2008	
	Based on Contributions to Highway Account			Based on Special Rule (Qualified States Only)		Minimum Share	
State	FY 2006 Highway Account Contributions ($000)	Share of Contributions	Share Based on Contributions (Share of Contributions times 92%)	Does State Qualify for Special Rule?	Share of Apportionments and High Priority Projects under TEA-21	Greater of Two Shares	
	(1)	(2)	(3)	(4)	(5)	(6)	The Equity Bonus (EB) is calculated after
TENNESSEE	818,963	2.4314%	2.2368%			2.2368%	Projects under TEA-21. In columns (4) and (5), we show whether a State qualifies for this provision(detail on next page) and its share of TEA-21 apportionments.
TEXAS	2,952,274	8.7648%	8.0636%	Yes	7.54262%	8.0636%	
UTAH	286,014	0.8491%	0.7812%	Yes	0.77359%	0.7812%	
VERMONT	72,054	0.2139%	0.1968%	Yes	0.44923%	0.4492%	
VIRGINIA	960,353	2.8511%	2.6230%			2.6230%	
WASHINGTON	618,937	1.8375%	1.6905%			1.6905%	
WEST VIRGINIA	225,074	0.6682%	0.6147%	Yes	1.11009%	1.1101%	Column (6) shows the greater of the two
WISCONSIN	612,349	1.8180%	1.6725%	Yes	1.95628%	1.9563%	shares--the one based on the 92.0% return
WYOMING	167,308	0.4967%	0.4570%	Yes	0.68588%	0.6859%	and the TEA-21 share. Each state will receive not High Priority Projects.
TOTAL	33,683,426	100%	92.0%	27	40.563024%	97.1141%	

Source: FHWA.

Table B-2. Step 2: Computing the Dollar Floor (Equity Bonus Apportionment - FY 2008)

Step 2: Compute Dollar Floor

120% of Average Annual TEA-21 Apportionments and High Priority Projects (HPP)

State	TEA-21 Aver. Ann. Apportionments and HPPs 1	120% of TEA-21 Average Annual 2
ALABAMA	558,328,105	669,993,726
ALASKA	326,827,381	392,192,857
ARIZONA	463,157,671	555,789,205
ARKANSAS	365,575,583	438,690,700
CALIFORNIA	2,553,243,954	3,063,892,745
COLORADO	334,594,734	401,513,680
CONNECTICUT	416,387,905	499,665,485
DELAWARE	121,404,732	145,685,678
DIST. OF COL.	108,507,402	130,208,882
FLORIDA	1,303,522,941	1,564,227,529
GEORGIA	985,048,097	1,182,057,716
HAWAII	141,958,070	170,349,683
IDAHO	212,310,656	254,772,788
ILLINOIS	927,169,304	1,112,603,165
INDIANA	660,387,364	792,464,836
IOWA	329,554,208	395,465,049
KANSAS	321,304,097	385,564,917
KENTUCKY	485,461,684	582,554,020

In addition to the two share based approaches described on previous pages, the Equity Bonus guarantees that each state will receive apportionments (including the EB) plus High Priority Projects equal to at least a certain percentage (120% for 2008) of its average annual TEA-21 apportionments and High Priority Projects. Note this floor is expressed in dollars, not in program shares.

Column (1) shows the average annual TEA-21 apportionments and High Priority Project allocations.

Column (2) shows the average annual Multiplied by 120%.

Step 2: Compute Dollar Floor

120% of Average Annual TEA-21 Apportionments and High Priority Projects (HPP)

State	TEA-21 Aver. Ann. Apportionments and HPPs	120% of TEA-21 Average Annual	
	1	2	
LOUISIANA	445,088,558	534,106,269	Regardless of the share calculations in step 1, no State will receive fewer dollars than the amount shown in column (2).
MAINE	146,044,554	175,253,465	
MARYLAND	443,219,686	531,863,623	
MASSACHUSETTS	515,085,233	618,102,280	
MICHIGAN	884,266,420	1,061,119,703	
MINNESOTA	410,879,135	493,054,962	
MISSISSIPPI	344,740,210	413,688,252	
MISSOURI	661,682,742	794,019,290	
MONTANA	272,474,525	326,969,430	
NEBRASKA	213,215,560	255,858,672	
NEVADA	198,883,564	238,660,277	
NEW HAMPSHIRE	141,895,714	170,274,857	
NEW JERSEY	725,530,617	870,636,741	
NEW MEXICO	271,038,261	325,245,913	
NEW YORK	1,415,097,862	1,698,117,434	
NORTH CAROLINA	778,064,319	933,677,183	
NORTH DAKOTA	179,831,478	215,797,773	
OHIO	963,308,164	1,155,969,796	

Table B-2. (Continued)

Step 2:	Compute Dollar Floor	
	120% of Average Annual TEA-21 Apportionments and High Priority Projects (HPP)	
	TEA-21 Aver. Ann. Apportionments and HPPs	120% of TEA-21 Average Annual
State	1	2
OKLAHOMA	424,770,200	509,724,240
OREGON	339,813,375	407,776,050
PENNSYLVANIA	1,383,667,693	1,660,401,232
RHODE ISLAND	164,327,250	197,192,700
SOUTH CAROLINA	457,541,146	549,049,375
SOUTH DAKOTA	199,986,896	239,984,275
TENNESSEE	629,386,744	755,264,092
TEXAS	2,106,157,841	2,527,389,409
UTAH	216,012,661	259,215,193
VERMONT	125,440,355	150,528,425
VIRGINIA	711,843,995	854,212,794
WASHINGTON	491,625,367	589,950,440
WEST VIRGINIA	309,975,967	371,971,161
WISCONSIN	546,259,882	655,511,858
WYOMING	191,521,113	229,825,336
TOTAL	27,923,420,971	33,508,105,165

Source: FHWA.

Table B-3. Step 3: Raising States to the Dollar Floor

State	Apportionments (Excluding Equity Bonus) plus High Priority Projects (1)	Dollar Floor 120% of Average Annual TEA-Annual21 $ (2)	Greater of Column (1) or Column (2) (3)	In the previous step, we determined a minimum share and a dollar floor for each State.
ALABAMA	518,758,511	669,993,726	669,993,726	Note that the overall programs level--remains unknown. That is, minimum share of WHAT?
ALASKA	252,879,164	392,192,857	392,192,857	
ARIZONA	473,388,271	555,789,205	555,789,205	
ARKANSAS	372,867,639	438,690,700	438,690,700	First we compare the amount already apportioned
CALIFORNIA	2,862,999,103	3,063,892,745	3,063,892,745	to each State plus its High Priority Project funds
COLORADO	430,414,847	401,513,680	430,414,847	to the dollar floor from Step 2.
CONNECTICUT	385,900,595	499,665,485	499,665,485	
DELAWARE	142,910,640	145,685,678	145,685,678	
DIST. OF COL.	149,550,231	130,208,882	149,550,231	
FLORIDA	1,136,899,652	1,564,227,529	1,564,227,529	Column (1) shows the amount apportioned
GEORGIA	837,209,001	1,182,057,716	1,182,057,716	to each State, excluding the Equity Bonus, plus
HAWAII	153,257,829	170,349,683	170,349,683	its High Priority Project funds.
IDAHO	195,182,788	254,772,788	254,772,788	
ILLINOIS	1,003,228,485	1,112,603,165	1,112,603,165	

Table B-3. (Continued)

State	Apportionments (Excluding Equity Bonus) plus High Priority Projects (1)	Dollar Floor 120% of Average Annual TEA-Annual21 $ (2)	Greater of Column (1) or Column (2) (3)	In the previous step, we determined a minimum share and a dollar floor for each State.
INDIANA	592,678,227	792,464,836	792,464,836	Column (2) shows the dollar floor from Step 2,
IOWA	402,742,945	395,465,049	402,742,945	column (2).
KANSAS	365,424,382	385,564,917	385,564,917	In Column (3), we see the greater of the
KENTUCKY	520,142,182	582,554,020	582,554,020	two dollar figures ensuring that each
LOUISIANA	531,951,536	534,106,269	534,106,269	State is at or above the dollar floor.
MAINE	186,229,357	175,253,465	186,229,357	
MARYLAND	514,670,978	531,863,623	531,863,623	Nine States, shown in bold, were already
MASSACHUSETTS	579,819,034	618,102,280	618,102,280	above the floor. These are Colorado,
MICHIGAN	835,151,315	1,061,119,703	1,061,119,703	the District of Columbia, Iowa, Maine, Nebraska,
MINNESOTA	486,224,560	493,054,962	493,054,962	Oregon, Rhode Island, Vermont, and Washington.
MISSISSIPPI	393,655,210	413,688,252	413,688,252	These states are NOT adjusted
MISSOURI	670,568,742	794,019,290	794,019,290	downward. The Equity Bonus provision works
MONTANA	240,689,458	326,969,430	326,969,430	by distributing additional funds to States, not
NEBRASKA	260,348,979	255,858,672	260,348,979	by taking funds away from States.
NEVADA	227,911,436	238,660,277	238,660,277	
NEW HAMPSHIRE	142,548,878	170,274,857	170,274,857	
NEW JERSEY	727,027,441	870,636,741	870,636,741	
NEW MEXICO	280,609,925	325,245,913	325,245,913	
NEW YORK	1,475,237,149	1,698,117,434	1,698,117,434	
NORTH CAROLINA	750,618,511	933,677,183	933,677,183	

State	Apportionments (Excluding Equity Bonus) plus High Priority Projects	Dollar Floor 120% of Average Annual TEA-Annual21 $	Greater of Column (1) or Column (2)
	(1)	(2)	(3)
NORTH DAKOTA	216,549,092	215,797,773	216,549,092
OHIO	991,210,977	1,155,969,796	1,155,969,796
OKLAHOMA	464,998,785	509,724,240	509,724,240
OREGON	412,006,256	407,776,050	412,006,256
PENNSYLVANIA	1,356,402,848	1,660,401,232	1,660,401,232
RHODE ISLAND	203,618,492	197,192,700	203,618,492
SOUTH CAROLINA	431,888,278	549,049,375	549,049,375
SOUTH DAKOTA	218,563,429	239,984,275	239,984,275
TENNESSEE	618,721,850	755,264,092	755,264,092
TEXAS	1,997,563,619	2,527,389,409	2,527,389,409
UTAH	247,072,575	259,215,193	259,215,193
VERMONT	170,453,328	150,528,425	170,453,328
VIRGINIA	709,871,843	854,212,794	854,212,794
WASHINGTON	597,499,500	589,950,440	597,499,500
WEST VIRGINIA	337,062,132	371,971,161	371,971,161
WISCONSIN	473,219,956	655,511,858	655,511,858
WYOMING	217,171,882	229,825,336	229,825,336
TOTAL	28,763,571,843	33,508,105,165	33,617,973,053

Source: FHWA.

In the previous step, we determined a minimum share and a dollar floor for each State.

Table B-4. Step 4: Determine Program Level—First Attempt

STEP 4—FIRST ATTEMPT	Apportion-ments (Excluding EB) plus HPP Projects Raised To Floor	Share of National Total	Minimum Share (From Step 1)	Required Share for States Currently Below Required Share	Minimum Program for Other States	1st Try Results	In the previous step, we determined a minimum share and a dollar floor for each State. We then raised each State's funding to the calculated floor.
State	(1)	(2)	(3)	(4)	(5)	(6)	
ALABAMA	669,993,726	1.9930%	1.9995%	1.9995%		726,802,802	
ALASKA	392,192,857	1.1666%	1.1704%	1.1704%		425,447,070	
ARIZONA	555,789,205	1.6533%	1.9319%	1.9319%		702,236,235	
ARKANSAS	438,690,700	1.3049%	1.3092%	1.3092%		475,887,486	Column (1) shows the apportionments to each State thus plus High Priority Project funds after bringing each State up to the floor as required in step 3.
CALIFORNIA	3,063,892,745	9.1139%	9.2230%	9.2230%		3,352,504,893	
COLORADO	430,414,847	1.2803%	1.3745%	1.3745%		499,624,024	
CONNECTICUT	499,665,485	1.4863%	0.9265%		499,665,485	499,665,485	
DELAWARE	145,685,678	0.4334%	0.4348%	0.4348%		158,038,434	
DIST. OF COL.	149,550,231	0.4449%	0.3886%		149,550,231	149,550,231	Column (2) shows what share of the total each State has received thus far.
FLORIDA	1,564,227,529	4.6530%	5.0249%	5.0249%		1,826,502,229	
GEORGIA	1,182,057,716	3.5161%	3.6189%	3.6189%		1,315,457,881	
HAWAII	170,349,683	0.5067%	0.2283%		170,349,683	170,349,683	Column (3) repeats the minimum share in step 1.
IDAHO	254,772,788	0.7578%	0.7603%	0.7603%		276,375,090	
ILLINOIS	1,112,603,165	3.3095%	3.4697%	3.4697%		1,261,196,699	
INDIANA	792,464,836	2.3573%	2.5392%	2.5392%		922,997,060	In column (4) we show the minimum share states that have not yet achieved it through the initial apportionments and High Priority plus the amount added.

STEP 4—FIRST ATTEMPT	Apportion-ments (Excluding EB) plus HPP Projects Raised To Floor	Share of National Total	Minimum Share (From Step 1)	Required Share for States Currently Below Required Share	Minimum Program for Other States	1st Try Results	In the previous step, we determined a minimum share and a dollar floor for each State. We then raised each State's funding to the calculated floor.
State	(1)	(2)	(3)	(4)	(5)	(6)	
IOWA	402,742,945	1.1980%	1.1731%		402,742,945	402,742,945	
KANSAS	385,564,917	1.1469%	0.9185%		385,564,917	385,564,917	
KENTUCKY	582,554,020	1.7329%	1.7385%	1.7385%		631,949,044	
LOUISIANA	534,106,269	1.5888%	1.5940%	1.5940%		579,393,386	
MAINE	186,229,357	0.5540%	0.4624%		186,229,357	186,229,357	
MARYLAND	531,863,623	1.5821%	1.6008%	1.6008%		581,863,659	For states that are already (or above) the share, column (5) shows the dollar
MASSACHUSET	618,102,280	1.8386%	1.5263%		618,102,280	618,102,280	amount they have already received
MICHIGAN	1,061,119,703	3.1564%	2.8478%		1,061,119,703	1,061,119,703	from the initial apportionments and
MINNESOTA	493,054,962	1.4666%	1.6804%	1.6804%		610,805,140	High Priority Projects the amount
MISSISSIPPI	413,688,252	1.2306%	1.2346%	1.2346%		448,765,069	added (if any) to reach the floor set by.
MISSOURI	794,019,290	2.3619%	2.3696%	2.3696%		861,344,551	the Equity Bonus provision
MONTANA	326,969,430	0.9726%	0.9758%	0.9758%		354,693,318	
NEBRASKA	260,348,979	0.7744%	0.7636%		260,348,979	260,348,979	At this point an interative process starts to
NEVADA	238,660,277	0.7099%	0.7881%	0.7881%		286,478,072	determine the overall program level--the of the initial apportionments,
NEW	170,274,857	0.5065%	0.3812%		170,274,857	170,274,857	High Priority Projects, AND the Equity Bonus.
NEW JERSEY	870,636,741	2.5898%	2.5955%	2.5955%		943,440,065	
NEW MEXICO	325,245,913	0.9675%	0.9706%	0.9706%		352,823,664	

Table B-4. (Continued)

STEP 4—FIRST ATTEMPT	Apportion-ments (Excluding EB) plus HPP Projects Raised To Floor	Share of National Total	Minimum Share (From Step 1)	Required Share for States Currently Below Required Share	Minimum Program for Other States	1st Try Results	In the previous step, we determined a minimum share and a dollar floor for each State. We then raised each State's funding to the calculated floor.
State	(1)	(2)	(3)	(4)	(5)	(6)	
NEW YORK	1,698,117,434	5.0512%	3.6149%		1,698,117,434	1,698,117,434	First we set a target overall program level MIGHT meet all of the criteria set in the Bonus provision.
NORTH	933,677,183	2.7773%	2.7770%		933,677,183	933,677,183	
NORTH	216,549,092	0.6441%	0.6440%		216,549,092	216,549,092	
OHIO	1,155,969,796	3.4385%	3.5995%	3.5995%		1,308,405,933	
OKLAHOMA	509,724,240	1.5162%	1.5212%	1.5212%		552,943,993	Thus far, it appears that certain States will "floor states," that is, their program level be set based on the Equity Bonus dollar provision.
OREGON	412,006,256	1.2256%	1.2169%		412,006,256	412,006,256	
PENNSYLVANIA	1,660,401,232	4.9390%	3.5563%		1,660,401,232	1,660,401,232	
RHODE ISLAND	203,618,492	0.6057%	0.2219%		203,618,492	203,618,492	
SOUTH	549,049,375	1.6332%	1.6291%		549,049,375	549,049,375	
SOUTH	239,984,275	0.7139%	0.7162%	0.7162%		260,332,652	It also appears that the "share states," that the States whose program level will be on one of the Equity Bonus share minimums will make up 69.4613% of the overall at the national level.
TENNESSEE	755,264,092	2.2466%	2.2368%		755,264,092	755,264,092	
TEXAS	2,527,389,409	7.5180%	8.0636%	8.0636%		2,931,054,936	
UTAH	259,215,193	0.7711%	0.7812%	0.7812%		283,958,314	
VERMONT	170,453,328	0.5070%	0.4492%		170,453,328	170,453,328	
VIRGINIA	854,212,794	2.5409%	2.6230%	2.6230%		953,450,595	
WASHINGTON	597,499,500	1.7773%	1.6905%		597,499,500	597,499,500	These two facts provide a reasonable 1st for the total program level.

STEP 4— FIRST ATTEMPT	Apportion- ments (Excluding EB) plus HPP Projects Raised To Floor	Share of National Total	Minimum Share (From Step 1)	Required Share for States Currently Below Required Share	Minimum Program for Other States	1st Try Results	In the previous step, we determined a minimum share and a dollar floor for each State. We then raised each State's funding to the calculated floor.
State	(1)	(2)	(3)	(4)	(5)	(6)	
WEST VIRGINIA	371,971,161	1.1065%	1.1101%	1.1101%		403,510,767	These two facts provide a reasonable 1st for the total program level of
WISCONSIN	655,511,858	1.9499%	1.9563%	1.9563%		711,093,010	Column (6) shows the result of giving the "share states" their percentage of
WYOMING	229,825,336	0.6836%	0.6859%	0.6859%		249,312,332	the target.
TOTAL	33,617,973,053	100.0000%	97.1141%	69.4613%	11,100,584,42	36,349,272,823	
Target Program =	11,100,584,420 / (1-.694613)		36,349,272,823				

Source: FHWA.

Table B-5. Step 5: Determine Program Level—Second Attempt

STEP 5: SECOND ATTEMPT	1st Try Results	Share of National Total	Minimum Share (From Step 1)	Any State Below Minimum Share?	Required Share	Minimum Program for Other States	2nd Try Results	Now we evaluate the results of the 1st try to determine if the Equity Bonus requirements have been met.
State	(1)	(2)	(3)	(4)	(5)	(6)	(7)	
ALABAMA	726,802,802	1.9995%	1.9995%	No	1.9995%		757,478,838	
ALASKA	425,447,070	1.1704%	1.1704%	No	1.1704%		443,403,838	
ARIZONA	702,236,235	1.9319%	1.9319%	No	1.9319%		731,875,393	Column (1) shows the results of the try from the previous step.
ARKANSAS	475,887,486	1.3092%	1.3092%	No	1.3092%		495,973,184	
CALIFORNIA	3,352,504,893	9.2230%	9.2230%	No	9.2230%		3,494,003,466	

Table B-5. (Continued)

STEP 5: SECOND ATTEMPT	1st Try Results	Share of National Total	Minimum Share (From Step 1)	Any State Below Minimum Share?	Required Share	Minimum Program for Other States	2nd Try Results	Now we evaluate the results of the 1st try to determine if the Equity Bonus requirements have been met.
State	(1)	(2)	(3)	(4)	(5)	(6)	(7)	
COLORADO	499,624,024	1.3745%	1.3745%	No	1.3745%		520,711,566	Column (2) shows what share each of the overall program thus
CONNECTICU	499,665,485	1.3746%	0.9265%	No		499,665,485	499,665,485	far.
DELAWARE	158,038,434	0.4348%	0.4348%	No	0.4348%		164,708,734	
DIST. OF COL.	149,550,231	0.4114%	0.3886%	No		149,550,231	149,550,231	Column (3) shows the minimum share State as determined in step
FLORIDA	1,826,502,229	5.0249%	5.0249%	No	5.0249%		1,903,593,081	1.
GEORGIA	1,315,457,881	3.6189%	3.6189%	No	3.6189%		1,370,979,176	
HAWAII	170,349,683	0.4686%	0.2283%	No		170,349,683	170,349,683	Column (4) shows that 8 States that appeared to be "floor states"
IDAHO	276,375,090	0.7603%	0.7603%	No	0.7603%		288,040,003	are now states" and they are below the determined in step 1.
ILLINOIS	1,261,196,699	3.4697%	3.4697%	No	3.4697%		1,314,427,802	
INDIANA	922,997,060	2.5392%	2.5392%	No	2.5392%		961,953,831	
IOWA	402,742,945	1.1080%	1.1731%	Yes	1.1731%		444,392,976	
KANSAS	385,564,917	1.0607%	0.9185%	No		385,564,917	385,564,917	We repeat the adjustment process At the bottom of coiumn(7), we target program level.
KENTUCKY	631,949,044	1.7385%	1.7385%	No	1.7385%		658,621,604	
LOUISIANA	579,393,386	1.5940%	1.5940%	No	1.5940%		603,847,738	
MAINE	186,229,357	0.5123%	0.4624%	No		186,229,357	186,229,357	
MARYLAND	581,863,659	1.6008%	1.6008%	No	1.6008%		606,422,274	Column (7) shows the result
MASSACHUSET	618,102,280	1.7005%	1.5263%	No		618,102,280	618,102,280	giving states their minimum program level.
MICHIGAN	1,061,119,703	2.9192%	2.8478%	No		1,061,119,703	1,061,119,703	

STEP 5: SECOND ATTEMPT	1st Try Results	Share of National Total	Minimum Share (From Step 1)	Any State Below Minimum Share?	Required Share	Minimum Program for Other States	2nd Try Results	Now we evaluate the results of the 1st try to determine if the Equity Bonus requirements have been met.
State	(1)	(2)	(3)	(4)	(5)	(6)	(7)	
MINNESOTA	610,805,140	1.6804%	1.6804%	No	1.6804%		636,585,283	
MISSISSIPPI	448,765,069	1.2346%	1.2346%	No	1.2346%		467,706,016	
MISSOURI	861,344,551	2.3696%	2.3696%	No	2.3696%		897,699,166	
MONTANA	354,693,318	0.9758%	0.9758%	No	0.9758%		369,663,796	
NEBRASKA	260,348,979	0.7162%	0.7636%	Yes	0.7636%		289,267,678	
NEVADA	286,478,072	0.7881%	0.7881%	No	0.7881%		298,569,401	
NEW	170,274,857	0.4684%	0.3812%	No		170,274,857	170,274,857	
NEW JERSEY	943,440,065	2.5955%	2.5955%	No	2.5955%		983,259,671	
NEW MEXICO	352,823,664	0.9706%	0.9706%	No	0.9706%		367,715,229	
NEW YORK	1,698,117,434	4.6717%	3.6149%	No		1,698,117,434	1,698,117,434	
NORTH	933,677,183	2.5686%	2.7770%	Yes	2.7770%		1,052,018,625	
NORTH	216,549,092	0.5957%	0.6440%	Yes	0.6440%		243,975,787	
OHIO	1,308,405,933	3.5995%	3.5995%	No	3.5995%		1,363,629,587	
OKLAHOMA	552,943,993	1.5212%	1.5212%	No	1.5212%		576,282,001	
OREGON	412,006,256	1.1335%	1.2169%	Yes	1.2169%		461,021,822	
PENNSYLVANI	1,660,401,232	4.5679%	3.5563%	No		1,660,401,232	1,660,401,232	
RHODE	203,618,492	0.5602%	0.2219%	No		203,618,492	203,618,492	
SOUTH	549,049,375	1.5105%	1.6291%	Yes	1.6291%		617,162,628	
SOUTH	260,332,652	0.7162%	0.7162%	No	0.7162%		271,320,466	
TENNESSEE	755,264,092	2.0778%	2.2368%	Yes	2.2368%		847,394,203	
TEXAS	2,931,054,936	8.0636%	8.0636%	No	8.0636%		3,054,765,446	
UTAH	283,958,314	0.7812%	0.7812%	No	0.7812%		295,943,291	
VERMONT	170,453,328	0.4689%	0.4492%	No		170,453,328	170,453,328	

Table B-5. (Continued)

STEP 5: SECOND ATTEMPT	1st Try Results	Share of National Total	Minimum Share (From Step 1)	Any State Below Minimum Share?	Required Share	Minimum Program for Other States	2nd Try Results	Now we evaluate the results of the 1st try to determine if the Equity Bonus requirements have been met.
State	(1)	(2)	(3)	(4)	(5)	(6)	(7)	
VIRGINIA	953,450,595	2.6230%	2.6230%	No	2.6230%		993,692,713	
WASHINGTON	597,499,500	1.6438%	1.6905%	Yes	1.6905%		640,424,080	
WEST	403,510,767	1.1101%	1.1101%	No	1.1101%		420,541,673	
WISCONSIN	711,093,010	1.9563%	1.9563%	No	1.9563%		741,105,986	
WYOMING	249,312,332	0.6859%	0.6859%	No	0.6859%		259,835,013	
TOTAL	36,349,272,82	100.0000%	97.1141%		81.5924%	6,973,446,999	37,883,460,068	
Target Program	$6,973,446,999 / (1-.815924)		37,883,460,068					

Source: FHWA.

Table B-6. Step 6: Determine Program Level—Third Attempt

Step 6: Third Attempt State	2nd Try Results	Share of National Total	Minimum Share (From Step 1)	Any State Below Minimum Share?	Required Share	Minimum Program for Other States	3rd Try Results	Now we evaluate the results of the 2nd try to determine if the Equity Bonus requirements have been met.
	(1)	(2)	(3)	(4)	(5)	(6)	(7)	
ALABAMA	757,478,838	1.9995%	1.9995%	No	1.9995%		759,755,497	
ALASKA	443,403,838	1.1704%	1.1704%	No	1.1704%		444,736,522	
ARIZONA	731,875,393	1.9319%	1.9319%	No	1.9319%		734,075,100	Column (1) shows the results of the try from the previous step.

Step 6: Third Attempt State	2nd Try Results	Share of National Total	Minimum Share (From *Step 1)*	Any State Below *Minimum* Share?	Required Share	Minimum Program for Other States	3rd Try Results	Now we evaluate the results of the 2nd try to determine if the Equity Bonus requirements have *been met.*
	(1)	(2)	(3)	(4)	(5)	(6)	(7)	
ARKANSAS	495,973,184	1.3092%	1.3092%	No	1.3092%		497,463,869	
CALIFORNIA	3,494,003,466	9.2230%	9.2230%	No	9.2230%		3,504,504,955	
COLORADO	520,711,566	1.3745%	1.3745%	No	1.3745%		522,276,604	Column (2) shows what share each
CONNECTICUT	499,665,485	1.3190%	0.9265%	No		499,665,485	499,665,485	of the overall program thus far.
DELAWARE	164,708,734	0.4348%	0.4348%	No	0.4348%		165,203,778	
DIST. OF COL.	149,550,231	0.3948%	0.3886%	No		149,550,231	149,550,231	Column (3) shows the minimum
FLORIDA	1,903,593,081	5.0249%	5.0249%	No	5.0249%		1,909,314,473	share State as determined in step 1.
GEORGIA	1,370,979,176	3.6189%	3.6189%	No	3.6189%		1,375,099,756	
HAWAII	170,349,683	0.4497%	0.2283%	No		170,349,683	170,349,683	Column (4) shows that ! State that
IDAHO	288,040,003	0.7603%	0.7603%	No	0.7603%		288,905,729	appeared to be a "floor state" is now state" and is below the
ILLINOIS	1,314,427,802	3.4697%	3.4697%	No	3.4697%		1,318,378,413	minimum determined in step 1.
INDIANA	961,953,831	2.5392%	2.5392%	No	2.5392%		964,845,056	
IOWA	444,392,976	1.1731%	1.1731%	No	1.1731%		445,728,632	
KANSAS	385,564,917	1.0178%	0.9185%	No		385,564,917	385,564,917	At the bottom of column (7), we target program level.
KENTUCKY	658,621,604	1.7385%	1.7385%	No	1.7385%		660,601,141	
LOUISIANA	603,847,738	1.5940%	1.5940%	No	1.5940%		605,662,648	
MAINE	186,229,357	0.4916%	0.4624%	No		186,229,357	186,229,357	Column (7) shows the result of giving states" their minimum level of $37,997,321,644.
MARYLAND	606,422,274	1.6008%	1.6008%	No	1.6008%		608,244,922	

Table B-6. (Continued)

Step 6: Third Attempt State	2nd Try Results	Share of National Total	Minimum Share (From *Step 1)*	Any State Below *Minim um* Share?	Required Share	Minimum Program for Other States	3rd Try Results	Now we evaluate the results of the 2nd try to determine if the Equity Bonus requirements have *been met.*
	(1)	(2)	(3)	(4)	(5)	(6)	(7)	
MASSACHUSETT	618,102,280	1.6316%	1.5263%	No		618,102,280	618,102,280	
MICHIGAN	1,061,119,703	2.8010%	2.8478%	Yes	2.8478%		1,082,078,920	
MINNESOTA	636,585,283	1.6804%	1.6804%	No	1.6804%		638,498,588	
MISSISSIPPI	467,706,016	1.2346%	1.2346%	No	1.2346%		469,111,742	
MISSOURI	897,699,166	2.3696%	2.3696%	No	2.3696%		900,397,268	
MONTANA	369,663,796	0.9758%	0.9758%	No	0.9758%		370,774,848	
NEBRASKA	289,267,678	0.7636%	0.7636%	No	0.7636%		290,137,093	
NEVADA	298,569,401	0.7881%	0.7881%	No	0.7881%		299,466,773	
NEW HAMPSHIRE	170,274,857	0.4495%	0.3812%	No		170,274,857	170,274,857	
NEW JERSEY	983,259,671	2.5955%	2.5955%	No	2.5955%		986,214,931	
NEW MEXICO	367,715,229	0.9706%	0.9706%	No	0.9706%		368,820,425	
NEW YORK	1,698,117,434	4.4825%	3.6149%	No		1,698,117,434	1,698,117,434	
NORTH	1,052,018,625	2.7770%	2.7770%	No	2.7770%		1,055,180,546	
NORTH	243,975,787	0.6440%	0.6440%	No	0.6440%		244,709,075	
OHIO	1,363,629,587	3.5995%	3.5995%	No	3.5995%		1,367,728,078	
OKLAHOMA	576,282,001	1.5212%	1.5212%	No	1.5212%		578,014,060	
OREGON	461,021,822	1.2169%	1.2169%	No	1.2169%		462,407,458	
PENNSYLVANIA	1,660,401,232	4.3829%	3.5563%	No		1,660,401,232	1,660,401,232	
RHODE ISLAND	203,618,492	0.5375%	0.2219%	No		203,618,492	203,618,492	
SOUTH	617,162,628	1.6291%	1.6291%	No	1.6291%		619,017,556	
SOUTH	271,320,466	0.7162%	0.7162%	No	0.7162%		272,135,940	
TENNESSEE	847,394,203	2.2368%	2.2368%	No	2.2368%		849,941,110	

Step 6: Third Attempt State	2nd Try Results	Share of National Total	Minimum Share (From *Step 1)*	Any State Below *Minim um* Share?	Required Share	Minimum Program for Other States	3rd Try Results	Now we evaluate the results of the 2nd try to determine if the Equity Bonus requirements have *been met.*
	(1)	(2)	(3)	(4)	(5)	(6)	(7)	
TEXAS	3,054,765,446	8.0636%	8.0636%	No	8.0636%		3,063,946,772	
UTAH	295,943,291	0.7812%	0.7812%	No	0.7812%		296,832,771	
VERMONT	170,453,328	0.4499%	0.4492%	No		170,453,328	170,453,328	
VIRGINIA	993,692,713	2.6230%	2.6230%	No	2.6230%		996,679,331	
WASHINGTON	640,424,080	1.6905%	1.6905%	No	1.6905%		642,348,923	
WEST VIRGINIA	420,541,673	1.1101%	1.1101%	No	1.1101%		421,805,643	
WISCONSIN	741,105,986	1.9563%	1.9563%	No	1.9563%		743,333,435	
WYOMING	259,835,013	0.6859%	0.6859%	No	0.6859%		260,615,967	
TOTAL	37,883,460,068	100.0000%	97.1141%		84.4401%	5,912,327,296	37,997,321,644	
Target Program =	5,912,327,296 / (1-.844401)		37,997,321,644					

Source: FHWA.

Table B-7. Step 7: Determine Program Level—Forth Attempt

Step 7: Forth Attempt	3rd Try Results	Share of National Total	Minimum Share(From Step 1)	Any State Below Minimum?	Required Share	Minimum Program for Other States	4th Try Results	Now we evaluate the results of the3rd try to determine if the Equity Bonus requirements have been met.
State	(1)	(2)	(3)	(4)	(5)	(6)	(7)	
ALABAMA	759,755,497	1.9995%	1.9995%	No	1.9995%		759,787,520	
ALASKA	444,736,522	1.1704%	1.1704%	No	1.1704%		444,755,267	
ARIZONA	734,075,100	1.9319%	1.9319%	No	1.9319%		734,106,040	Column (1) shows the results
ARKANSAS	497,463,869	1.3092%	1.3092%	No	1.3092%		497,484,836	of the 3rd try from the previous
CALIFORNIA	3,504,504,955	9.2230%	9.2230%	No	9.2230%		3,504,652,664	step.
COLORADO	522,276,604	1.3745%	1.3745%	No	1.3745%		522,298,617	Column (2) shows what share each State of the overall
CONNECTICUT	499,665,485	1.3150%	0.9265%	No			499,665,485	program thus far.

Table B-7. (Continued)

Step 7: Forth Attempt	3rd Try Results	Share of National Total	Minimum Share(From Step 1)	Any State Below Minimum?	Required Share	Minimum Program for Other States	4th Try Results	Now we evaluate the results of the3rd try to determine if the Equity Bonus requirements have been met.
State	(1)	(2)	(3)	(4)	(5)	(6)	(7)	
DELAWARE	165,203,778	0.4348%	0.4348%	No	0.4348%		165,210,741	
DIST. OF COL.	149,550,231	0.3936%	0.3886%	No			149,550,231	Column (3) shows the minimum share State as determined in 1.
FLORIDA	1,909,314,473	5.0249%	5.0249%	No	5.0249%		1,909,394,947	step 1.
GEORGIA	1,375,099,756	3.6189%	3.6189%	No	3.6189%		1,375,157,714	
HAWAII	170,349,683	0.4483%	0.2283%	No			170,349,683	Column (4) shows that 1 State that had appeared to be
IDAHO	288,905,729	0.7603%	0.7603%	No	0.7603%		288,917,906	a "floor state" is now a
ILLINOIS	1,318,378,413	3.4697%	3.4697%	No	3.4697%		1,318,433,981	state" and is below the minimum share determined in step 1.
INDIANA	964,845,056	2.5392%	2.5392%	No	2.5392%		964,885,722	
IOWA	445,728,632	1.1731%	1.1731%	No	1.1731%		445,747,419	
KANSAS	385,564,917	1.0147%	0.9185%	No		385,564,917	385,564,917	At the bottom of column (7), we
KENTUCKY	660,601,141	1.7385%	1.7385%	No	1.7385%		660,628,984	target program level.
LOUISIANA	605,662,648	1.5940%	1.5940%	No	1.5940%		605,688,176	
MAINE	186,229,357	0.4901%	0.4624%	No			186,229,357	Column (7) shows the result of giving the states" their
MARYLAND	608,244,922	1.6008%	1.6008%	No	1.6008%		608,270,558	minimum program level and
MASSACHUSETT	618,102,280	1.6267%	1.5263%	No			618,102,280	"share states" their percentage
MICHIGAN	1,082,078,920	2.8478%	2.8478%	No	2.8478%		1,082,124,528	of the program level of
MINNESOTA	638,498,588	1.6804%	1.6804%	No	1.6804%		638,525,500	$37,998,923,162.
MISSISSIPPI	469,111,742	1.2346%	1.2346%	No	1.2346%		469,131,514	
MISSOURI	900,397,268	2.3696%	2.3696%	No	2.3696%		900,435,218	
MONTANA	370,774,848	0.9758%	0.9758%	No	0.9758%		370,790,475	
NEBRASKA	290,137,093	0.7636%	0.7636%	No	0.7636%		290,149,322	
NEVADA	299,466,773	0.7881%	0.7881%	No	0.7881%		299,479,395	

Step 7: Forth Attempt	3rd Try Results	Share of National Total	Minimum Share(From Step 1)	Any State Below Minimum?	Required Share	Minimum Program for Other States	4th Try Results	Now we evaluate the results of the 3rd try to determine if the Equity Bonus requirements have been met.
State	(1)	(2)	(3)	(4)	(5)	(6)	(7)	
NEW HAMPSHIRE	170,274,857	0.4481%	0.3812%	No			170,274,857	
NEW JERSEY	986,214,931	2.5955%	2.5955%	No	2.5955%		986,256,498	
NEW MEXICO	368,820,425	0.9706%	0.9706%	No	0.9706%		368,835,970	
NEW YORK	1,698,117,434	4.4690%	3.6149%	No			1,698,117,434	
NORTH	1,055,180,546	2.7770%	2.7770%	No	2.7770%		1,055,225,020	
NORTH	244,709,075	0.6440%	0.6440%	No	0.6440%		244,719,389	
OHIO	1,367,728,078	3.5995%	3.5995%	No	3.5995%		1,367,785,726	
OKLAHOMA	578,014,060	1.5212%	1.5212%	No	1.5212%		578,038,422	
OREGON	462,407,458	1.2169%	1.2169%	No	1.2169%		462,426,947	
PENNSYLVANIA	1,660,401,232	4.3698%	3.5563%	No			1,660,401,232	
RHODE ISLAND	203,618,492	0.5359%	0.2219%	No			203,618,492	
SOUTH	619,017,556	1.6291%	1.6291%	No	1.6291%		619,043,646	
SOUTH	272,135,940	0.7162%	0.7162%	No	0.7162%		272,147,410	
TENNESSEE	849,941,110	2.2368%	2.2368%	No	2.2368%		849,976,933	
TEXAS	3,063,946,772	8.0636%	8.0636%	No	8.0636%		3,064,075,912	
UTAH	296,832,771	0.7812%	0.7812%	No	0.7812%		296,845,282	
VERMONT	170,453,328	0.4486%	0.4492%	Yes	0.4492%		170,702,522	
VIRGINIA	996,679,331	2.6230%	2.6230%	No	2.6230%		996,721,339	
WASHINGTON	642,348,923	1.6905%	1.6905%	No	1.6905%		642,375,997	
WEST VIRGINIA	421,805,643	1.1101%	1.1101%	No	1.1101%		421,823,421	
WISCONSIN	743,333,435	1.9563%	1.9563%	No	1.9563%		743,364,765	

Table B-7. (Continued)

Step 7: Forth Attempt	3rd Try Results	Share of National Total	Minimum Share(From Step 1)	Any State Below Minimum?	Required Share	Minimum Program for Other States	4th Try Results	Now we evaluate the results of the 3rd try to determine if the Equity Bonus requirements have been met.
State	(1)	(2)	(3)	(4)	(5)	(6)	(7)	
WYOMING	260,615,967	0.6859%	0.6859%	No	0.6859%		260,626,951	
TOTAL	37,997,321,644	100.0000%	97.1141%		84.8894%	5,741,873,96 7	37,998,923,16 2	
Target Program =	5,741,873,967 / (1-.848894)		37,998,923,162					

Source: FHWA.

Table B-8. Determine Program Level—Fifth Attempt

Step 8: Fifth Attempt	4th Try Results	Share of National Total	Minimum Share (From Step 1)	State Below Minimum ?	Rate of Return	Now we evaluate the results of the 4th try to determine if the Equity Bonus requirements have been met.
State	(1)	(2)	(3)	(4)	(5)	
ALABAMA	759,787,520	1.9995%	1.9995%	No	102.0%	
ALASKA	444,755,267	1.1704%	1.1704%	No	328.8%	
ARIZONA	734,106,040	1.9319%	1.9319%	No	92.0%	Column (1) shows the results of the 4th
ARKANSAS	497,484,836	1.3092%	1.3092%	No	103.7%	try from the previous step.
CALIFORNIA	3,504,652,664	9.2230%	9.2230%	No	92.0%	
COLORADO	522,298,617	1.3745%	1.3745%	No	92.0%	Column (2) shows what share each State has
CONNECTICUT	499,665,485	1.3149%	0.9265%	No	130.6%	of the overall program thus far.

Step 8: Fifth Attempt	4th Try Results	Share of National Total	Minimum Share (From Step 1)	State Below Minimum ?	Rate of Return	Now we evaluate the results of the 4th try to determine if the Equity Bonus requirements have been met.
State	(1)	(2)	(3)	(4)	(5)	
DELAWARE	165,210,741	0.4348%	0.4348%	No	163.8%	
DIST. OF COL.	149,550,231	0.3936%	0.3886%	No	465.4%	Column (3) shows the minimum share for each
FLORIDA	1,909,394,947	5.0249%	5.0249%	No	92.0%	State as determined in step 1.
GEORGIA	1,375,157,714	3.6189%	3.6189%	No	92.0%	
HAWAII	170,349,683	0.4483%	0.2283%	No	180.7%	Column (4) shows all States are at or above the
IDAHO	288,917,906	0.7603%	0.7603%	No	146.9%	minimum share determined in step 1.
ILLINOIS	1,318,433,981	3.4697%	3.4697%	No	92.0%	
INDIANA	964,885,722	2.5392%	2.5392%	No	92.0%	Column (5) shows the rate of return as defined
IOWA	445,747,419	1.1731%	1.1731%	No	92.0%	in the Equity Bonus. This is the ratio of the
KANSAS	385,564,917	1.0147%	0.9185%	No	101.6%	share of apportionments and High Priority Project
KENTUCKY	660,628,984	1.7385%	1.7385%	No	94.7%	allocations in 2008 to the share of contributions
LOUISIANA	605,688,176	1.5940%	1.5940%	No	94.1%	to the Highway Account in 2006. Note that
MAINE	186,229,357	0.4901%	0.4624%	No	97.5%	no State has a rate of return less than 92%
MARYLAND	608,270,558	1.6008%	1.6008%	No	92.0%	
MASSACHUSETTS	618,102,280	1.6266%	1.5263%	No	98.1%	
MICHIGAN	1,082,124,528	2.8478%	2.8478%	No	92.0%	
MINNESOTA	638,525,500	1.6804%	1.6804%	No	92.0%	
MISSISSIPPI	469,131,514	1.2346%	1.2346%	No	93.6%	
MISSOURI	900,435,218	2.3696%	2.3696%	No	96.4%	
MONTANA	370,790,475	0.9758%	0.9758%	No	213.6%	
NEBRASKA	290,149,322	0.7636%	0.7636%	No	99.9%	
NEVADA	299,479,395	0.7881%	0.7881%	No	92.0%	
NEW HAMPSHIRE	170,274,857	0.4481%	0.3812%	No	108.1%	
NEW JERSEY	986,256,498	2.5955%	2.5955%	No	92.0%	

Table B-8. (Continued)

Step 8: Fifth Attempt	4th Try Results	Share of National Total	Minimum Share (From Step 1)	State Below Minimum ?	Rate of Return	Now we evaluate the results of the 4th try to determine if the Equity Bonus requirements have been met.
State	(1)	(2)	(3)	(4)	(5)	
NEW MEXICO	368,835,970	0.9706%	0.9706%	No	107.3%	
NEW YORK	1,698,117,434	4.4689%	3.6149%	No	113.7%	
NORTH CAROLINA	1,055,225,020	2.7770%	2.7770%	No	92.0%	
NORTH DAKOTA	244,719,389	0.6440%	0.6440%	No	201.6%	
OHIO	1,367,785,726	3.5995%	3.5995%	No	92.0%	
OKLAHOMA	578,038,422	1.5212%	1.5212%	No	97.6%	
OREGON	462,426,947	1.2169%	1.2169%	No	99.8%	
PENNSYLVANIA	1,660,401,232	4.3696%	3.5563%	No	113.0%	
RHODE ISLAND	203,618,492	0.5359%	0.2219%	No	222.2%	
SOUTH CAROLINA	619,043,646	1.6291%	1.6291%	No	92.0%	
SOUTH DAKOTA	272,147,410	0.7162%	0.7162%	No	195.9%	
TENNESSEE	849,976,933	2.2368%	2.2368%	No	92.0%	
TEXAS	3,064,075,912	8.0636%	8.0636%	No	92.0%	
UTAH	296,845,282	0.7812%	0.7812%	No	92.0%	
VERMONT	170,702,522	0.4492%	0.4492%	No	210.0%	
VIRGINIA	996,721,339	2.6230%	2.6230%	No	92.0%	
WASHINGTON	642,375,997	1.6905%	1.6905%	No	92.0%	
WEST VIRGINIA	421,823,421	1.1101%	1.1101%	No	166.1%	
WISCONSIN	743,364,765	1.9563%	1.9563%	No	107.6%	
WYOMING	260,626,951	0.6859%	0.6859%	No	138.1%	
TOTAL	37,998,923,162	100.0000%	97.1141%		100.0%	

Source: FHWA.

Table B-9. Step 9--Determine Equity Bonus

Step 9	Overall Program Level	Initial Apportionments and High Priority Projects	Equity Bonus	All of the preceding steps have been to determine the overall program level that is required by the Equity Bonus provision to ensure that both the minimum share and dollar floor provisions are met
State	(1)	(2)	(3)	
ALABAMA	759,787,520	518,758,511	241,029,009	
ALASKA	444,755,267	252,879,164	191,876,103	
ARIZONA	734,106,040	473,388,271	260,717,769	
ARKANSAS	497,484,836	372,867,639	124,617,197	
CALIFORNIA	3,504,652,664	2,862,999,103	641,653,561	The actual Equity Bonus is the amount of
COLORADO	522,298,617	430,414,847	91,883,770	additional funding that must be added to
CONNECTICUT	499,665,485	385,900,595	113,764,890	each State's initial apportionments and High
DELAWARE	165,210,741	142,910,640	22,300,101	Priority Projects to reach the determined
DIST. OF COL.	149,550,231	149,550,231	-	program level.
FLORIDA	1,909,394,947	1,136,899,652	772,495,295	
GEORGIA	1,375,157,714	837,209,001	537,948,714	Column (1) shows the final program level
HAWAII	170,349,683	153,257,829	17,091,854	determined in step 7 (and confirmed in step 8).
IDAHO	288,917,906	195,182,788	93,735,118	
ILLINOIS	1,318,433,981	1,003,228,485	315,205,495	Column (2) shows the total each State received
INDIANA	964,885,722	592,678,227	372,207,495	in initial apportionments for the programs
IOWA	445,747,419	402,742,945	43,004,474	included in the Equity Bonus calculation--IM
KANSAS	385,564,917	365,424,382	20,140,535	NHS, STP, Bridge, CMAQ, Rec. Trails, ADHS,
KENTUCKY	660,628,984	520,142,182	140,486,802	Metro Planning, HSIP, Safe Routes to School,
LOUISIANA	605,688,176	531,951,536	73,736,639	Rail-Highway Grade Crossing, Border--and for High
MAINE	186,229,357	186,229,357	-	Priority Projects.
MARYLAND	608,270,558	514,670,978	93,599,581	

Table B-9. (Continued)

Step 9	Overall Program Level	Initial Apportionments and High Priority Projects	Equity Bonus	All of the preceding steps have been to determine the overall program level that is required by the Equity Bonus provision to ensure that both the minimum share and dollar floor provisions are met
State	(1)	(2)	(3)	
MASSACHUSETTS	618,102,280	579,819,034	38,283,246	Column (3) shows the difference between the
MICHIGAN	1,082,124,528	835,151,315	246,973,213	overall program level and the initial apportionments
MINNESOTA	638,525,500	486,224,560	152,300,940	and High Priority Project funding. This is the
MISSISSIPPI	469,131,514	393,655,210	75,476,304	Equity Bonus. Note that 3 States receive no
MISSOURI	900,435,218	670,568,742	229,866,476	Equity Bonus funds in FY 2008. These States
MONTANA	370,790,475	240,689,458	130,101,018	received sufficient funds from their initial
NEBRASKA	290,149,322	260,348,979	29,800,344	apportionments and High Priority Projects so
NEVADA	299,479,395	227,911,436	71,567,959	that no additional funds were required to meet
NEW HAMPSHIRE	170,274,857	142,548,878	27,725,978	the share and dollar floor provisios of the
NEW JERSEY	986,256,498	727,027,441	259,229,057	Equity Bonus.
NEW MEXICO	368,835,970	280,609,925	88,226,045	
NEW YORK	1,698,117,434	1,475,237,149	222,880,285	
NORTH CAROLINA	1,055,225,020	750,618,511	304,606,509	
NORTH DAKOTA	244,719,389	216,549,092	28,170,297	
OHIO	1,367,785,726	991,210,977	376,574,749	
OKLAHOMA	578,038,422	464,998,785	113,039,637	
OREGON	462,426,947	412,006,256	50,420,691	
PENNSYLVANIA	1,660,401,232	1,356,402,848	303,998,383	
RHODE ISLAND	203,618,492	203,618,492	-	
SOUTH CAROLINA	619,043,646	431,888,278	187,155,368	
SOUTH DAKOTA	272,147,410	218,563,429	53,583,981	
TENNESSEE	849,976,933	618,721,850	231,255,084	
TEXAS	3,064,075,912	1,997,563,619	1,066,512,293	

Step 9	Overall Program Level	Initial Apportionments and High Priority Projects	Equity Bonus	All of the preceding steps have been to determine the overall program level that is required by the Equity Bonus provision to ensure that both the minimum share and dollar floor provisions are met
State	(1)	(2)	(3)	
UTAH	296,845,282	247,072,575	49,772,707	
VERMONT	170,702,522	170,453,328	249,194	
VIRGINIA	996,721,339	709,871,843	286,849,496	
WASHINGTON	642,375,997	597,499,500	44,876,497	
WEST VIRGINIA	421,823,421	337,062,132	84,761,289	
WISCONSIN	743,364,765	473,219,956	270,144,809	
WYOMING	260,626,951	217,171,882	43,455,069	
TOTAL	37,998,923,162	28,763,571,843	9,235,351,320	

Source: FHWA.

Table B-10. Step 10—Further Breakdown of Equity Bonus

Step 10:	Equity Bonus	Percent of National Total	$639 Million Exempt from Obligation Limitation	$2 Billion Subject to Special No-Year Limitation	Remainder Subject to Formula Limitation	
State	(1)	(2)	(3)	(4)	(5)	
ALABAMA	241,029,009	2.6099%	16,676,955	52,197,042	172,155,012	Column (1) shows the Equity Bonus amount for each State from step 9.
ALASKA	191,876,103	2.0776%	13,276,033	41,552,529	137,047,541	
ARIZONA	260,717,769	2.8230%	18,039,233	56,460,823	186,217,713	
ARKANSAS	124,617,197	1.3493%	8,622,345	26,986,997	89,007,855	Column (2) shows the percent of total for each State.
CALIFORNIA	641,653,561	6.9478%	44,396,430	138,955,961	458,301,170	

Table B-10. (Continued)

Step 10:	Equity Bonus	Percent of National Total	$639 Million Exempt from Obligation Limitation	$2 Billion Subject to Special No-Year Limitation	Remainder Subject to Formula Limitation	Step 10:
State	(1)	(2)	(3)	(4)	(5)	State
COLORADO	91,883,770	0.9949%	6,357,498	19,898,273	65,627,999	
CONNECTICUT	113,764,890	1.2318%	7,871,467	24,636,830	81,256,593	Each year $639 million of the Equity Bonus
DELAWARE	22,300,101	0.2415%	1,542,959	4,829,291	15,927,851	is exempt from the obligation limitation that
DIST. OF COL.	-	0.0000%	-	-	-	otherwise applies to the Federal-aid Highway
FLORIDA	772,495,295	8.3645%	53,449,455	167,290,939	551,754,902	Program. Each State receives a proportional
GEORGIA	537,948,714	5.8249%	37,221,023	116,497,726	384,229,964	share of this desirable treatment for its
HAWAII	17,091,854	0.1851%	1,182,597	3,701,398	12,207,860	Equity Bonus funds. This is shown in column
IDAHO	93,735,118	1.0150%	6,485,594	20,299,199	66,950,325	(3).
ILLINOIS	315,205,495	3.4130%	21,809,274	68,260,640	225,135,581	Each year $2 billion of the Equity Bonus
INDIANA	372,207,495	4.0302%	25,753,280	80,604,946	265,849,269	is subject to special no-year obligation limitation
IOWA	43,004,474	0.4657%	2,975,508	9,313,013	30,715,953	that never expires instead of the usual 1-year
KANSAS	20,140,535	0.2181%	1,393,537	4,361,618	14,385,381	obligation limitation that applies to most of the
KENTUCKY	140,486,802	1.5212%	9,720,374	30,423,705	100,342,723	Federal-aid Highway Program. Each State
LOUISIANA	73,736,639	0.7984%	5,101,886	15,968,345	52,666,407	receives a proportional share of this desirable
MAINE	-	0.0000%	-	-	-	treatment for its Equity Bonus funds. Each
MARYLAND	93,599,581	1.0135%	6,476,216	20,269,847	66,853,517	State's amount of the $2 billion is shown in
MASSACHUSETTS	38,283,246	0.4145%	2,648,843	8,290,588	27,343,815	column (4).
MICHIGAN	246,973,213	2.6742%	17,088,238	53,484,314	176,400,661	The remainder of the Equity Bonus is program-
MINNESOTA	152,300,940	1.6491%	10,537,802	32,982,165	108,780,973	matically distributed to the six core programs.
MISSISSIPPI	75,476,304	0.8173%	5,222,255	16,345,086	53,908,964	These funds lose their identity as Equity Bonus
MISSOURI	229,866,476	2.4890%	15,904,612	49,779,693	164,182,171	funds and take on the characteristics of the
MONTANA	130,101,018	1.4087%	9,001,775	28,174,568	92,924,675	program to which they are distributed. This
NEBRASKA	29,800,344	0.3227%	2,061,905	6,453,538	21,284,901	portion of the Equity Bonus is subject to and
NEVADA	71,567,959	0.7749%	4,951,834	15,498,698	51,117,427	shares the formula limitation.

Step 10:	Equity Bonus	Percent of National Total	$639 Million Exempt from Obligation Limitation	$2 Billion Subject to Special No-Year Limitation	Remainder Subject to Formula Limitation
State	(1)	(2)	(3)	(4)	(5)
NEW HAMPSHIRE	27,725,978	0.3002%	1,918,379	6,004,315	19,803,285
NEW JERSEY	259,229,057	2.8069%	17,936,228	56,138,429	185,154,400
NEW MEXICO	88,226,045	0.9553%	6,104,418	19,106,159	63,015,468
NEW YORK	222,880,285	2.4133%	15,421,233	48,266,769	159,192,283
NORTH CAROLINA	304,606,509	3.2983%	21,075,924	65,965,332	217,565,253
NORTH DAKOTA	28,170,297	0.3050%	1,949,121	6,100,536	20,120,640
OHIO	376,574,749	4.0775%	26,055,453	81,550,714	268,968,581
OKLAHOMA	113,039,637	1.2240%	7,821,286	24,479,770	80,738,581
OREGON	50,420,691	0.5460%	3,488,641	10,919,063	36,012,987
PENNSYLVANIA	303,998,383	3.2917%	21,033,847	65,833,637	217,130,899
RHODE ISLAND	-	0.0000%	-	-	-
SOUTH CAROLINA	187,155,368	2.0265%	12,949,402	40,530,211	133,675,755
SOUTH DAKOTA	53,583,981	0.5802%	3,707,511	11,604,102	38,272,368
TENNESSEE	231,255,084	2.5040%	16,000,691	50,080,409	165,173,985
TEXAS	1,066,512,293	11.5482%	73,792,683	230,963,015	761,756,595
UTAH	49,772,707	0.5389%	3,443,806	10,778,736	35,550,165
VERMONT	249,194	0.0027%	17,242	53,965	177,987
VIRGINIA	286,849,496	3.1060%	19,847,304	62,119,888	204,882,303
WASHINGTON	44,876,497	0.4859%	3,105,034	9,718,417	32,053,046
WEST VIRGINIA	84,761,289	0.9178%	5,864,689	18,355,834	60,540,766
WISCONSIN	270,144,809	2.9251%	18,691,496	58,502,335	192,950,978

Note that the 2% State Planning and Research setaside applies to all Equity Bonus funds, but the setaside is deducted from the portion of the Equity Bonus that is programmatically distributed.

Table B-10. (Continued)

Step 10:	Equity Bonus	Percent of National Total	$639 Million Exempt from Obligation Limitation	$2 Billion Subject to Special No-Year Limitation	Remainder Subject to Formula Limitation	Step 10:
State	(1)	(2)	(3)	(4)	(5)	State
WYOMING	43,455,069	0.4705%	3,006,685	9,410,594	31,037,791	
TOTAL	9,235,351,320	100.0000%	639,000,000	2,000,000,000	6,596,351,320	

Source: FHWA.

Table B-11. Which Equity Bonus Rule Prevailed?

	No Equity Bonus Needed?	Floor State? (120% of TEA-21 Average Annual)	92% Minimum Rate of Return State?	TEA-21 Share State?	
State	(1)	(2)	(3)	(4)	
ALABAMA				Yes	This sheet shows which of the 3 Equity Bonus
ALASKA				Yes	rules was the final determining factor for each
ARIZONA			Yes		State that received Equity Bonus.
ARKANSAS				Yes	
CALIFORNIA			Yes		Column (1) shows the 3 States that received
COLORADO			Yes		no Equity Bonus for the year. The amount
CONNECTICUT		Yes			of apportionments and High Priority Project
DELAWARE				Yes	funding they received were sufficient to
DIST. OF COL.	Yes				pass the three Equity Bonus tests without
FLORIDA			Yes		adding any additional funds in the form of
GEORGIA			Yes		the Equity Bonus.
HAWAII		Yes			Column (2) shows the States for which the
IDAHO				Yes	Equity Bonus was determined based on the
ILLINOIS			Yes		dollar floor of 120% of the average annual
INDIANA			Yes		apportionments and High Priority Project.

State	No Equity Bonus Needed? (1)	Floor State? (120% of TEA-21 Average Annual) (2)	92% Minimum Rate of Return State? (3)	TEA-21 Share State? (4)
IOWA			Yes	
KANSAS		Yes		
KENTUCKY				Yes
LOUISIANA				Yes
MAINE	Yes			
MARYLAND			Yes	
MASSACHUSETTS		Yes		
MICHIGAN			Yes	
MINNESOTA			Yes	
MISSISSIPPI				Yes
MISSOURI				Yes
MONTANA				Yes
NEBRASKA				Yes
NEVADA			Yes	
NEW HAMPSHIRE			Yes	
NEW JERSEY		Yes	Yes	Yes
NEW MEXICO		Yes		
NEW YORK				
NORTH CAROLINA				
NORTH DAKOTA				Yes
OHIO			Yes	
OKLAHOMA				Yes
OREGON				Yes
PENNSYLVANIA		Yes		
RHODE ISLAND	Yes			

Column (3) shows the States for which the Equity Bonus was determined based on the minimum relative return of 92% on the State's share of contributions to the Highway Account of the Highway Trust Fund.

Column (4) shows the States for which the Equity Bonus was determined based of their share of apportionments and High Priority Project funding under TEA-21. While 27 States were eligible for con-sideration under the "special rule," the "special rule" provided the best result for only 20 of those States.

Table B-11. (Continued)

State	No Equity Bonus Needed? (1)	Floor State? (120% of TEA-21 Average Annual) (2)	92% Minimum Rate of Return State? (3)	TEA-21 Share State? (4)	State
SOUTH CAROLINA			Yes		
SOUTH DAKOTA				Yes	
TENNESSEE			Yes		
TEXAS			Yes		
UTAH			Yes		
VERMONT				Yes	
VIRGINIA			Yes		
WASHINGTON			Yes		
WEST VIRGINIA				Yes	
WISCONSIN				Yes	
WYOMING				Yes	
TOTAL	3	7	21	20	

Source: FHWA.

End Notes

[1] The highway trust fund has two accounts the highway account and the mass transit account. The focus of the donordonee controversy is on the flow of funds to and from the highway account.

[2] Available at: http://www.fhwa.dot.gov/policy/ohim/hs06/pdf/fe221.pdf.

[3] CRS Report R40053, *Surface Transportation Program Reauthorization Issues for the 111th Congress*, coordinated by John W. Fischer.

[4] Apportioned programs are so called because each state gets "a portion" of the authorized amount by formula.

[5] Devolution generally refers to the shifting of federal programmatic responsibility, as well as shifting the fuel taxes that helps support these responsibilities, to the state level.

[6] This assumes all other attributes of the equity guarantee are held constant. This is not always the case. For example, tax changes can change states' relative shares and could affect the calculation of total program size discussed later in this report.

[7] The tire tax is on tires with rated capacity over 3,500 pounds. The heavy vehicle use tax is on trucks with a gross vehicle weight over 55,000 pounds.

[8] For a detailed discussion of the estimation and attribution process, see *Attribution and Apportionment of Federal Highway Tax Revenues: Process Refinements*, by the Center for Transportation Analysis, Federal Highway Administration, Washington, 2002. 36 p. This report also includes FHWA's time-line for data improvements. These improvements were, in part, a response to a General Accounting Office report, *Highway Funding: Problems With Highway Trust Fund Information Can Affect State Highway Funds,* GAO/RCED/AIMD-00-148, June 2000, pp. 1-62. See also the Federation of Tax Administrators Motor Fuel Tax Section, [http://www.taxadmin.org/fta/mf/].

[9] [http://www.fhwa.dot.gov/policy/ohim/hs02/fe221b.htm].

[10] U.S. Senate, *Report of the Secretary of the Treasury [Albert Gallatin], on the Subject of Public Roads and Canals; Made in Pursuance of a Resolution of the Senate, of March 2, 1807*, (Washington, C.R. Weightman, reprinted by Sentry Press, 1968), p. 65-75. Secretary Gallatin estimated budget surplus at $5.5 million and suggested that an annual $2 million peacetime appropriation would not be burdensome. However, following the imposition of trade restrictions under the embargo of 1807, revenues fell from $17 million in 1808 to $7.7 million in 1809 and recovered only slightly in 1810. Spending during the War of 1812 nearly tripled the public debt (Census Bureau, *Historical Statistics*, 1104).

[11] Ibid, p.68-69. Sectional jealousy/conflict was only one reason for the rejection of the canal and road plan. Other reasons included the view that retiring the national debt was more important and the view by some that the plan exceeded the authority of the federal government under the Constitution.

[12] "Federal Money for Local Roads," *Good Roads Magazine*, vol. 11, June 3, 1916, pp. 231-232. The Federal Aid Road Act of 1916 was passed to support nonurban roads. Senator Lippitt's table may actually have encouraged support for the bill since it made it clear that the majority of states would be net beneficiaries of the bill.

[13] Richard F. Weingroff, *"Clearly Vicious as a Matter of Policy": the Fight Against Federal-Aid*, Federal Highway Administration, Washington, DC, August 2005, pp. 175-233. See also Porter K. Wheeler, *Highway Assistance Programs: a Historical Perspective*, Congressional Budget Office, Washington DC, January 1978, pp. 6-29.

[14] Department of Transportation, Federal Highway Administration., Office of Highway Policy Information, *Highway Statistics Series*, Washington, DC, http://www.fhwa.dot.gov/policy/ohpi/hss/hsspubs.cfm.

[15] Herman B. Leonard and Jay H. Walder, *The Federal Budget and the States: Fiscal Year 1999* (Cambridge, MA, Taubman Center for State and Local Government, 2000), 125 p. See also, Curtis S. Dubay, *Federal Tax Burdens andExpenditures by State: Which States Gain the Most from Federal Fiscal Operations?*, Tax Foundation, 2006. Available at: http://www.taxfoundation.org/publications/show/62.html.

[16] Most of the general fund revenues transferred to the highway account, until 1998, were for interest on the unexpended balance of the highway account. There has also been significant programmatic spending, however. See Table FA-5 in FHWA's annual *Highway Statistics* series, which includes data on general fund spending on highways. [http://www.fhwa.dot.gov/policy/ohim/hs06/htm/fa5.htm] This issue is further complicated by some highway user taxes having been deposited in the general fund for deficit reduction during the 1990s.

[17] Gerald Prante and Andrew Chamberlain, *Putting Taxes on the Map: Federal Tax Burdens by City, County, Congressional District and State*, Tax Foundation, Special Report no. 150, Washington, DC, March 2007, p. 8, http://www.taxfoundation.org/publications/show/2278.html.

[18] Office of Highway Information Policy, *Highway Statistics 2007*, Federal Highway Administration, Washington, DC, 2008, http://www.fhwa.dot.gov/policyinformation/statistics/2007/fe221.cfm. The percentage-in/percentage out method was first added to FE-221 in the 2007 edition.

[19] These terms are not official terms used by the FHWA but are terms of art used by congressional staff in discussing donor-donee issues.

[20] Arizona is a good example of how a state that can be a donee state under dollar-in/dollar-out, both historically and during a particular fiscal year, but be a donor state under the percentage-in/percentage-out calculation.

[21] Ronald D. Utt, *Highway Trust Fund Inequities Will Get Worse in Future Years*, Heritage Foundation, Web Memo no. 2100, October 9, 2008, http://www.heritage.org/research/smartgrowth/wm2100.cfm.

[22] Congressional Budget Office, *Highway Trust Fund Projections: SAFETEA-LU Run 2007-2018*, Washington, DC, January 7, 2009, p. 1.

[23] President Barack Obama, *A New Era of Responsibility: Renewing America's Promise*, Office of Management and Budget, Washington, WA, 2009, pp. 91-92. http://www.whitehouse.gov/omb/assets/fy2010_ new_era/A _New_Era_of_Responsibility2.pdf.

[24] The so-called firewalls were created in TEA-21 by amendment of the Balanced Budget and Emergency Deficit Control Act of 1985 (Gramm-Rudman-Hollings Balanced Budget Act; P.L. 99-177).

[25] *Transportation Weekly*, "President Proposes Ending Budget Firewalls, Contract Authority: Would Give Appropriations Committees Full Control of Spending," vol. 10, no. 13 (March 3, 2009), p. 7.

[26] See Wheeler, Porter K., *Highway Assistance Programs: a Historical Perspective*, Congressional Budget Office, 1978, 86 p. See also archived CRS Report 91-12 E, *Matching Federal Aid for Highways: Rationale from Post Roads to Interstates*, by J.F. Hornbeck. 23 p.

[27] The fuel taxes were 2 cents per gallon prior to passage of the Federal Highway Revenue Act of 1956. The act raised the tax to 3 cents effective July 1, 1956. The tax was again raised in 1959 to 4 cents effective October 1, 1959.

[28] This is not to say that there is no cost to the states in participating in the Federal-Aid Highway Program. Federal administrative, labor, and environmental requirements add significant costs to federal highway projects in some states.

[29] Utt, Ronald D., *Restoring Regional Equity to the Federal Highway Trust Fund*, Heritage Foundation, Backgrounder no. 2074, Washington, DC, October 9, 2007., pp. 2-4, http://www.heritage.org /Research /SmartGrowth/bg2074.cfm.

[30] Utt, Ronald D., *Highway Trust Fund Inequities Will Get Worse in Future Years*, Heritage Foundation, 2008, Web Memo No. 2100. Available at: http://www.heritage.org/Research/SmartGrowth/wm2100.cfm

[31] From 1956 through FY2007 the $643 billion in tax and fee payments into the fund is roughly 89% of the total $719 billion apportioned or allocated from the HTF. Complicating this issue further, some highway tax revenues have been directed to the general fund. For example, in the early years of the HTF the already existing 10% excise tax on new automobiles continued to be credited to the general fund. Also, from FY1990 through FY1996 a portion of fuel taxes was directed to the general fund for purposes of deficit reduction. These revenues had nothing to do with the HTF, however.

[32] Prante, Gerald and Andrew Chamberlain, *Putting Taxes on the Map: Federal Tax Burdens by City, County, Congressional District and State*, Tax Foundation, Special Report no. 150, Washington, DC, March 2007, p. 8, http://www.taxfoundation.org/publications/show/2278.html.

[33] *Transportation Weekly*, "Infrastructure Stimulus: "Use It or Lose It" vs. Regular Funding Distribution, Planning Processes," vol. 10, no. 4 (December 24, 2008), p. 4.

[34] *Transportation Weekly*, "In-Depth Analysis: Earmarked Highway Projects: Their History, Their Nature and Their Role in Highway Legislation," Apr. 10, 2002, p.3.

[35] Most of the rest of the federal-aid highway programs that are " below the line" are formula programs whose funding is administered by the states' departments of transportation.

[36] U.S. Government Accountability Office, *Highway Bridge Program: Clearer Goals and Performance Measures Needed for a More Focused and Sustainable Program*, GAO-08-1043, September 2008, p. 22.

[37] The State Highway Alliance for Real Equity (SHARE) has distanced itself from advocates of a transit guarantee and has a policy statement on its website [http://www.sharestates.org]: "The SHARE Coalition and its predecessors have been organized over the last twenty years in an effort to improve their rate of return in the highway program funds. SHARE specifically focuses on the highway program and has made a deliberate decision not to address transit equity issues."

[38] As mentioned previously, "devolution," during the 1990s, generally referred to the shifting of federal programmatic responsibility and funding resources to the states. The relinquishing of a share of the federal tax

on gasoline to finance programs returned to state responsibility was a 1987 recommendation of the Advisory Commission on Intergovernmental Relations in its report *Devolving Selected Federal-Aid Highway Programs and Revenue Bases: a Critical Appraisal,* A-108 (Washington, D.C.:U.S. GPO, 1987).

[39] Representative Jeff Flake introduced a bill with similar attributes, H.R. 3113, the Transportation Empowerment Act, on September 17, 2003. The bill was referred to the House Subcommittee on Highways, Transit, and Pipelines on September 18, 2003. There was no further action on the bill. On May 12, 2005, Rep. Flake reintroduced a version of the bill H.R. 2284. Senator Jim Demint introduced S. 2823, the Transportation Empowerment Act, on Apr. 7, 2008.

[40] Utt, Ronald D., *Highway Trust Fund Inequities Will Get Worse in Future Years*, Heritage Foundation, Washington, DC, 2008, http://www.heritage.org/Research/SmartGrowth/wm2100.cfm.

[41] STAA also established the Mass Transit Account of the HTF but did not make it subject to the minimum guarantee. The donor-donee discussion is limited to the highway account of the HTF and does not take into consideration federal mass transit funding which is also paid for by federal fuel taxes but is deposited into a separate account. Although, typically, donee states in the Northeast are more transit dependent, some highway donor states get significant federal transit funding, while some donee states, especially the large "pass-through" Western States get relatively little.

[42] P.L. 105-178, Sec. 1104. Also 23 U.S.C. Sec. 105.

[43] TEA-21 authorizes such sums as may be necessary for FY1998-FY2003 for MG.

[44] 23 U.S.C. 105 (c) (1).

[45] P.L. 105-178 Sec. 1103. Also 23 U.S.C. 104.

[46] See Earle, Geoff, Once and Future ISTEA, *Governing Magazine*, Feb. 1998; *Congress Daily*, STEP-21 Coalition Claims Victory, National Journal: Congress Daily, Oct. 3, 1997.

[47] Brown, Jeffrey, *Donor States v.s. Donee States: the Geopolitical Struggle Over Federal Highway Dollars*, Florida State University, Tallahassee, FL, [2003?], 19 p. This paper provides a regression analysis of rate-of-return for FY1990, FY1995, and FY2000.

[48] The following tables were provided by the Federal Highway Administration.

In: Surface Transportation
Editor: David M. Boche

ISBN: 978-1-61470-855-1

Chapter 4

FEDERALISM ISSUES IN SURFACE TRANSPORTATION POLICY: PAST AND PRESENT*

Robert Jay Dilger

SUMMARY

American federalism, which shapes the roles, responsibilities, and interactions among and between the federal government, the states, and local governments, is continuously evolving, adapting to changes in American society and American political institutions. The nature of federalism relationships in surface transportation policy has also evolved over time, with the federal government's role becoming increasingly influential, especially since the Federal-Aid to Highway Act of 1956 which authorized the interstate highway system. In recent years, state and local government officials, through their public interest groups (especially the National Governors Association, National Conference of State Legislatures, National Association of Counties, National League of Cities, U.S. Conference of Mayors, and American Association of State Highway and Transportation Officials) have lobbied for increased federal assistance for surface transportation grants and increased flexibility in the use of those funds. They contend that they are better able to identify surface transportation needs in their states than federal officials and are capable of administering federal grant funds with relatively minimal federal oversight. They also argue that states have a long history of learning from one another. In their view, providing states flexibility in the use of federal funds results in better surface transportation policy because it enables states to experiment with innovative solutions to surface transportation problems and then share their experiences with other states. Others argue that the federal government has a responsibility to ensure that federal funds are used in the most efficient and effective manner possible to promote the national interest in expanding national economic growth and protecting the environment. In their view, providing states increased flexibility in the use of federal funds diminishes the federal government's ability to ensure that national needs are met.

* This is an edited, reformatted and augmented version of a Congressional Research Service 7-5700 publication R40431, dated April 20, 2011.

Still others have argued for a fundamental restructuring of federal and state government responsibilities in surface transportation policy, with some responsibilities devolved to states and others remaining with the federal government.

Congressional attention to federalism issues in surface transportation policy tends to increase during reauthorizations of the federal highway and mass transit program. The current highway and mass transit program, the Safe, Accountable, Flexible, and Efficient Transportation Equity Act of 2005: A Legacy for Users (SAFETEA; P.L. 109-59), after being extended several times, is set to expire on September 30, 2011. Its reauthorization is expected to generate considerable legislative activity during the 112th Congress. Issues addressed by Congress in the recent past, and expected to receive continued attention, include SAFETEA's funding level and financing, especially proposals addressing the Highway Trust Fund's fiscal sustainability, state funding guarantees, and congressional earmarks.

This report provides an historical perspective on contemporary federalism issues in surface transportation policy that are likely to be addressed by Congress during the 112th Congress, including possible devolution of programmatic responsibility to states and proposals to change state maintenance-of-effort requirements and state cost matching requirements.

INTRODUCTION

American federalism, which shapes the roles, responsibilities, and interactions among and between the federal government, the states, and local governments, is continuously evolving, adapting to changes in American society and American political institutions. The nature of federalism relationships in surface transportation policy has also evolved over time, with the federal government's role becoming increasingly influential, especially since the Federal-Aid to Highway Act of 1956 which authorized the interstate highway system.

In recent years, state and local government officials, through their public interest groups (especially the National Governors Association, National Conference of State Legislatures, National Association of Counties, National League of Cities, U.S. Conference of Mayors, and American Association of State Highway and Transportation Officials) have lobbied for increased federal assistance for surface transportation grants and increased flexibility in the use of those funds. They contend that they are better able to identify surface transportation needs in their states than federal officials and are capable of administering federal grant funds with relatively minimal federal oversight. They also argue that states have a long history of learning from one another. In their view, providing states flexibility in the use of federal funds results in better surface transportation policy because it enables states to experiment with innovative solutions to surface transportation problems and then share their experiences with other states. Others argue that the federal government has a responsibility to ensure that federal funds are used in the most efficient and effective manner possible to promote the national interest in expanding national economic growth and protecting the environment. In their view, providing states increased flexibility in the use of federal funds diminishes the federal government's ability to ensure that national needs are met. Still others have argued for a fundamental restructuring of federal and state government responsibilities in surface transportation policy, with some responsibilities devolved to states and others remaining with the federal government.

Congressional attention to federalism issues in surface transportation policy tends to increase during reauthorizations of the federal highway and mass transit program. The authorization for the current highway and mass transit program, the $286 billion, Safe, Accountable, Flexible, and Efficient Transportation Equity Act of 2005: A Legacy for Users (SAFETEA; P.L. 109-59), was set to expire on September 30, 2009, but has been extended several times. Its reauthorization is now set to expire on September 30, 2011.[1] Issues addressed by Congress in the recent past, and expected to continue to receive attention, include funding levels and financing, especially proposals addressing the Highway Trust Fund's fiscal sustainability, state funding guarantees, and congressional earmarks.[2]

This report provides an historical perspective on contemporary federalism issues in surface transportation policy that may be addressed by Congress during the 112th Congress, including possible devolution of programmatic responsibility to states and proposals to change state maintenance-of-effort requirements and state cost matching requirements.

RECENT PROPOSALS AFFECTING FEDERAL, STATE, AND LOCAL GOVERNMENT ROLES AND RESPONSIBILITIES IN SURFACE TRANSPORTATION POLICY

Several bills have been introduced during the 112th and recent Congresses that would fundamentally change existing federal, state, and local government roles and responsibilities in surface transportation policy. For example, Senator Jim DeMint and Representative Jeff Flake introduced legislation during the 109th Congress and Senator DeMint introduced legislation in the 110th Congress (S. 2823, the Transportation Empowerment Act) that would phase-out most of the federal fuel and excise taxes that support the Highway Trust Fund over five years; preserve federal responsibility for interstate highways, transportation facilities on public lands, national transportation research and safety programs, and emergency transportation assistance; and devolve most other surface transportation programs to states.[3] Senator Kay Bailey Hutchison and Representative Jeff Flake introduced legislation during the 112th Congress (H.R. 632 and S. 252, the Highway Fairness and Reform Act of 2011) that would permit a governor to waive the state's right to receive apportioned or allocated funds under the federal-aid highway program and receive instead a prorated amount of the taxes appropriated to the Highway Trust Fund (other than from the Mass Transit Account), which are attributable to highway users in the state. The state would have to have an interstate maintenance program; submit to the Department of the Transportation a plan describing the purposes, projects, and uses for the funding and the federal-aid highway programmatic requirements the state elects to continue; agree to obligate program amounts exclusively for projects that would be eligible for surface transportation program funding; and continue to suballocate surface transportation program funds to urbanized and other areas using certain formulae and rules. In addition, during previous reauthorizations some congressional Members from "donor" states (states whose highway users pay more in estimated federal highway tax revenue to the Highway Trust Fund than that state receives from the program) advocated program devolution as a means to achieve program efficiencies and to address what they viewed as an inequitable distribution of federal surface transportation funds to states.[4]

As will be discussed, recent reauthorizations have focused a great deal of attention on resolving disagreements among donor and donee states concerning the distribution of the program's funds. Because many donor states are located in the South and the Mid-West and many donee states are located in the Northeast, Pacific Rim, and sparsely populated Western states, recent reauthorizations have taken on a regional perspective, pitting states from one region against another. Although most governors and state legislative leaders have been united in their advocacy of additional federal funding with minimal restrictions on the use of those funds, the donor-donee debates in recent reauthorizations have divided them.

In addition to legislative efforts to change federalism relationships in surface transportation policy, two SAFETEA-mandated, non-partisan commissions (the National Surface Transportation Policy and Revenue Study Commission and the National Surface Transportation Infrastructure Financing Commission) issued recommendations that, if enacted, would lead to significant changes in existing federalism relationships in surface transportation policy.

In December 2007, the National Surface Transportation Policy and Revenue Study Commission released *Transportation for Tomorrow*, a report on the status of nation's surface transportation system. The Commission concluded that "the current Federal surface transportation programs should *not* be "re-authorized" in their current form [emphasis in original]."[5] Instead, it recommended a "new user-financed Federal surface transportation program" that is "performance-driven, outcome-based, generally mode-neutral, and refocused to pursue activities of genuine national interest."[6] The Commission made numerous specific policy recommendations to achieve these goals, including some that would fundamentally change federalism relationships in surface transportation policy. For example, it recommended that 108 federal surface transportation programs be consolidated into 10 programs, with each of the new programs focused on a national goal and organized along functional categories, such as congestion relief, rural accessibility, saving lives, environmental stewardship, and energy security, as opposed to the current practice of organizing most programs by transportation mode. It also recommended that the project development and selection process be streamlined, including changes to the National Environmental Policy Act Process, and that the planning process be refocused from the current "bottom-up" approach to a more "top-down" approach. Under this new planning approach, the U.S. Department of Transportation (DOT) would work with various stakeholders to establish "appropriate performance standards critical to serve the national interest under the targeted new program structure." DOT would also establish "national transportation targets ... to advance critical national goals for condition of transportation infrastructure, efficiency and mobility, safety, rural accessibility, environmental quality, energy conservation, access to Federal lands, and research."[7]

In February 2009, the National Surface Transportation Infrastructure Financing Commission released, *Paying Our Way: A New Framework for Transportation Finance*. The report concluded that "the federal Highway Trust Fund faces a near-term insolvency crisis, exacerbated by recent reductions in federal motor fuel tax revenues and truck–related user fee receipts" and that baseline revenue projections for the Highway Trust Fund fall short of anticipated transportation needs by nearly $400 billion in 2010-2015, and about $2.3 trillion through 2035.[8] It recommended a 10 cents per gallon increase in the federal gasoline tax, a 15 cents per gallon increase in the federal diesel tax, and "commensurate increases" in all special fuels taxes and indexing these rates to inflation to address the Highway Trust Fund's immediate revenue shortfalls. For the long-term, it recommended a shift from the present reliance on federal fuel taxes to fund federal surface transportation programs to a "federal funding system based on more direct forms of "user pay" charges, in the form of a charge for each mile driven (commonly referred to as a vehicle miles traveled or VMT fee system)."[9]

The Highway Trust Fund's sustainability, and the means employed to retain sustainability, could have a significant impact on federalism relationships in surface transportation policy. For example, some have argued that states should be provided additional flexibility to use tolling and other congestion pricing strategies to both combat traffic congestion and generate additional revenue for surface transportation projects.[10] Others have suggested that sustainability should be achieved by having the federal government supplement Highway Trust Fund revenue with funding from the general fund account. If that took place, it could change the nature of the donor-donee debate, as some of the donor states are donee states in terms of overall federal tax and spending flows. Others have advocated an increase in federal fuel taxes to achieve sustainability in the Highway Trust Fund.[11] State officials have historically opposed federal fuel tax increases because, as a practical matter, such increases make it more difficult for states to increase their state fuel taxes, and in principle, they view such increases as an infringement on state sovereignty. Secretary of Transportation Ray LaHood indicated in February 2009 that he had interest in exploring alternative means to ensure the Highway Trust Fund's sustainability, including the possibility of a VMT tax, but other Obama Administration officials indicated that the President had no interest in imposing a VMT tax.[12] Still others have proposed taxing oil or transactions in oil futures and options as a means to achieve sustainability in the Highway Trust Fund.[13]

Several other organizations have also advocated changes in federalism relationships in surface transportation policy. For example, the National Conference of State Legislatures has argued that "The Congress should not re-enact SAFETEA-LU and must look at surface transportation anew, authorizing a new program that better meets current and future needs for interstate mobility."[14] It argued that Congress should articulate a new national vision for surface transportation that focuses on "legitimate federal objectives: interstate commerce and freight mobility; interstate movement of people; national defense and homeland security; safety; environmental and air quality preservation and improvements; and research and innovation" and heeds "the Tenth Amendment and not intervene in or interfere with state-specific transportation priorities."[15]

This will not be the first time that Congress has considered proposals to alter federalism relationships in surface transportation policy. Congress has debated the federal role in transportation policy since the nation's formation in 1789. The following sections provide a historical perspective on contemporary federalism issues in surface transportation policy, focusing on efforts to devolve programmatic responsibility to states, change state maintenance-ofeffort requirements, and alter federal reimbursement matching rates.

THE FEDERAL GOVERNMENT'S ROLE IN SURFACE TRANSPORTATION POLICY: 1789-1956

When the nation was formed in 1789, there was considerable debate concerning whether Congress had constitutional authority to provide direct, cash assistance for surface transportation projects. That uncertainty created a conceptual framework that initially limited congressional options for federal involvement in surface transportation policy. Over time, that conceptual framework has evolved in response to changes in American society and in the American political system. Today, the federal government has a prominent role in surface transportation policy, providing about $52 billion annually for highway and mass transit grants, including $41.8 billion for highways and $10.2 billion for mass transit.[16] This spending represents about one-quarter of total government expenditures on highways and mass transit and nearly half (45%) of government highway and mass transit capital expenditures.[17]

The following section examines the evolution of the federal role in surface transportation policy since the nation's formation in 1789 to 1956, the year the Federal-Aid to Highway Act of 1956, which authorized the interstate highway system's construction, was adopted. The discussion focuses on key provisions, and arguments presented, affecting federalism issues in surface transportation policy in selected Federal-Aid to Highway Acts, starting with The Federal-Aid Road Act of 1916.

Constitutional Limits on Congressional Options

Article 1, Section 8 of the U.S. Constitution provides Congress authority "To establish Post Offices and post Roads."[18] When the Constitution was ratified in 1789, the prevailing view was that because other types of transportation projects were not listed in the Constitution that they were excluded purposively, suggesting that other transportation projects were either meant to be a state or local government responsibility, or outside the scope of governmental authority altogether. Nevertheless, during the 1800s there were congressional efforts, primarily from representatives from western states, to adopt legislation to provide federal cash assistance for various types of transportation projects other than post roads to encourage western migration and promote interstate commerce. Most of these efforts failed, primarily due to sectional divisions within the Congress which, at that time, made it difficult to build coalitions large enough to adopt programs that targeted most of its assistance to western states, opposition from Members of Congress who viewed reducing the national debt as a higher priority, and opposition from Members who viewed the provision of cash assistance for transportation projects, other than for post roads, a violation of states' rights, as articulated in the Tenth Amendment: "The powers not delegated to the United States by the Constitution, nor prohibited by it to the States, are reserved to the States respectively, or to the people."[19]

During the 1800s, instead of authorizing cash assistance to states for internal improvements, Congress typically authorized federal land grants to states. The federal land was subsequently auctioned to raise money for internal improvements. For example, in 1823 Ohio received a federal land grant of 60,000 acres along the Maumee Road to raise revenue to improve that road. In 1827, Ohio received another federal land grant of 31,596 acres to raise revenue for the Columbus and Sandusky Turnpike.[20]

In 1841, nine states (Ohio, Indiana, Illinois, Alabama, Missouri, Mississippi, Louisiana, Arkansas, and Michigan), and, with three exceptions, all subsequent newly admitted states were designated land grant states and guaranteed at least 500,000 acres of federal land to be auctioned to support transportation projects, including roads, railroads, bridges, canals and improvement of water courses, that expedited the transportation of the United States mail and military personnel and munitions.[21] By 1900, over 3.2 million acres of federal land was donated to these states to support wagon road construction. Congress also authorized the donation of another 4.5 million acres of federal land to Illinois, Indiana, Michigan, Ohio and Wisconsin to raise revenue for canal construction and 2.225 million acres to Alabama, Iowa and Wisconsin to improve river navigation. In addition, states were provided 37.8 million acres for railroad improvements and 64 million acres for flood control.[22] States were provided wide latitude in project selection and federal oversight and administrative regulations were minimal.

Balancing Constitutional Concerns and Constituent Interests: The Federal-Aid Road Act of 1916

Congressional interest in providing federal cash assistance for surface transportation increased during the early 1900s, primarily due to the lobbying efforts of the "Good Roads" movement, initially started by bicycle enthusiasts, that gained momentum as automobile ownership in the United States increased rapidly, from 8,000 registered motor vehicles in 1900 to over 2 million by 1915. Often finding themselves stuck in the mud, the public's demand for improved roads intensified. Although most of the lobbying for public investment in roads was directed at state and local government officials, several organizations, including the American Automobile Association, formed in 1902, the National Grange, which advocated public investment in farm-tomarket roads, and the American Association of State Highway Officials (AASHO, renamed the American Association of State Highway and Transportation Officials, AASHTO, in 1973) lobbied Congress for federal road assistance.[23] In 1912, their efforts led to the establishment of the Joint Committee on Federal Aid in the Construction of Post Roads, chaired by Senator Jonathan Bourne, Jr., to consider proposals to expand federal assistance for post roads.

The Joint Committee's final report, issued on November 25, 1914, did not recommend specific legislation. However, it created the groundwork for the Federal-Aid Road Act of 1916, named by the now defunct U.S Advisory Commission on Intergovernmental Relations (ACIR) as the federal government's most significant intergovernmental grant program enacted prior to the New Deal era.[24]

The Joint Committee argued that federal assistance for post roads was constitutional because "federal aid to good roads will accomplish several of the objectives indicated by the Framers of the Constitution – establish post roads, regulate commerce, provide for the common defense, and promote the general welfare. Above all, it will promote the general welfare."[25] It also argued that federal assistance for paved post roads would generate significant economic benefits for the nation, as much as $504 million annually in reduced freight hauling costs alone, given the emergence of the "auto truck" for hauling freight short distances.[26]

The Federal-Aid Road Act of 1916 authorized $75 million over five years to improve rural, post roads. Funding was prohibited in communities with populations over 2,500 and was offered to states on a 50-50 cost matching basis. Funding was limited to post roads to avoid constitutional challenges based on the Tenth Amendment's language concerning powers reserved to states. State officials did not object to this federal intrusion into what was then considered one of their domestic policy areas because the program was voluntary and funds were directed to rural areas. At that time, state apportionment rules allocated most state legislative seats to representatives from rural areas. Also, many farmers used rural, post roads to get their produce to market. It was politically difficult at that time for state politicians to object to a federal subsidy for agriculture when most constituents were farmers.[27]

Balancing States Rights, Interstate Commerce Powers, and Constituent Interests: The Federal Highway Act of 1921

Constituent demand for public investment in roads and highways continued to expand as automobile ownership increased across the nation. Motor vehicle registrations reached 10.4 million in 1921. AAA and AASHO lobbied for expanded federal assistance for road construction, but recommended that the increased funding be used in different ways. During the reauthorization of the Federal Aid Road Act of 1916 Congress faced the same fundamental question in 1921 that it faces today: what role should the federal government have in surface transportation policy?

At that time, AAA advocated the creation of a federal highway commission to design and oversee the construction of a proposed 50,000-mile federal highway system.[28] AASHO advocated the continuation of the reliance on states to design and oversee program operations and the use of the grant device to supplement state road development. AASHO argued that state officials were better positioned than federal bureaucrats to make project selection decisions, having superior knowledge of "its populations and its valuations, and a lot of intricate and small things that a commission here in Washington can not know."[29] Importantly, AASHO also advocated an expansion of grants-in-aid eligibility to roads "divided into two classes, primary or interstate roads and secondary or intercounty roads."[30] AASHO argued that its plan had elements similar to a federal highway system while, at the same time, "takes care of the immediate needs of the largest number of rural communities, recognizing the fact that fully half of the wealth of this country is rural and the modern means of transportation, the automobile and truck, are half in the possession of the farmer."[31]

In an historic decision that continues to influence congressional debate today, Congress adopted AASHO's state-centered approach in the Federal Highway Act of 1921. The act left project selection in the hands of state officials and rejected the idea of creating a direct spending program for surface transportation projects. Congress rejected AAA's federal-centered approach primarily because the use of the grant device was believed to be the best means to avoid constitutional objections that could be raised in the direct provision of domestic services. Because grants are voluntary, it was generally believed that state and local government officials were much less likely to challenge the legality of a federal grant program than a federal direct spending program.[32]

Congress also increased federal funding to $75 million annually, maintained the 50-50 cost matching basis, and expanded grants-in-aid eligibility to non-post roads. In recognition of constitutional concerns, eligibility was limited to a Primary System of federal-aid highways, not to exceed 7% of all roads in the state. At least three-sevenths of this system had to consist of roads that were interstate in character. Up to 60% of federal-aid funds could be used on interstate routes. By retaining the federal-aid concept, the act appeased advocates of rural, farm-to-market roads. State highway agencies could be counted on to consider local concerns when deciding the mix of projects.[33]

Congress also established in the Federal Highway Act of 1921 that constitutional concerns about states rights still constrained program eligibility, but that congressional authority to regulate interstate commerce and promote the general welfare also had a role in determining program eligibility. As in the past, the prevailing view was that post roads were eligible for federal assistance because they were mentioned as a federal responsibility in the Constitution. Now, the prevailing view was that highways that were interstate in character and expedited the completion of an "adequate and connected system of highways" were also eligible for federal assistance because of their connection to Congressional authority to regulate interstate commerce and promote the general welfare.[34] Indicative of the expansion of the program's scope, the program's title was changed from the Federal-Aid Road Act to the Federal Highway Act.

Expanding the Federal Role: The Federal-Aid Highway Act of 1944

During subsequent reauthorizations of the Federal Highway Act AASHO and the American Municipal Association and its constituent state leagues of municipalities lobbied Congress to increase federal funding and to expand program eligibility to include secondary and urban highways.[35] They argued that all roads were interconnected, forming a single national surface transportation system. In their view, if any portion of that system was in disrepair or lacked sufficient capacity to carry traffic, then the entire national surface transportation system was affected adversely. As Frederick MacMillin, then-executive secretary of the League of Wisconsin Municipalities, testified before the House Committee on Roads in 1944, "while rural highways may not be all that is desired, it is generally conceded now that urban links have become the bottleneck in our highway system."[36] They also argued that Congress should add urban road construction to the program because urban motorists contributed more in federal gasoline and automotive-related excise taxes than they received in funding.

Trucking organizations opposed the expansion of program eligibility to secondary and urban highways because they worried that expanding the Federal-Aid system might result in higher gasoline taxes and fees. Farm organizations also opposed the expansion of program eligibility because they worried that expanding the system might result in less money for farm-to-market roads.[37]

At that time, traffic congestion was not the nation's most pressing issue. Millions of Americans were overseas fighting in War World War II, mandatory gasoline rationing was in place, and civilian automobile production had been halted in 1942 to allow automotive assembly plants to be converted to producing war materials. Nevertheless, there were more than 30 million registered motor vehicles on the nation's roads, and federal, state, and local government officials knew that traffic congestion, especially in and around the nation's largest cities, would be a salient political issue for elected officials at all levels of government once the War was over. Most highway-related organizations, led by AAA, supported the creation of an interstate system of highways, similar to those already present in several European countries, to relieve traffic congestion. The idea of creating an interstate system in the United States had been discussed for several years. For example, Thomas H. MacDonald,

Chief of the U.S. Bureau of Public Works, advocated the construction of a special system of direct interregional highways in 1939.[38] However, there was no consensus on how to finance it. For example, the National Governors Conference (now the National Governors Association) opposed the use of the federal gasoline taxes to fund interstate highways as an infringement on their sovereign taxing powers.

Although lobby organizations were divided on whether the highway program's scope should be expanded to include secondary and urban highways, Congress was aware that national demographic shifts in the nation had heightened the political relevance of urban areas, as Americans increasingly left rural America in search of employment in the nation's cities, and later its suburbs. At the beginning of the century, about 40% of the U.S. population lived in metropolitan areas. By the time the twentieth century ended, that figure had doubled to about 80%. As a result of the on-going transformation of the nation from a primarily rural nation to an urban one, both major political parties sought political advantage in gaining a political foothold in urban America. Funding urban highways was one of the avenues Congress chose to achieve that goal.

The three-year, $1.5 billion Federal-Aid Highway Act of 1944 expanded federal surface transportation funding eligibility by adding three new programs to the existing Federal-Aid Highway Primary System: a Federal-Aid Highway Secondary System, comprised of principal secondary and feeder routes, including farm-to-market roads, rural mail and public school bus routes, local rural roads, and county and township roads, either outside of municipalities or inside of municipalities of less than 5,000 population; urban extensions of the Federal-Aid Highway Primary System in municipalities and other urban places having a population of 5,000 or more; and an interstate highway network, not to exceed 40,000 miles, to be called the National System of Interstate Highways.[39]

The Primary System was authorized at $225 million annually, the Secondary System at $150 million annually, and the urban extension program at $125 million annually, all on a 50-50 cost matching basis. Routes for the National System of Interstate Highways were designated the following year, but budgetary pressures related to World War II precluded the expenditure of more than token amounts for the interstate system's construction.

One of the more significant effects of the Federal-Aid Highway Act of 1944 on federalism relationships in surface transportation policy was Congress's abandonment of constitutional constraints on program eligibility. Congressional Members and hearing witnesses no longer mentioned states rights as a factor limiting congressional options to the funding of post roads and roads with direct influence on interstate commerce. Now, states, through AASHO and, to an increased extent following the adoption of the Federal-Aid Highway Act of 1956, the National Governors Association, were actively lobbying Congress for increased federal assistance. The congressional focus was on determining the best means to expedite traffic flow and promote economic prosperity, within the constraints of available federal resources and a federalism framework. The result was the expansion of program eligibility, with each of the new programs focused on the needs of specific constituencies. The Primary System focused on projects that addressed county transportation needs. The Secondary System focused on projects that addressed rural America's transportation needs. The urban highway extension program focused on projects that addressed urban America's transportation needs. The Interstate Highway System, given is expansive scope, addressed transportation needs throughout the nation.

The Interstate Highway System Redefines Federalism Relationships in Surface Transportation Policy: The Federal-Aid Highway Act of 1956

The $25 billion, 13-year Federal-Aid Highway Act of 1956 authorized the construction of the then-41,000 mile National System of Interstate and Defense Highways, with a 1972 target completion date. For the next thirty-five years, federal surface transportation policy focused on the completion of the interstate system.

Financing the interstate system had been a key sticking point for many years. Motorist and trucking organizations opposed tolls to finance the system. Governors and highway-related organizations, including AAA, opposed raising federal fuel taxes to finance the system. A special panel formed by the Eisenhower Administration in 1954, the Advisory Committee on a National Highway Program, recommended that thirty-year bonds, financed by federal fuel taxes, be used to finance the system. However, that proposal failed to achieve congressional approval, primarily because Senator Harry Byrd, Chair of the Senate Committee on Finance, wanted a pay-as-you-go financing system that avoided interest charges. The funding impasse was resolved by The Highway Revenue Act of 1956, which created the Highway Trust Fund to finance the system. A relatively small increase in the federal gasoline tax, from two to three cents per gallon, appeased governors and AAA. Governors continued to oppose the federal fuel tax on principle, but recognized that using federal fuel taxes to fund interstate highways was the only viable political option available. One factor contributing to their support was that all Highway Trust Fund revenue was dedicated to highways. In the past, one-third to one-half of federal gasoline revenue had been diverted to other uses. Providing a 90% reimbursement for interstate system expenses also played a role in attracting gubernatorial support. Prohibiting tolls on interstate highways, with an exception for the 2,447 miles of toll roads already in operation, appeased motorist and trucking organizations.[40]

The Federal-Aid Highway Act of 1956 was a defining moment in surface transportation policy because it expanded and solidified the federal government's role in shaping the nation's transportation system. The act elevated the role of federal and state highway department officials in determining the scope and nature of the nation's highway system. Local government officials and urban planners still had a role, but the overall design and location of the interstate system, and increasingly, of primary and secondary highways, were decided by federal and state officials whose goals of promoting national economic growth and expediting traffic flow sometimes conflicted with those held by local government officials who were also interested in clearing slums and other blighted areas, and promoting local economic development. In addition, federal and state highway engineers imposed professional, uniform road construction and design standards throughout the nation. Some local government officials resented the imposition of these standards because they increased construction costs and impinged on their autonomy.[41]

The Federal Government's Role in Surface Transportation Policy: 1956-1991

From 1956 to 1991, state and local government officials focused their efforts in surface transportation policy on maximizing the provision of federal assistance and minimizing federal involvement in how they used federal funds. Specifically, they opposed efforts to increase federal fuel taxes to pay for the increasing cost to complete the interstate highway system on the grounds that any such increases infringed on their sovereign authority to tax fuel by making it more difficult for them to raise state fuel taxes. They also opposed efforts to divert federal Highway Trust Fund revenue to other uses, including mass transit and deficit reduction; and opposed the proliferation of intergovernmental crossover sanctions requiring states to take specific actions, such as limiting highway speeds, removing certain highway billboards, and imposing uniform alcohol standards for determining drunk driving, or lose a portion of federal highway assistance. States also supported efforts to increase federal surface transportation funding levels and to increase the federal share of non-interstate highway expenses.

Debating Reimbursement Rates: The Federal-Aid to Highway Acts of 1970 and 1978

When the Federal-Aid Road Act of 1916 was debated, there was a general consensus that the federal reimbursement rate for expenses would be set at 50%. At that time, a 50-50 cost sharing arrangement was viewed as "an equitable apportionment of burdens, an automatic check upon the demands from the States for Federal appropriation, insures the accomplishment of tangible results, and affords a sound basis for the exercise by the Federal officials of the most searching scrutiny and a conservative policy of approval."[42]

As the federal intergovernmental grants-in-aid system matured, and federal cost sharing requirements became more varied both across and within policy areas, academics, stakeholders, and policymakers became increasingly interested in the impact federal cost sharing requirements had on state and local government budgetary behavior. Critics of federal grants with state or local government cost sharing requirements (particularly federal grants that had a 50% or higher state and local government cost sharing requirement) argued that cost sharing requirements distort state and local government budgetary decisions in favor of the federally assisted activity. In their view, because state and local government officials are better positioned than federal bureaucrats to identify and respond to state and local government needs, the distortion of state and local government decision-making resulting from the imposition of cost matching requirements led to the non-optimal use of public funds. They argued that lowering state cost matching requirements, or eliminating them altogether, would result in less distortion of state and local government budgetary decisions and would maximize the public interest. Others argued that providing federal funds with very low or no cost matching requirements may lure state and local governments into programmatic activities that they could not afford if the federal assistance was later withdrawn, or could result in spending on projects that never could have stood on their own merits. Still others argued that the imposition of state and local government cost sharing requirements are an appropriate means to stimulate state and local government spending in areas deemed to be in the national interest. In their view, federal cost sharing requirements should be proportional to the extent to which the aided activity aligns with an identified national interest. In academic terms, "the danger of distortion and waste of resources occurs when the cost-sharing requirement is more generous to the recipient government than is justified by the degree of spillover or national interest characterizing the aided state or local government activity."[43]

In 1970, several organizations, including AASHO and the American Road Builders Association, joined state and local governments in advocating an increase in the federal share of expenses for non-interstate highways. They argued that increased highway maintenance costs and "increasing requirements for non-Federally aided state highway improvements" were making it more difficult for states to meet the federal government's 50% matching requirement for non-interstate highways.[44] Representatives of the National League of Cities and U.S. Conference of Mayors argued that the focus on interstate highway construction had led the nation to neglect urban highway systems and that the cost of improving urban highways had increased dramatically, justifying an increase in the reimbursement rate for non-interstate highways.[45] The National Association of Counties argued that because the interstate system was nearing completion that Congress should focus additional resources on non-interstate highways and increase the federal share of expenses to 70% for any additions to the interstate system and for all other federally aided highways. In their view, increasing the reimbursement rate to 70% was justified because "many States and most local governments are finding it increasingly difficult to come up with 50 percent matching funds."[46] Congress subsequently increased the federal share of expenses for non-interstate highways from 50% to 70% in the Federal-Aid Highway Act of 1970.

In 1978, states advocated another increase in the federal share of expenses for non-interstate highways, arguing that rising gasoline prices had led motors to drive less and, coupled with improvements in automotive fuel economy, had caused state fuel tax revenue to fall, making it more difficult for them to find state funds to meet their 30% share of expenses. The National Association of Counties argued that some local governments were also having difficulty participating in the program because of the required matching rate.[47] Secretary of Transportation Brock Adams indicated that the Carter Administration also supported an increase in the federal share of expenses for non-interstate highways, arguing that "we find about 70 percent is a breaking point, the States are simply unable to raise sufficient money to match Federal moneys and then the program languishes.... we would like to establish uniformity in percentages of grants, whether it is 75-25 or 80-20."[48] Congress subsequently increased the federal share of expenses for non-interstate highways from 70% to 75% in the Federal-Aid Highway Act of 1978.[49]

The following sections discuss several efforts during this time period to "sort out" or devolve federal surface transportation programs to state and local governments. This discussion is pertinent given recent proposals to sort out federal-state responsibilities in surface transportation policy.

Efforts to "Sort-out" Governmental Responsibilities in Surface Transportation Policy: Presidents Nixon's and Reagan's New Federalism Proposals

During the 1960s and 1970s, the number of federal grants to state and local governments, including those provided for surface transportation, increased dramatically. The total number of federal grants to state and local governments increased from 132 in 1960 to 387 in 1968, the year before President Richard Nixon became President, and to 539 in 1981, when President Ronald Reagan become President.[50]

The number of federal surface transportation grant programs funded by the Federal-Aid to Highway Act also increased. There were nine surface transportation programs in the Federal Highway Act of 1960: forest development roads and trails, forest highways, Indian Reservation Roads and Bridges, Park Roads and Trails, Parkway, Public Land Highways, Federal Aid Primary System, Federal Aid Secondary System and Federal-Aid Primary and Secondary Systems Extensions in Urban Areas.[51] In 1975, there were 37 programs: Interstate Highway System; Federal-Aid Highway Primary System in Rural Areas; Federal-Aid Secondary System in Rural Areas; Federal-Aid Urban Systems; Federal-Aid Primary and Secondary Systems Extensions in Urban Areas; Emergency Relief; Forest Highways; Priority Primary Routes; Special Urban High Density Traffic Program; Motor Vehicle Diagnostic Inspection Demonstration Projects; Off-System Road Projects; Railroad Safety; Carpool Demonstration Projects in Urban Areas; Surveys, Planning, Research and Development for Highway Programs; Public Land Highways; three grant programs for Highway Beautification; Education and Training Program for Highway Personnel; four grant programs for urban mass transportation; Transportation Planning in Urban Areas; Urban Area Traffic Operations Improvements; Bridges on Federal Dams; Economic Growth Center Development Highways; and ten grant programs for highway safety.[52]

During the 1970s and 1980s, there were several attempts to change federal, state, and local government roles in surface transportation policy. Presidents Nixon's and Reagan's efforts are particularly noteworthy as both were convinced that federal grants to state and local governments had become duplicative and wasteful, and both attempted to sort out the appropriate roles and responsibilities of each level of government in several programmatic areas, including surface transportation policy.[53] For example, in his 1971 State of the Union speech, President Nixon announced a plan to focus federal resources on areas of national interest by consolidating 129 federal grant programs in six functional areas, 33 in education, 26 in transportation, 12 in urban community development, 17 in manpower training, 39 in rural community development, and 2 in law enforcement, into six special revenue sharing programs. Unlike the categorical grants they would replace, the proposed special revenue sharing programs had no state matching requirements, relatively few auditing or oversight requirements, and the funds were distributed automatically without prior federal approval of plans for their use.[54]

President Nixon's proposal to consolidate 26 federal surface transportation programs into a special revenue sharing program failed to gain congressional approval, primarily because it generated opposition from interest groups affiliated with highway construction who worried that the programs' future funding would be compromised, and from state highway officials worried about losing programmatic influence to governors.[55] Nonetheless, President Nixon and his successor, President Gerald Ford, continued to oppose further expansion in the number of federal surface transportation programs and those numbers remained fairly stable for the remainder of the decade. When President Ronald Reagan entered office in 1981, there were 34 federal surface transportation programs funded by the Federal-Aid Highway Act, compared to 37 in 1975.[56]

President Reagan also wanted to change federal and state roles in surface transportation policy. In 1982, he proposed a $20 billion "swap" in which the federal government would return to states full responsibility for funding Aid to Families With Dependent Children (AFDC) (now Temporary Assistance for Needy Families) and food stamps in exchange for federal assumption of state contributions for Medicaid. He also proposed a temporary $28 billion trust fund or "super revenue sharing program" to replace 43 other grant programs, including all non-interstate highways, Appalachian highways and urban mass transit construction and operating grants. The trust fund, and federal taxes supporting it, would begin phasing out after four years leaving states the option of replacing federal tax support with their own funds to continue the programs or allowing the programs to expire.

Both the swap proposal and the proposed devolution of 43 federal programs failed to gain congressional approval. Both proposals were opposed by organizations who feared that if enacted, they would result in less funding for the affected programs. For example, the National Governors Association supported the federal take over of Medicaid, but objected to assuming the costs for AFDC and food stamps. The economy was weakening at that time and governors worried that they would not have the fiscal capacity necessary to support the programs without continued federal assistance.[57]

President Reagan's Surface Transportation Block Grant Proposals and Opposition to Highway"Demonstration Projects"

In 1983, President Reagan proposed the Federalism Block Grant Highway Act of 1983. It would have provided states the choice of continuing to receive funds for highway programs focused on local and state needs (Urban System, Secondary System, bridges other than Primary and high-cost bridges, highway safety, hazard elimination and rail-highway crossings) under existing statutory mechanisms or receiving them in the form of a block grant. The federal role in highway programs that focused on "the federal interest" (primary and interstate highways and bridges, as well as high-cost bridges) was to be continued.[58] In 1986, he proposed the Surface Transportation Reauthorization Act of 1986, which would have combined the Primary, Interstate reconstruction and Interstate construction programs into a single program. It would have also created a block grant for the remaining highway programs and mass transit. Neither proposal was approved by Congress.[59]

In 1987, President Reagan vetoed the Surface Transportation and Uniform Relocation Assistance Act of 1987 (STURAA), the last surface transportation authorization bill of the Interstate era. In the first, and only, veto of a federal-aid highway bill in the 20th Century, President Reagan cited several objections to the bill, but was especially critical of the bill's 121 "demonstration projects" which he considered wasteful. Members of Congress who wanted funds for a project in their state had adopted the practice of inventing a concept it would "demonstrate" indicating that it was part of an important research initiative. Using this idea, for example, funding for two parking lots became a demonstration of "methods of facilitating the transfer of passengers between different modes of transportation."[60] Congress initially sustained President Reagan's veto by a single vote in the Senate on April 1, 1987, but the following day one of the Senators who had voted to sustain the veto switched his vote, and the veto was overridden.[61]

The inclusion of demonstration projects in STURAA, and the inclusion of increasing numbers of congressionally earmarked projects in subsequent reauthorizations have implications for federalism relationships in surface transportation policy. Although many Members of Congress discuss their surface transportation earmarks with their state and local government officials prior to making their requests for an earmark, earmarks, by definition, reduce state and local government flexibility. The extent of congressional earmarks' impact on state and local government flexibility is related to how the earmarks are treated in the distribution of the program's funds. For example, congressional earmarks in SAFETEA's National Corridor Infrastructure Improvement Program ($1.9 billion), Projects of National and Regional Significance ($1.8 billion), Transportation Improvements ($2.5 billion), as well as discretionary programs earmarked during the annual appropriations process are all outside the scope of SAFETEA's Equity Bonus (EB) program. The EB program is designed to guarantee each state at least a 92% return on payments to the Highway Account in the Highway Trust Fund for those programs listed in the EB program (which includes all of the core formula programs as well as several other programs).[62] Because these earmarks are outside of the EB program's scope, they have no direct impact on the calculations that determine the distribution of the EB program's funds to states. As a result, although states have little discretion concerning how those earmarked funds are to be spent, the funds are considered additional funding, often referred to as being "above the line."

On the other hand, SAFETEA's High Priority Project (HPP) earmarks (nearly $15 billion) are included within the scope of SAFETEA's EB program, often referred to as being "below the line." As a result, these earmarks are counted in the calculations that determine the distribution of the EB program's funds to states, reducing the amount that each state receives through the EB program. Because EB program funding is distributed to states through the program's core formula programs, states receiving HPP earmarks not only have little discretion concerning how those earmarked funds are to be spent, but also experience a reduction in the amount of formula program funds that they would otherwise receive and rely on to implement their state transportation improvement plans. The issue is whether congressional earmarks, if continued, should be inside or outside the scope of the EB program. Keeping congressional earmarks outside, as opposed to inside, the EB program would place less of a restraint on state flexibility in regard to the funding received for the core formula programs, but it would also dilute the impact of a rate-of-return guarantee.[63]

Although President Reagan's New Federalism and block grant proposals were not adopted, he continued to advocate further reductions in the number of surface transportation programs, and had some success. There were 27 federal surface transportation programs funded by the Federal-Aid Highway program at the conclusion of his second term in office, compared to 34 at the outset of his presidency.[64] Among the programmatic changes that took place during his presidency was a reduction in mass transit operating assistance and a refocused emphasis on capital expenditures.

ACIR: The Geographic Range of Benefits Argument

In 1987, the now defunct U.S. Advisory Commission on Intergovernmental Relations (ACIR) recommended that Congress "move toward the goal of repealing all highway and bridge programs that are financed from the federal Highway Trust Fund, except for: (1) the Interstate highway system, (2) the portion of the bridge program that serves the Interstate system, (3) the emergency relief highway program, and (4) the federal lands highway program."[65] The Commission also recommended that Congress "relinquish an adequate share of the federal excise tax on gasoline" to enable states to finance the devolved programs.[66]

ACIR was one of the first organizations to offer specific criteria for defining areas of national interest and determining roles for federal, state and local government officials in surface transportation policy. ACIR conceded that all roads are physically interconnected. As noted earlier, the highway system's interconnectedness had been used as a rationale for expanding federal program eligibility in surface transportation policy. ACIR argued that while all roads are interconnected, "they differ systematically in the length of trips on them and in the travel purposes for which they are used."[67] ACIR argued that "most trips on Interstate highways are much longer than trips taken on the Secondary and Urban systems" and that "this fact argues that the Interstate network provides transportation benefits over a wider geographic range than Secondary and Urban systems."[68] ACIR went on to conclude that "This concept of the geographic range of highway benefits is a key test to determine which unit of government should bear responsibility for highway finance."[69]

ACIR argued that "roads that serve largely local purposes – helping to make quicker trips to the supermarket, for example – compete with financing for roads that provide truly national benefits – for instance, facilitating the interstate commerce and economic health on which the whole nation's welfare depends."[70] It recommended that the approximate geographical range of benefits associated with surface transportation programs supported the idea of incremental devolution, where roads that provide virtually no national benefits were devolved first and others that, on balance, provide some national benefits could be devolved later. ACIR noted that incremental devolution was "likely to be more palatable politically than a wrenching, once-and-for-all change."[71]

ACIR also introduced the notion of interstate spillovers, or externalities, as an example of the use of the geographic range of benefits criteria. Economists use the term spillover or externality to describe the market imperfection that results when producers and consumers in a market either do not bear all of the costs or do not reap all of the benefits of an economic activity. Wastewater and air pollution treatment are often used as examples where economic spillovers occur. The primary beneficiaries of cleaner water and air often live downstream or downwind from a pollution source, not those who live where the effluent or polluted air is treated. Those living at the source of the pollution have no, or little, incentive to pay for activities that primarily benefit those living downstream or downwind. Economists argue that services with spillover effects are not likely to be provided at optimal levels without some form of government intervention, typically by providing an incentive to the provider to undertake the service at optimal levels or by a mandate to do so.[72]

ACIR argued that highways, especially interstate highways, are subject to spillovers and the "best government for providing services is one with an appropriately large jurisdiction so that the jurisdiction can encompass the externalities."[73] It argued that

> an interstate spillover occurs when road benefits are not fully captured in-state, or are not fully captured by taxes and other charges levied by the providing state. The state budgetary process has little reason to value fully out-of-state benefits. An all too logical consequence might be underfinancing of roads with large out-of-state benefits relative to their in-state benefits. For example, by charging tolls on Interstate 80 (which is not currently permitted), Pennsylvania could reap the savings of fuel and time gained by the highway's efficient New York to Chicago routing, with the tolls defraying maintenance costs for efficient transportation. In this case, toll finance could internalize what would otherwise be an interstate spillover, namely the region-wide advantages of a direct, swift, well-maintained superhighway. However, it the hypothetical tolls on Interstate 80 were set too high in relation to the additional cost incurred by additional use (e.g., wear or perhaps the need for extra lanes)

motorists would be overcharged. In effect, they would be paying twice, through both tolls and taxes, and the interstate motorist would be exploited.[74]

ACIR also advocated the principle of fiscal equivalence to sort out surface transportation financing. It argued that "Those who benefit from the government function should pay for it" and that jurisdictions that pay for a function and receive its benefits have an incentive to make "judicious fiscal choices, neither skimping on valuable public investment nor squandering other person's tax dollars."[75] It went on to argue that "without fiscal equivalence, highway beneficiaries who do not pay their fair share are motivated to exaggerate their demands, if successful they improve their services at the expense of others."[76]

ACIR noted that "over time, considerable national standardization has been developed in the highway transportation system" largely due to the efforts of "transportation officials (notably AASHTO)" and that such standardization "most likely would continue after devolution, even if direct, federal control were limited to the Interstate system."[77] It argued that the benefits of standardization, such as for safety requirements, "serve both the national and local goals."[78]

Applying these principles, ACIR argued that the "great preponderance of the Interstate System ... merits continued federal support."[79] However, the "national role of the Primary system has been greatly reduced by the Interstate system," and "with well functioning Interstate and Primary systems, the national benefits of the federal-aid Urban system are contained, by and large, within individual states or metropolitan areas."[80] Also, "by and large, Secondary highways are even more appropriate for state-local financing and control than the Urban system" because "most Secondary roads are only lightly traveled, because of shifts in population and the presence of alternative routes that are designed to higher standards."[81]

ACIR argued that it was "doubtful" that any general principle of fiscal federalism governs the award of funds through demonstration projects" but noted that highway demonstration projects "rarely convey important national benefits."[82] It also argued that certain bridge safety programs serve a "coordinating as well as an operational safety function that is not appropriate for devolution" but programs to widen bridges to remove traffic bottlenecks may be appropriate for devolution if the bridge's traffic is primarily local in nature.[83]

The Federal Government's Role in Surface Transportation Policy: The Post-Interstate Era

There have been three reauthorizations of the Federal-Aid Highway Act since 1987, the $151 billion, six-year, Intermodal Surface Transportation Efficiency Act of 1991 (ISTEA, P.L. 102- 240) signed by President George H.W. Bush on December 18, 1991, the $203.4 billion, six-year Transportation Equity Act for the 21st Century (TEA-21, P.L. 105-178), signed by President Bill Clinton on June 9, 1998, and the $286 billion, Safe, Accountable, Flexible, and Efficient Transportation Equity Act of 2005: A Legacy for Users (SAFETEA, P.L. 109-59) signed by President George W. Bush on August 10, 2005 and set to expire on September 30, 2009.[84] The following discussion examines the major federalism issues involved in each of these reauthorizations, focusing on federalism issues that may be discussed during SAFETEA's reauthorization, including efforts to sort out appropriate roles for federal, state, and local governments in surface transportation policy, change state maintenance-of-effort requirements, and alter federal reimbursement rates.

Congress Sets a New Direction for Federalism Relationships in Surface Transportation Policy: ISTEA

Although most lobbying organizations involved in the 1991 reauthorization of the Surface Transportation and Uniform Relocation Assistance Act of 1987 had not changed their positions on federal surface transportation policy, circumstances had changed a great deal. From 1956 to 1991, there had been a shared consensus among policymakers and lobbying organizations that the highway program's primary goal was to build the Interstate System. Now that the Interstate system was, for all practical matters, complete, that consensus no longer existed. During reauthorization, President George H. W. Bush, the House, and Senate advocated fundamentally different approaches to structuring federalism relationships in surface transportation policy.

President George H. W. Bush shared President Reagan's view that the intergovernmental system had become duplicative and wasteful and targeted surface transportation policy as an area in need of reform. On February 13, 1991, he announced a five-year, $105 billion reauthorization proposal for the Federal-Aid Highway program, called the Surface Transportation Assistance Act (H.R. 1351, S. 610). It included a 40% increase in funding for highways ($88.5 billion) and a marginal increase for mass transit ($16.5 billion). His proposal was guided by two fundamental principles, that state and local government officials should have greater influence on project selection and federal financial assistance should reflect the program's geographic range of benefits. In his words, "Our approach will provide States and localities with flexibility to select which highways will receive targeted Federal dollars, and States and localities will be able to choose whether to spend Federal dollars on transit or highway solutions. As never before, we are encouraging creative new financing and management by the States."[85]

Using the geographic range of benefits principle, he recommended that the Interstate, Primary, Secondary and Urban Highway programs be replaced by two programs: a $43.5 billion, 150,000 mile National Highway System (NHS) consisting of highways with significance for national defense or that carried goods and people across state lines and a $22.2 billion urban and rural highway block grant for other federally funded roads (about 716,000 miles at that time).[86] Because the block grant consisted of roads lacking national significance, he recommended that it receive less funding than the proposed national highway system and its reimbursement rate lowered from 75% to 60%. The federal reimbursement rate for highways in the national highway system would remain the same, 90% for interstate highways and 75% for primary highways. He also recommended that states be allowed to shift funds between urban and rural highways, from urban and rural highways to mass transit and, with the exception for new mass transit starts, from mass transit to urban and rural highways.[87] Because the President believed that mass transit's benefits accrue primarily within state and metropolitan areas, in addition to proposing that mass transit funding be increased only marginally, to $16.5 billion over five years, he also recommended that the federal reimbursement rate for mass transit capital expenses be reduced from 80% to 60%, and for new starts from 75% to 50%.

Senator Daniel Patrick Moynihan, Chair of the Senate Committee on Environment and Public Works' Subcommittee on Water Resources, Transportation, and Infrastructure, led the Senate's reauthorization effort. The Senate bill took a fundamentally different approach to federalism relationships in surface transportation policy than what was offered by the President.[88] Senator Moynihan had a close working relationship with the Surface Transportation Project, a coalition of urban, environmental and intermodal transportation advocates, and crafted a bill, S. 965, the Surface Transportation Efficiency Act of 1991 (later incorporated into S. 1204 with the same title), that would have shifted the focus of federal policy away from highway construction toward maintenance, placed greater emphasis on mass transit and intermodal solutions to traffic congestion, further decentralized programmatic authority to states and metropolitan planning organizations in the project development process, increased public participation in the project development process, and strengthened environmental protections. Specifically, the Senate bill authorized funding at $123 billion, with almost half of the bill's highway funds ($44.7 billion) for a Surface Transportation Program, which would allow states to fund a broad range of surface transportation projects, including construction, restoration, and operational improvements for highways and bridges; capital and operating costs for mass transit, rail, and magnetic levitation systems; carpool projects and parking and bicycle facilities and programs; and surface transportation research and development programs. The bill also including $21 billion for mass transit.[89]

The Senate bill rejected the geographic range of benefits argument in the determination of federal reimbursement rates. Instead of lowering cost matching rates for transportation projects lacking a national interest, the Senate bill would have "leveled the playing field" by setting reimbursement rates at 80% for maintaining and improving transportation facilities, and 75% for new construction. The financial incentive to fund new construction over maintenance was to be eliminated by giving maintenance a higher reimbursement rate than new construction.

The Bush Administration indicated that it could not support S. 965 because it did not include its recommended National Highway System, and did not focus federal resources on highways of national interest. Dr. Thomas Larson, Administrator of the Federal Highway Administration, testified before the Senate Committee on Environment and Public Works that "While we are moving to the post-Interstate construction era, we are not yet ready for a post-highway transportation economy."[90] He added that "50 strong state programs will not necessarily provide a strong national program, and the experience in the European Community and the experience that we've had in working with the 50 States in response to the House Public Works [Committee's] charge that we develop an illustrative national [highway] system suggests that there is a need for Federal oversight of coordination."[91] To avoid a presidential veto, the Senate bill was amended on the Senate floor to include funding for a National Highway System.

The House bill (H.R. 2950, the Intermodal Surface Transportation Efficiency Act of 1991) took yet another approach to structuring federalism relationships in surface transportation policy, incorporating some elements of the Administration's proposal and some elements from the Senate bill. It authorized $151 billion for the program, including $32 billion for mass transit. It included funding for a National Highway System (up to 155,000 miles, plus or minus 15%, to be designated within two years) and, although it did not go as far as the Senate bill in providing states additional programmatic flexibility, it would have provided states added flexibility to shift funds among existing highway programs, including for mass transit purposes. It accepted Senator Moynihan's "level playing field argument" and set federal reimbursement rates at 80% for most programs, and 90% to 95% for interstate highways, with the higher reimbursement rate offered to states with relatively large amounts of federal land.

The $151 billion, six-year, Intermodal Surface Transportation Efficiency Act of 1991 (ISTEA,P.L. 102-240), subsequently adopted by Congress, represented a compromise between the House and Senate approaches to federalism relationships in surface transportation policy. ISTEA was authorized at the House level, $46 billion more than the President had requested, and nearly doubled the amount the Administration requested for mass transit, providing $119 billion for highways and $32 billion for mass transit. ISTEA replaced the Interstate, Primary, Secondary and Urban Highway programs with two programs: a $21 billion, 155,000 mile National Highway System (NHS), including all interstate routes, a large percentage of urban and rural principal arterials, the defense strategic highway network, and strategic highway connectors; and a $23.9 billion Surface Transportation Program (STP) for all roads not functionally classified as local or rural minor collector. ISTEA retained separate programs and authorizations for Interstate Highways ($7.2 billion), Interstate Maintenance ($17 billion), Bridge Replacement and Rehabilitation ($16.1 billion), and created a new, $6 billion Congestion Mitigation and Air Quality Improvement Program.

ISTEA's impact on federalism relationships in surface transportation policy was particularly noteworthy for several reasons. First, it increased state programmatic authority to shift funds among existing programs, allowing states to shift up to half of their NHS funds to other highway programs and mass transit and up to 100% with the approval of the Secretary of the U.S. Department of Transportation. Second, ISTEA enhanced the role of Metropolitan Planning Organizations (MPOs) in project selection by requiring states to reserve approximately $9 billion of STP funds for the use of MPOs representing urban areas with populations of 200,000 or more. Third, ISTEA mandated a new style of performance planning for managing and monitoring highway pavement conditions, bridge maintenance, highway safety programs, traffic congestion mitigation, transit facility and equipment maintenance, and intermodal transportation facilities and systems. In addition, statewide transportation improvement plans, both for the long-term and for a shorter-term, were required for the first time, in addition to metropolitan transportation improvement plans that had been required since 1962. Fourth, ISTEA rejected the application of the geographic range of benefits argument in setting reimbursement rates. Instead, it "leveled the playing field" by retaining interstate reimbursement rates at 90% for interstate construction and maintenance (with up to 95% for states with relatively large amounts of federally owned land) and increased reimbursement rates to 80% for most non-interstate highway and mass transit projects. This change removed the financial incentive to fund highways over mass transit, and new construction over maintenance.[92]

Debating Program Devolution and Continuing the Expansion of State Programmatic Flexibilities: TEA-21

In 1995, there were 633 federal grants-in-aid programs, including 618 categorical grants and 15 block grants.[93] There were 30 surface transportation grant programs, 28 categorical grants and 2 block grants. Several prominent members of President Bill Clinton's Administration, including Alice Rivlin, Director of the Office of Management and Budget, advocated a sorting out of intergovernmental responsibilities to reduce expenses and improve government performance. However, President Bill Clinton proposed more modest intergovernmental reforms. For example, his ISTEA reauthorization proposal, the six-year, $174.5 billion, National Economic Crossroads Transportation Efficiency Act (NEXTEA, H.R. 1268, S. 468), would have retained and increased funding for virtually all ISTEA programs (providing $139 billion for highways and $35.5 billion for mass transit). It also included $4.7 billion for Amtrak and would have made Amtrak eligible for STP funding.

During ISTEA's reauthorization, Congress addressed efforts to devolve programmatic authority to states and to expand state authority to "flex" federal funding among existing programs, but it focused most of its attention on resolving differences related to the program's allocation of resources among states. The STEP 21 Coalition, representing the "donor" states of Alabama, Arizona, Arkansas, Florida, Georgia, Indiana, Kentucky, Louisiana, Michigan, Minnesota, Mississippi, Missouri, Nebraska, North Carolina, Oklahoma, Oregon, South Carolina, Tennessee, Texas, Virginia, and Wisconsin, advocated a minimum 95 cents return per dollar their highway users contributed to the Highway Trust Fund. They also wanted to merge the interstate maintenance program and portions of the bridge program into the national highway system and create a Streamlined Surface Transportation Block Grant program which would receive about 60% of the program's highway funding and could be used for all existing program activities.[94] The Alliance for ISTEA Renewal (U.S. Conference of Mayors, National Association of Counties, National League of Cities, American Public Transit Association, Association of Metropolitan Planning Organizations and the Surface Transportation Policy Project) wanted to prevent the redirection of federal fuel tax revenue from the Highway Trust Fund, but otherwise recommended relatively minor changes to ISTEA. California, Ohio, South Carolina, and Michigan endorsed efforts by Representative John Kasich in the House and Senator Connie Mack in the Senate to devolve most non-interstate highway and mass transit programs to states. Their Surface Transportation and Transit Empowerment Act (H.R. 3045 and S. 1497) would have returned "to the individual States maximum discretionary authority and fiscal responsibility for all elements of the national transportation systems that are not within the direct purview of the Federal Government."[95]

The proposed Surface Transportation and Transit Empowerment Act did not generate the level of congressional attention provided to the state donor-donee debate. Nonetheless, the arguments presented both for and against its adoption are relevant today given that the devolution issue may be considered during SAFETEA's reauthorization. However, current fiscal conditions are much different today than in 1997 and 1998. It could be argued that the current economic fiscal crisis may limit the states' fiscal capacity to assume responsibility for federal surface transportation projects if they were asked, as they were in 1997 and 1998, to increase state fuel taxes to fund those projects.

At a House subcommittee hearing on ISTEA's reauthorization in 1997, Senator Mack defended his devolution proposal, arguing that "the simple fact is that states now have the technical capability to build their own roads and, frankly, they know better than Washington what their transportation needs are. A continued role for the federal government is appropriate in certain areas, such as the maintenance of the interstate highway system or limited coordination functions."[96] He added:

> current policy has been unable to keep up with our Nation's growing infrastructure needs. One reason for this is that we have not been getting as much out of our transportation dollars as we used to. For instance, since 1956 Federal Highway Administration costs have grown from 7 percent to 21 percent today. Moreover, studies suggest the elimination of Federal mandates and restrictions would increase States' real purchasing power for transportation projects by 20 percent.[97]

Representative Kasich stated at the hearing that Ohio was one of 32 states at that time that received less from ISTEA than its highway users paid into the Highway Trust Fund. He added that the governors of Michigan, Ohio, California, South Carolina and Florida, all states that received less ISTEA funding at that time than their highway users paid into the Highway Trust Fund, had endorsed his bill. He argued that "if you let us keep our money and get rid of all the Federal bureaucracy and all the Federal rules, we'll be able to actually have more highway construction."[98]

On April 1, 1998, Representative Kasich offered his bill as an amendment in the nature of a substitute to BESTEA (Building Efficient Surface Transportation and Equity Act of 1998), the House ISTEA reauthorization bill. During floor debate, Representative E. G. "Bud" Shuster, Chair of the House Committee on Transportation and Infrastructure, rose in opposition to the amendment, arguing:

> while this would simply turn things back to the States, ironically there is a greater need for us to have a coordinated, tied-together national transportation system than ever. Why? Because more people and more goods are moving interstate than ever before.[99]

He also argued that "Indeed, there is a greater need to have this tied together than ever before. Our bill not only does that, but it also gives flexibilities to the States and the cities by saying that 50 percent of the funding in each category can be flexibly moved about to other categories."[100] He added that "It is very important, also, to recognize that, of the money that comes to Washington now, only 1 percent stays here down at the Department of Transportation for administrative purposes, 88 percent goes back to the States to be spent, 5 percent goes to the Secretary of Transportation to be sent back to the States for high cost discretionary projects, 5 percent goes back to the States through the congressional projects, and only 1 percent stays in Washington."[101] He concluded by arguing:

> Further, State regulations, which in many cases are as onerous, if not more onerous, than Federal regulations, would obviously stay in place. Indeed, we have no assurance whatsoever that, if we turn this back to the States, that the States would pass and increase their gas taxes. Indeed, I am told that, on the average, each State would have to pass the State gas tax increasing it by 15 cents per gallon. So what assurance do we have? No, this is simply destroying what must be a national program which is to tie our country together from a transportation point of view. For those reasons, I say we should defeat this amendment.[102]

Representative James Oberstar also opposed the amendment, arguing that it would:

> ... take us back to a time that none of us here could possibly imagine, a time when some States started roads, others did not, they built it up to a certain point and then it stopped. Bridges were started and then stopped. If we followed the gentleman's logic all the way through, we would have bridges go halfway across a river because one State would want to build it and the other State would not or would run out of money, or we would have roads that go up to a State's border and the other State would say "Well, we don't think that we want to build a road there." ... [the amendment] would have us in chaos. ... This is a vote for the past, not a vote for the future. ... If we are going to be a Nation, and if my colleagues believe in the Constitution that said a responsibility of the Congress shall be to build post roads, that it shall have authority over interstate and foreign commerce, then it is our duty to promote interstate and foreign commerce, and the way to do it is through transportation.103

The amendment was defeated, 98-318.[104]

Much of the remaining congressional debate on ISTEA's reauthorization focused on the state return-on-investment (state donor-donee) issue, ending the diversion of revenue generated by 4.3 cents per gallon of the gasoline tax from the Highway Trust Fund to the general revenue account for deficit reduction (enacted in 1993), and the inclusion of congressional earmarks.

The \$203.4 billion, six-year Transportation Equity Act for the 21st Century (TEA-21, P.L. 105- 178), signed by President Clinton on June 9, 1998, effectively ended the diversion of highway trust fund revenue for deficit reduction by authorizing \$167.1 billion for highways and \$36.3 billion for mass transit, roughly equivalent to the amount of revenue expected to be generated by the Highway Trust Fund. TEA-21 also created a three-part state minimum guarantee program. First, each state was guaranteed a percentage share (set forth in tabular form) for the apportioned programs: Interstate Maintenance Program, National Highway System Program, Surface Transportation Program, Highway Bridge Replacement and Rehabilitation Program, Congestion Mitigation and Air Quality Program, Metropolitan Planning, Recreational Trails Program, Appalachian Development Highway System Program and Minimum Guarantee, as well as High Priority Projects. Second, each state was guaranteed at least 90.5% of the amount its highway users paid into the Highway Trust Fund (based on the most recent year for which the data are available, typically from two fiscal years before). Third, each state was guaranteed that as part of the minimum guarantee it will receive at least \$1 million in minimum guarantee funds.

Although efforts to devolve surface transportation programs to states failed, TEA-21 retained ISTEA's programmatic flexibilities and increased them further by reducing from 16 to 7 the number of required planning factors to be used by states and MPOs when selecting projects, and increasing the role of local elected government officials in project selection. Congress did not accept the President's proposed language making Amtrak eligible for STP funding, but it did make Amtrak eligible for Congestion Mitigation and Air Quality Improvement funding.

Balancing State Program Flexibilities with the Need to Address National Interests: SAFETEA

On May 14, 2003, President George W. Bush announced his Administration's TEA-21 reauthorization proposal, the six-year, $247 billion, Safe, Accountable, Flexible and Efficient Transportation Equity Act of 2003 (SAFETEA, H.R. 2088, S. 1072). One of the bill's stated goals was to change federalism relationships in surface transportation policy by eliminating "program silos" that can alter state and local government decisions based on the availability of funds.[105] The bill proposed to accomplish this by eliminating most discretionary highway grant programs and making those funds available under the core formula highway grant programs; creating a new Highway Safety Improvement Program, in place of the existing Surface Transportation Program safety set-aside; and merging several highway safety programs into a new General Performance Grant and a new Safety Belt Performance Grant. It also would have merged mass transit grants into three main programs: an Urbanized Area Formula Grant, which would have included the existing Urbanized Area Formula Grant and the Fixed Guideway Modernization program; a Major Capital Investments Program, which would have included the New Starts program and non-fixed guideway corridor improvements, such as Bus Rapid Transit; and State-Administered Programs, which would have included the Rural, Elderly and Disabled, Job Access and Reverse Commute, and New Freedom Initiative programs.[106]

Although Congress did consider proposals to change federalism relationships in surface transportation policy during TEA-21's reauthorization, most of its attention, once again, was focused on resolving disagreements over funding levels and how funds were to be distributed among states.[107] Donor states, mainly those with growing populations located in the South and Southwest, wanted TEA-21's state minimum guarantee increased from 90.5% to 95% of the amount their highway users contributed to the Highway Trust Fund. Several donor states, including Arizona, California, Florida, North Carolina and Texas, also wanted to increase the scope of the guarantee by increasing the range of programs included when calculating each state's share.

Donee states did not object to a higher minimum guarantee in principle, but only if it did not reduce their funding. However, because the President threatened to veto any substantial funding increase above his initial recommendation of $247 billion and Congress lacked the votes to override his veto on this issue, it became virtually impossible to increase the state minimum funding guarantee without reducing funding for at least some states. Unable to reach agreement, Congress extended TEA-21 for short periods 12 times before finally passing the $286 billion Safe, Accountable, Flexible, and Efficient Transportation Equity Act - A Legacy for Users (SAFETEA) on July 29, 2005. It was signed by President Bush on August 10, 2005. It was only after the President removed his veto threat (partly due to a 2004 change in the tax treatment of ethanol fuel, which was expected to generate an additional $18.9 billion for the Highway Trust Fund) and the program's overall funding level was increased to $286 billion that the impasse over the minimum guarantee was resolved.

SAFETEA created an Equity Bonus (EB) program that ensures that states receive a specified percentage of the revenue their highway users contribute to the highway account of the Highway Trust Fund for programs listed in the EB program. The guaranteed rate was set at 91.5% for FY2007, and 92% for FYs 2008 and 2009. SAFETEA also includes a guaranteed overall increase for all states over the previous reauthorization bill, and a number of "hold harmless" provisions intended to mitigate the impact on certain donee states of the shift in funding to donor states. Meeting all of these requirements is done by providing a spending overlay across all of the programs listed in the EB program in a way that gives spending increases to all states, but larger increases to donor states. The EB program is the largest formula program in SAFETEA ($41 billion over five years).[108] In an important concession to donor states, funds for members projects were included in the funds that are distributed by the equity bonus formula.

Balancing its interest in ensuring that the program meets national needs with its interest in continuing to expand state programmatic flexibility, Congress did not adopt President Bush's recommendation to eliminate discretionary programs and reduce the number of formula programs in SAFETEA. Instead, SAFETEA added three new formula programs: the previously described core formula Highway Safety Improvement Program ($7.5 billion), the Coordinated Border Infrastructure Program, which replaced a TEA-21 discretionary program of the same name, and the Safe Routes to School Program. Also, a new discretionary transportation improvement program, a redefined national corridor infrastructure program (formerly part of the national corridor planning and development and coordinated border infrastructure program), and a new program for projects of national or regional significance were added. SAFETEA retained TEA-21's provisions that had expanded state authority to shift funds among core, formula-driven highway programs and between highways and mass transit. It also included a new provision allowing states to transfer certain discretionary program funds for administration of highway projects and mass transit projects. It also enhanced environmental streamlining regulations, changed clean air conformity regulations, funding for transit new starts, expanded reliance on innovative financing and tolls and spending on congressional high priority projects.

MOEs and the American Recovery and Reinvestment Act of 2009

P.L. 111-5, the American Recovery and Reinvestment Act of 2009 (ARRA), included $27.5 billion for highway, bridge and road projects, $8.4 billion for mass transit and $8.6 billion for discretionary grants to states to help fund capital costs associated with intercity rail services, with an emphasis on developing high-speed rail services. As a condition for the receipt of funding for these programs, the law includes a state maintenance-of-effort (MOE) requirement that requires the Governor of each state to certify to the Secretary of Transportation that

> the State will maintain its effort with regard to State funding for the types of projects that are funded by the appropriation. As part of this certification, the Governor shall submit to the Secretary of Transportation a statement identifying the amount of funds the State planned to expend from State sources as of the date of enactment of this Act during the period beginning on the date of enactment of this Act through September 30, 2010, for the types of projects that are funded by the appropriation.[109]

States are required to submit a report on their activities not later than 90 days after the act's enactment and an updated report not later than 180 days, one year, two years, and three years after enactment. States that are unable to maintain the level of effort will be prohibited by the Secretary of Transportation from receiving additional funds "pursuant to the redistribution of the limitation on obligations for Federal-aid highway and highway safety construction programs that occurs after August 1 for fiscal year 2011."[110]

Because state budgets are fungible and nominal state revenue tends to increase over time, when states receive federal financial assistance they typically have several budgetary options. They can choose to not make any budgetary adjustments other than to supplement existing spending levels with the federal assistance, or they can choose to substitute all or a portion of the federal funds received for existing state funds and use the savings to spend in other areas, reduce taxes, or increase their state "rainy day" funds. An examination of grants-in-aid listed in the Catalog of Federal Domestic Assistance revealed that 33 federal grants to state and local governments have state spending MOE requirements to prevent states from substituting federal funds for existing state funds.

An analysis completed by the Government Accountability Office in 2004 found that "state and local governments have used roughly half of the increases in federal highway grants since 1982 to substitute for funding they would otherwise have spent from their own resources. In addition, our model estimated that the rate of grant substitution increased significantly over the past two decades, rising from about 18 cents on the dollar during the early 1980s to roughly 60 cents on the dollar during the 1990s."[111]

Because state revenue growth has declined in recent years, it could be argued that states facing a budgetary shortfall are not likely to substitute federal funds received from the economic recovery plan for existing state funds. Instead, it could be argued that at least some states, particularly those facing budgetary shortfalls, might have a difficult time finding state revenue to maintain their previous spending levels. In either case, state MOE requirements may become an issue during SAFETEA's reauthorization and will be the subject of congressional interest and oversight during ARRA's implementation.

States have traditionally opposed state MOE requirements as an infringement on their sovereignty. For example, on January 15, 2008 the National Governors Association, National Conference of State Legislatures, and State Higher Education Executive Officers sent a letter to the chairs and ranking Members of the House Committee on Education and Labor and Senate Committee on Health, Education, Labor, and Pensions opposing a proposed MOE mandate in the College Opportunity and Affordability Act (H.R. 4137) because they believed that it infringed on state autonomy:

> Governors, legislators, and higher education officials share your desire to help make higher education accessible and affordable for students and families. They also share your concern with the rising cost of higher education, and are committed to making higher education easily accessible and affordable to all our citizens.
>
> That said, state budgeting decisions should be made by state officials. The decision to fund a new building or campus, expand student aid, help low-income families to access health care, or improve high schools, must remain with the officials closest to the needs of their specific communities.[112]

Opponents of state MOE requirements also argue that during prosperous times MOEs discourage increased state spending in areas receiving federal assistance. For example, on July 31, 2008 the National Governors Association opposed a state MOE requirement in the Higher Education Opportunity Act (P.L. 110-315) because it would penalize states that increased spending during good economic times and decreased them during economic downturns:

> Governors must balance their budgets in both good and bad economic times. This mandate means that states will be unable to make major increases or invest one-time surpluses in higher education during good times because they will be penalized if forced to reduce spending during difficult times. In the end, this will increase the cost of college for students and their families.[113]

Advocates of state MOE requirements argue that states should not be allowed to substitute federal assistance for existing state and local government spending. In their view, federal assistance should either supplement current state spending in the functional area receiving federal assistance or encourage states to increase their current level of spending in that area. For example, in 1978 the now-defunct U.S. Advisory Commission on Intergovernmental Relations (ACIR) argued that

> Maintenance-of-effort requirements and matching ratios should be considered together. Without an effective maintenance-of-effort requirement, a categorical grant with no matching requirements likely will result in reduced spending from recipients' own funds for the aided function.[114]

Federal Reimbursement Rates and the American Recovery and Reinvestment Act of 2009

ARRA set federal reimbursement rates for funding received from the act for several programs, including highway, bridge and road projects, transit capital assistance, fixed guideway infrastructure investment, and capital assistance for high speed rail corridors and intercity passenger rail service, at up to 100%. It remains to be seen if ARRA's up to 100% reimbursement rate will be viewed as a precedent for re-opening discussions of SAFETEA's reimbursement rates, or it will be viewed as an aberration designed to meet a special economic circumstance.

One possibility is that the states' ability or inability to meet ARRA's transportation MOE requirements may have an effect on congressional views concerning any proposals to increase the federal share of expenses in SAFETEA's programs or to waive, as Senator Bernard Sanders' and Representative Peter Welch's legislation (S. 198, H.R. 491) proposed to do for FY2009, "any requirement that would otherwise require a state or local government to contribute non-federal funds toward the cost of a covered transportation program or activity authorized by SAFTETEA or an amendment made by that Act."[115]

SAFETEA Reauthorization Efforts During the 111th Congress

As mentioned previously, in February 2009, the Obama Administration indicated that it was interested in exploring alternative means to ensure the long-term sustainability of the Highway Trust Fund. However, concerned that the congressional agenda already included several high-profile issues, including health care reform, global warming, and appropriations legislation, and still considering the various proposed options for funding surface transportation projects, the Obama Administration announced on June 17, 2009, that instead of pursuing a comprehensive reauthorization of SAFETEA, it supported a cash infusion of $20 billion to replenish the Highway Trust Fund to avert a revenue shortfall later that year and the enactment of an 18-month reauthorization of SAFETEA, without major programmatic changes. The Administration asserted that an 18-month extension of existing legislation would provide "Congress the time it needs to fully deliberate the direction of America's transportation priorities."[116]

Senator Barbara Boxer, chair of the Senate Environment and Public Works, endorsed the Administration's call for a 18-month extension of SAFETEA, stating at a congressional hearing on June 25, 2009, that "we have a lot of issues on the table in terms of a long-term solution to our funding" and an 18-month extension "provided a level of funding certainty" for state and local government transportation officials that was preferable to a shorter-term extension.[117]

Representative James Oberstar, then-chair of the House Committee on Transportation and Infrastructure, and others in the House preferred a comprehensive reauthorization bill. On June 18, 2009, Representative Oberstar, then-ranking member John Mica, and others on the House Committee on Transportation and Infrastructure released a draft of a six-year, $450 billion SAFETEA reauthorization bill.[118] The proposal would have also authorized an additional $50 billion to develop 11 high-speed rail corridors linking major metropolitan regions within the United States. The committee's Subcommittee on Highways and Transit held a hearing on the proposal on June 24, 2009.

The proposal, which was not formally introduced as a bill, would have provided $337.4 billion for highway construction, $99.8 billion for mass transit, and $12.6 billion for highway and motor carrier safety. It also would have

- consolidated funding in four, core formula categories: highway and bridge systems, highway safety; improved capacity; and congestion and greenhouse gas emissions;
- focused the majority of transit funding in four core categories: repair, restoration, mobility and access, and planning;
- required states and local governments to establish transportation plans with specific performance standards, measure their progress annually in meeting these standards, and periodically adjust their plans as necessary to achieve specific goals;
- created a national infrastructure bank to leverage transportation funding; and
- consolidated or terminated more than 75 transportation programs.

Congress subsequently passed legislation that transferred an additional $21.7 billion in general fund revenues associated with transportation-related activities to the Highway Trust Fund.[119] Congress also passed four short-term SAFETEA reauthorizations during the 111th Congress.[120]

On September 6, 2010, President Obama proposed a six-year reauthorization of surface transportation programs, with $50 billion in "upfront investment in our nation's infrastructure" to "help jump-start additional job creation."[121] The Administration did not provide an estimate for the total amount of funding for the reauthorization, but indicated that the $50 billion would represent a significant portion of any increase above current levels. The proposal called for

- the establishment of an infrastructure bank "to leverage federal funding and focus on investments of national and regional significance that often fall through the cracks in the current siloed transportation programs."[122]
- the integration of high-speed rail on an equal footing into the surface transportation program "to ensure a sustained and effective commitment to a national high speed rail system over the next generation."[123]
- consolidating more than 100 different programs and focusing on using performance measurement and "race-to-the-top" style competitive pressures to drive investment toward better policy outcomes.[124]
- increasing funding for safety, environmental sustainability, economic competitiveness, and livability projects, "helping to build communities where people have choices about how to travel, including options that reduce oil consumption, lower greenhouse gas emissions, and expand access to job opportunities and housing that's affordable."[125]

Congress did not act on the proposal.

SAFETEA Reauthorization Efforts During the 112th Congress

On March 3, 2011, Congress passed another short-term SAFETEA reauthorization bill and President Obama signed it into law on March 4, 2011. The latest extension is set to expire on September 30, 2011.[126] Both the House Committee on Transportation and Infrastructure and the Senate Committee on Environment and Public Works continue to hold hearings on SAFETEA's reauthorization and to consult with the Obama Administration.[127]

CONCLUSION

Congress has debated the federal role in surface transportation policy since the nation's formation in 1789. A review of the historical record suggests that the debate over the federal role in surface transportation policy has been influenced by factors both internal and external to the institution. Internally, the background, personalities, and ideological preferences of congressional leaders such as Senator Harry Byrd, Senator Daniel Patrick Moynihan, and Representative E. G. "Bud" Shuster have had a profound impact on the development of federal-state-local government relationships in surface transportation policy over time. The norms, customs, and traditions of the House and Senate have also had an influence. For example, the decentralized nature of decision-making in both the House and the Senate has compartmentalized decisions into more manageable pieces, but, arguably, has made it more difficult for Congress to develop broad-based policies that cut across committee jurisdictions or to enact proposals to consolidate programs or devolve programmatic authority to states as these actions might upset existing power relationships and require the consent of several committees and committee chairs. For example, in the House of Representatives, programmatic and funding distribution issues are under the jurisdiction of the Committee on Transportation and Infrastructure, but tax and Highway Trust Fund issues are under the jurisdiction of the Committee on Ways and Means. In the Senate, most programmatic and funding distribution issues are under the jurisdiction of the Committee on Environment and Public Works for highways and other aspects of Title 23, but are under the Committee on Banking, Housing, and Urban Affairs for transit. Tax and Highway Trust Fund issues are under the jurisdiction of the Committee on Finance. In the Senate, most safety issues are under the jurisdiction of either the Committee on Environment and Public Works or the Committee on Commerce, Science, and Transportation. The size of the 59-member House Committee on Transportation and Infrastructure may also have an impact on federal-state-local relationships in surface transportation policy as each Member has a natural tendency to attempt to maximize surface transportation resources for their home district. Arguably, the committee's unusually large size could make it more difficult to eliminate congressional earmarks or to achieve committee approval for program consolidations or devolution of programmatic authority because such changes are often viewed as jeopardizing existing funding streams and the ability of Members to claim and receive credit for helping their constituents.[128]

Externally, interest groups representing both the private and public sectors have historically been united in their advocacy of additional federal funding, but have been divided over how program funds should be allocated, both among states and among transportation modes. Congress has tended to arbitrate the differences among these varied interests by balancing the need to promote the national interest with the recognition that, for the most part, state and local government officials have proven over time to be relatively capable administrators of surface transportation programs. As a result, Congress has rejected efforts to devolve programmatic authority to states. Instead, it has adopted policies that have expanded state programmatic flexibility while, at the same time, promote the national interest by requiring state and local governments to adhere to federal guidelines for managing the project development process and monitoring highway and bridge conditions, highway safety programs, traffic congestion mitigation programs, transit facility and equipment maintenance programs, as well as intermodal transportation facilities and systems.

Presidents, perhaps reflecting their role in representing the national interest as a whole and, perhaps, at least in part, because several Presidents had formerly served as governors, have tended to be more supportive of program consolidation and devolution of programmatic authority in surface transportation policy than Congress. This has been especially the case when the President's ideology favored smaller government. Typically, presidential efforts to consolidate surface transportation programs have faced strong opposition from private sector interest groups worried that program consolidation will result in less funding for the consolidated programs over time, and from Members worried that consolidation could lead to less funding for specific programs that are important to them.

Perhaps the most difficult factor to account for in the development of federalism relationships in surface transportation policy over time has been the changing nature of American society and expectations concerning personal mobility. Once a rural society with relatively limited expectations concerning personal mobility, America is now a primarily urban/suburban society where automobile ownership and the personal mobility that automobile ownership brings is not only a powerful social status symbol but also a necessity.

Obtaining a drivers' license is now a major life-altering event, signifying for millions of American teenagers each year the transition from childhood to adulthood. Because the American bond with the automobile is strong, moving away from a primary focus on building and constructing highways towards a "more balanced" intermodal transportation approach has been made more difficult for policymakers at all levels of government. Moreover, given the public's relatively high expectations concerning personal mobility, Congress has been reluctant to consolidate or devolve surface transportation programs to states, at least in part, because some Members worry that if states are provided additional authority and fail to meet public expectations, that they might be held accountable for that failure on election day. In their view, a more prudent, risk-adverse approach is to provide states additional programmatic flexibility, but retain a federal presence through both program oversight and the imposition of federal guidelines to ensure that states do not stray too far from national objectives.

It remains to be seen how all of these factors will play out during SAFETEA's reauthorization. One certainty is that Congress will play the key role in determining the future of federalism relationships in surface transportation policy. Another is that those relationships will continue to evolve over time, adopting to changes in American society and in Congress.

End Notes

[1] P.L. 111-118, the Department of Defense Appropriations Act, 2010; P.L. 111-144, the Temporary Extension Act of 2010, P.L. 111-147; the Hiring Incentives to Restore Employment Act; P.L. 111-322, the Continuing Appropriations and Surface Transportation Extensions Act, 2011; and P.L. 112-5, the Surface Transportation Extension Act of 2011.

[2] See CRS Report R41512, *Surface Transportation Program Reauthorization Issues for the 112th Congress*, coordinated by Robert S. Kirk; and CRS Report R40451, *The Donor-Donee State Issue: Funding Equity in Surface Transportation Reauthorization*, by Robert S. Kirk.

[3] During the 109th Congress, Senator DeMint introduced the Transportation Empowerment Act in the Senate on April 4, 2006 (S. 2512). It was referred to the Senate Committee on Finance. Rep. Flake introduced a companion bill in the House on April 26, 2006 (H.R. 5205). It was referred to the House Committee on Ways and Means, the House Committee on the Budget, and the House Committee on Transportation and Infrastructure and its Subcommittee on Highways, Transit and Pipelines. During the 110th Congress Senator DeMint introduced an updated version of the Transportation Empowerment Act on April 7, 2008 (S. 2823). It was referred to the Senate Committee on Finance.

[4] For further analysis, see CRS Report R40451, *The Donor-Donee State Issue: Funding Equity in Surface Transportation Reauthorization*, by Robert S. Kirk.

[5] National Surface Transportation Policy and Revenue Study Commission, *Transportation for Tomorrow*, Washington, DC: National Surface Transportation Policy and Revenue Study Commission, December 2007, Volume 1, p. 9.

[6] Ibid., Volume 1, p. 10.

[7] Ibid., Volume 1, pp. 11, 12.

[8] National Surface Transportation Infrastructure Financing Commission, *Paying Our Way: A New Framework for Transportation Finance* (Washington, DC: National Surface Transportation Infrastructure Financing Commission, February 2009), pp. 3, 4.

[9] Ibid., p. 7.

[10] For further analysis, see CRS Report RL33995, *Surface Transportation Congestion: Policy and Issues*, by William J. Mallett; and U.S. Government Accountability Office, *Highway Trust Fund: Improved Solvency Mechanisms and Communication Needed to Help Avoid Shortfalls in the Highway Account*, GAO-09-316, February 6, 2009, pp. 19-21, http://www.gao.gov/new.items/d09316.pdf.

[11] The National Commission on Fiscal Responsibility and Reform, "The moment of Truth," Washington, DC, December 2010, p. 24, http://www.fiscalcommission.gov/sites/fiscalcommission.gov/files/documents/TheMomentofTruth12_1_2010.pdf.

[12] Washington Post Editorial, "Mr. LaHood's Good Idea: The transportation chief's mileage tax shouldn't be a nonstarter," *The Washington Post*, February 23, 2009, p. A18.

[13] H.R. 3379, the Lopsided Oil Prices Act of 2009; and U.S. Congress, House Committee on Transportation and *Authorization in Sustaining Economic Recovery*, 111th Cong., 1st sess., July 16, 2009, H.Hrg. 111-50 (Washington: GPO, 2009), p. 15.

[14] National Conference of State Legislatures, "2010-2011 Policies for the Jurisdiction of the Transportation Committee - Surface Transportation Federalism," http://www.ncsl.org/Default.aspx?TabID=773&tabs=855,30,674#Surface_Transportation.

[15] Ibid.

[16] See CRS Report R40805, *Transportation, Housing and Urban Development, and Related Agencies (THUD): FY2010 Appropriations*, by David Randall Peterman and Maggie McCarty.

[17] U.S. Department of Transportation, Research and Innovative Technology Administration, Bureau of Transportation Statistics, *National Transportation Statistics*, Washington, DC, June 2009, Table 3-29a, http://www.bts.gov/publications/national_transportation_statistics/html/table_03_29a.html; U.S. Congres sional Budget Office and Joint Committee on Taxation, *Subsidizing Infrastructure Investment with Tax-Preferred Bonds*, Washington, DC, October 2009, p. 2, http://www.cbo.gov/ftpdocs/106xx/doc10667/ 10-26-TaxPreferredBonds.pdf; and Peter Orszag, Director, Congressional Budget Office, "Testimony, Current and Future Investment in Infrastructure," before the Committee on the Budget and the Committee on Transportation and Infrastructure, U.S. House of Representatives, May 8, 2008, p. 4, http://www.cbo .gov/ftpdocs/91xx/doc9136/05-07-Infrastructure_Testimony.pdf.

[18] Constitution of the United States, text available on the National Archives website: http://www.archives.gov /exhibits/charters/constitution_transcript.html.

[19] Constitution of the United States, text available on the National Archives website: http://www.archives .gov/exhibits/charters/bill_of_rights_transcript.html.

[20] Thomas Aquinas Burke, "Ohio Lands – A Short History," 8th Edition, (Columbus: Ohio: State Auditor's Office, September 1996),.http://freepages.history.rootsweb.ancestry.com/~maggie/ohio-lands/ohl5. html# WROT LNDS.

[21] Benjamin Horace Hibbard, *A History of the Public Land Policies* (New York: The Macmillan Company, 1924), pp. 228-233. Note: Maine and West Virginia were not eligible for the guarantee because they were formed out of other states and Texas was ineligible because it was considered a sovereign nation when admitted to the Union. Also, five states, Wisconsin, Alabama, Iowa, Nevada and Oregon, subsequently were permitted to use their proceeds from federal land sales solely for public education.

[22] Matthias Nordberg Orfield, *Federal Land Grants to the States With Special Reference to Minnesota* (Minneapolis, MN: Bulletin of the University of Minnesota, 1915), pp. 77- 111, 115-118; Morton Grodzins, *The American System* (Chicago: Rand McNally, 1966), p. 35; Gary M. Anderson and Dolores T. Martin, "The Public Domain and Nineteenth Century Transfer Policy," *Cato Journal* 6:3 (Winter 1987): 908-910; John Bell Rae, "Federal Land Grants in Aid of Canals," *The Journal of Economic History* 4:2 (November 1944): 167, 168, and U.S. Department of Transportation, Federal Highway Administration, *America's Highways, 1776/1976* (Washington, DC: GPO, 1976), 24. Note: 26 states received federal land grants during the 1800s.

[23] John B. Rae, *The Road and Car in American Life* (Cambridge, MA: MIT Press, 1971), pp. 33-39, 49; and Robert Jay Dilger, "Moving the Nation: Governors and the Development of American Transportation Policy," in *A Legacy of Innovation: Governors and Public Policy*, ed. Ethan G. Sribnick (Philadelphia: University of Pennsylvania Press, 2008), p. 172.

[24] U.S. Advisory Commission on Intergovernmental Relations, *Categorical Grants: Their Role and Design*, A-52 (Washington, DC: GPO, 1978), p. 16.

[25] U.S. Congress, House Committee on Roads, *Federal Aid to Good Roads: Report of the Joint Committee on Federal Aid in the Construction of Post Roads*, 63rd Cong., 3rd sess., November 25, 1914 (Washington, DC: GPO, 1915), p.14.

[26] Ibid., pp. 14-17.

[27] "Postwar Highway Program," in *Congress and the Nation, 1945-1964* (Washington, DC: Congressional Quarterly Press, 1965), pp. 525-527.

[28] U.S. Congress, Senate Committee on Post Offices and Post Roads, *Interstate Highway System*, Hearing on S. 1355, 77th Cong., 1st sess., May 13, 1921 (Washington, DC: GPO, 1921), pp. 76-97; and U.S. Congress, Senate Committee on Post Offices and Post Roads, *Interstate Highway System*, Hearing on S. 1355, 77th Cong., 1st sess., June 2, 1921 (Washington, DC: GPO, 1921), pp. 536-540.

[29] U.S. Congress, Senate Committee on Post Offices and Post Roads, *Interstate Highway System*, Hearing on S. 1355, 77th Cong., 1st sess., May 19, 1921 (Washington, DC: GPO, 1921), p. 181.

[30] Ibid., p. 173.

[31] Ibid., p. 175.

[32] U.S. Advisory Commission on Intergovernmental Relations (ACIR), *Categorical Grants: Their Role and Design*, A-52 (Washington, DC: GPO, 1978), pp. 51, 52.

[33] Richard F. Weingroff, "The Federal-State Partnership at Work," *Public Roads* 60:1 (Summer 1996): 7, http://www.tfhrc.gov/pubrds/summer96/p96su7.htm.

[34] John B. Rae, *The Road and Car in American Life* (Cambridge, MA: MIT Press, 1971), pp. 36-39; and Bruce E. Seely, *Building the American Highway System: Engineers as Policy Makers* (Philadelphia: Temple University Press, 1987), pp. 72-80.

[35] U.S. Congress, House Committee on Roads, *Federal-Aid Road Act, Summary of Hearings on H.R. 2426*, 78th Cong., 2nd sess., 1944 (Washington, DC: GPO, 1944), pp. 3-6; and Mark H. Rose, *Interstate: Express Highway Politics, 1939-1989, Revised Edition* (Knoxville, TN: The University of Tennessee Press, 1990), pp. 22-28.

[36] U.S. Congress, House Committee on Roads, *Federal-Aid Road Act, Summary of Hearings on H.R. 2426*, 78th Cong., 2nd sess., 1944 (Washington, DC: GPO, 1944), pp. 4-6.

[37] Ibid.; and Mark H. Rose, *Interstate: Express Highway Politics, 1939-1989, Revised Edition* (Knoxville, TN: The University of Tennessee Press, 1990), pp. 22-28.

[38] Richard F. Weingroff, "The Genie In The Bottle: The Interstate System and Urban Problems, 1939-1957," *Public Roads* 64:2 (September/October 2000), http://www.tfhrc.gov/pubrds/septoct00/urban.htm.

[39] U.S. Congress, House Committee of Conference, *Federal Highway Act of 1944*, Conference Report to Accompany S. 2105, 78th Cong., 2nd sess., December 11, 1944, pp. 2, 3.

[40] Robert Jay Dilger, "Moving the Nation: Governors and the Development of American Transportation Policy," in *A Legacy of Innovation: Governors and Public Policy*, ed. Ethan G. Sribnick (Philadelphia: University of Pennsylvania Press, 2008), p. 177.

[41] Mark H. Rose, *Interstate: Express Highway Politics, 1939-1989, Revised Edition* (Knoxville, TN: The University of Tennessee Press, 1990), pp. 95-104.

[42] U.S. Congress, Senate Committee on Post Offices and Post Roads, *Federal Aid in the Construction of Rural Post Roads*, Report to accompany H.R. 7617, 64th Cong., 1st sess., March 10, 1916 (Washington, DC: GPO, 1916), p. 21.

[43] ACIR, *Categorical Grants: Their Role and Design*, A-52 (Washington, DC: GPO, 1978), p. 176.

[44] U.S. Congress, Senate Committee on Public Works, Subcommittee on Roads, Statement of Burton F. Miller, Executive Vice President, American Road Builders' Association, *Federal Highway Act of 1970, Part 3*, hearing on S. 4055 and S. 4260, 91st Cong., 2nd sess., September 9, 1970 (Washington: GPO, 1970), p. 1224.

[45] U.S. Congress, Senate Committee on Public Works, Subcommittee on Roads, *Federal Highway Act of 1970 and Miscellaneous Bills, Part 2*, 91st Cong., 2nd sess., July 14 and 15, 1970 (Washington: GPO, 1970), pp. 603-608.

[46] U.S. Congress, Senate Committee on Public Works, Subcommittee on Roads, *Federal Highway Act of 1970 and Miscellaneous Bills, Part 1*, 91st Cong., 2nd sess., July 13 1970 (Washington: GPO, 1970), p. 512.

[47] U.S. Congress, Senate Committee on Environment and Public Works, Subcommittee on Transportation, Statement of Milton Johnson, on behalf of the National Association of Counties, *Federal Aid Highway Act of 1978*, hearing on Federal Aid Highway Act of 1978, 95th Cong., 1st sess., July 26, 1977 (Washington: GPO, 1977), p. 121.

[48] U.S. Congress, Senate Committee on Environment and Public Works, Subcommittee on Transportation, Statement of Brock Adams, Secretary of Transportation, *Federal Aid Highway Act of 1978*, hearing on Federal Aid Highway Act of 1978, 95th Cong., 1st sess., July 26, 1977 (Washington: GPO, 1977), p. 67.

[49] Ibid., 178-181.

[50] Robert Jay Dilger, "The Expansion and Centralization of American Governmental Functions," in *American Intergovernmental Relations Today: Perspectives and Controversies*, ed. Robert Jay Dilger (Englewood Cliffs, NJ: Prentice-Hall, Inc., 1986), p. 18.

[51] U.S. Congress, Senate Committee on Public Works, Subcommittee on Public Roads, *Federal-Aid Highway Act of 1960*, hearing on H.R. 10495, 86th Cong., 2nd sess., June 9, 1960 (Washington: GPO, 1960), p. 2.

[52] ACIR, *Categorical Grants: Their Role and Design*, A-52 (Washington, DC: GPO, 1978), pp. 118, 129; and ACIR, *A Catalog of Federal Grant-In-Aid Programs to State and Local Governments: Grants Funded FY 1975*. A-52A (Washington, DC: GPO, 1977), pp. 13-15.

[53] Claude E. Barfield, *Rethinking Federalism: Block Grants and Federal, State, and Local Responsibilities* (Washington, DC: American Enterprise Institute for Public Policy Research, 1981), p. 3.
[54] Ibid.
[55] Timothy Conlan, *New Federalism: Intergovernmental Reform From Nixon to Reagan* (Washington, DC: The Brookings Institution, 1988), pp. 36-38.
[56] ACIR, *A Catalog of Federal Grant-In-Aid Programs to State and Local Governments: Grants Funded FY 1981*, M-133 (Washington, DC: GPO, 1982), pp. 26-28.
[57] Timothy J. Conlan and David B. Walker, "Reagan's New Federalism: Design, Debate and Discord," *Intergovernmental Perspective* 8:4 (Winter 1983): 6-15, 18-22; and Timothy Conlan, *New Federalism: Intergovernmental Reform From Nixon to Reagan* (Washington, DC: The Brookings Institution, 1988), pp. 182-198.
[58] Elizabeth Parker, Major Proposals to Restructure the Highway Program," *Transportation Quarterly*, 45:1 (January 1991): 55-66, http://www.fhwa.dot.gov/infrastructure/restructure.htm.
[59] Ibid.
[60] Richard F. Weingroff, "President Ronald Reagan and the Surface Transportation and Uniform Relocation Assistance Act of 1987," U.S. Department of Transportation, Federal Highway Administration, http://www .fhwa.dot.gov/infrastructure/rw01e.cfm.
[61] Ibid. Note: Senator Terry Sanford switched his vote.
[62] The following programs are included in SAFETEA's EB program: Interstate Maintenance, National Highway System, Surface Transportation Program, Bridge and Bridge Maintenance, Congestion, Mitigation, and Air Quality, Highway Safety Improvement Program, Recreational Trails, Appalachian Development Highway System, High Priority Projects, Metropolitan Planning, Coordinated Border Infrastructure Program, Safe Routes to School Program, and the Rail-Highway Grade Crossing program. For further analysis, see CRS Report R40451, *The Donor-Donee State Issue: Funding Equity in Surface Transportation Reauthorization*, by Robert S. Kirk; and CRS Report RL33119, *Safe, Accountable, Flexible, Efficient Transportation Equity Act—A Legacy for Users (SAFETEA-LU or SAFETEA): Selected Major Provisions*, coordinated by John W. Fischer.
[63] For further analysis, see CRS Report R40053, *Surface Transportation Program Reauthorization Issues for the 111th Congress*, coordinated by John W. Fischer.
[64] ACIR, *Characteristics of Federal Grant-In-Aid Programs to State and Local Governments Funded FY 1991*, M-182 (Washington, DC: GPO, 1992), pp. 24, 28; and ACIR, *Characteristics of Federal Grant-In-Aid Programs to State and Local Governments Funded FY 1981*, M-133 (Washington, DC: GPO, 1982), pp. 26-29.
[65] ACIR, *Devolving Selected Federal-Aid Highway Programs and Revenue Bases: A Critical Appraisal*, A-108 (Washington, DC: GPO, 1987), p. 2.
[66] Ibid.
[67] Ibid., 27.
[68] Ibid.
[69] Ibid.
[70] Ibid., p. 28.
[71] Ibid.
[72] ACIR, *Categorical Grants: Their Role and Design*, A-52 (Washington, DC: GPO, 1978), p. 51.
[73] ACIR, *Devolving Selected Federal-Aid Highway Programs and Revenue Bases: A Critical Appraisal*, A-108 (Washington, DC: GPO, 1987), p 29.
[74] Ibid., pp. 29, 30.
[75] Ibid., p. 28.
[76] Ibid.
[77] Ibid., p. 30.
[78] Ibid.
[79] Ibid.
[80] Ibid., pp. 30, 31.
[81] Ibid., p. 31.
[82] Ibid.
[83] Ibid., pp. 31, 32.
[84] Because SAFETEA's enactment took place late in FY2005, it could be argued that a more useful representation of its funding is that it provided $244 billion in spending authority from FY2005 through FY2009. See CRS

Report R41512, *Surface Transportation Program Reauthorization Issues for the 112th Congress*, coordinated by Robert S. Kirk.

85 President George H.W. Bush, "Remarks Announcing Proposed Transportation Legislation," *Public Papers of President George H.W. Bush*, February 13, 1991, http://bushlibrary.tamu.edu/research/public_ papers. php?id=2703&year=1991&month=2.

86 Samuel Skinner, Secretary, Department of Transportation, *Intermodal Surface Transportation Efficiency Act of 1991 – A Summary* (Washington, DC: U.S. Department of Transportation, 1991), http://ntl.bts. gov/DOCS/ste.html.

87 Mike Mills, "Administration Asks States to Carry the Transit Load," *Congressional Quarterly Weekly Report*, March 9, 1991, pp. 599, 600.

88 U.S. Department of Transportation, Federal Highway Administration, Highway History, Richard F. Weingroff, "National Highway System: Imagining The Future," http://www.fhwa.dot.gov/infrastructure/nhsorigins.cfm. Note: Senator Quentin Burdick, Chair, Committee on Environment and Public Works, was in failing health at the time and allowed Senator Moynihan to take the lead.

89 S. 965, Surface Transportation Efficiency Act of 1991 (Introduced in Senate) and S. 1204, Surface Transportation Efficiency Act of 1991 (Engrossed as Agreed to or Passed by Senate).

90 U.S. Congress, Senate Committee on Environment and Public Works, *Pending Highway Legislation*, hearing on S. 823 and S. 965, 102nd Cong., 1st sess., May 14, 1991, S. Hrg. 102-142 (Washington: GPO, 1991), p. 339.

91 Ibid., p. 282.

92 Mike Mills, "Highway and Transit Overhaul is Cleared for President," *Congressional Quarterly Weekly Report*, November 30, 1991, pp. 3518-3522; Kirk Victor, "Skinner's Final Act," *National Journal*, December 14, 1991, pp. 3016-3019; and Bruce D. McDowell, "Reinventing Surface Transportation: New Intergovernmental Challenges," *Intergovernmental Perspective* 18:1 (Winter 1982): 6-8, 18.

93 ACIR, Characteristics of Federal Grant-in-Aid Programs to State and Local Governments: Grants Funded FY 1995, M-195 (Washington, DC: GPO, 1995), p. 3.

94 For further analysis, CRS Report R40451, *The Donor-Donee State Issue: Funding Equity in Surface Transportation Reauthorization*, by Robert S. Kirk.

95 Rep. John Kasich, "Building Efficient Surface Transportation And Equity Act of 1998," House debate, *Congressional Record*, vol. 144, part 4 (April 1, 1998), p. 5723.

96 U.S. Congress, House Committee on Transportation and Infrastructure, Subcommittee on Surface Transportation, *Reauthorization of the Intermodal Surface Transportation Efficiency Act (ISTEA): Comprehensive Reauthorization Proposals*, 105th Cong., 1st sess., February 12, 1997 (Washington, DC: GPO, 1997), p. 11.

97 Ibid.

98 Ibid., pp. 12, 13.

99 Rep. Bud Shuster, "Building Efficient Surface Transportation and Equity Act of 1998," House debate, *Congressional Record*, vol. 144, part 4 (April 1, 1998), p. 5728.

100 Ibid.

101 Ibid.

102 Ibid.

103 Rep. James Oberstar, "Building Efficient Surface Transportation And Equity Act of 1998," House debate, *Congressional Record*, vol. 144, part 4 (April 1, 1998), p. 5730.

104 Rep. John Kasich, "Building Efficient Surface Transportation And Equity Act of 1998," House debate, *Congressional Record*, vol. 144, part 4 (April 1, 1998), pp. 5723-5734.

105 U.S. Congress, Senate Committee on Banking, Housing, and Urban Affairs, *The Administration's Proposal for Reauthorization of the Federal Public Transportation Program*, Hearing on the Reauthorization of the Public Transportation Title of the Transportation Equity Act For the Twenty-First Century (TEA-21), 108th Cong., 1st sess., June 10, 2003, S. Hrg. 108-640 (Washington, DC: GPO, 2004), pp. 17, 18.

106 U.S. Congress, House Committee on Transportation and Infrastructure, Subcommittee on Highways, Transit and Pipelines, *Overview of the Administration's Proposed Reauthorization Bill (SAFETEA)*, Hearing on the Safe, Accountable, Flexible, and Efficient Transportation Equity Act (SAFETEA) of 2003, 108th Cong., 1st sess., May 15, 2003, Committee Serial No. 108-26 (Washington, DC: GPO, 2003).

107 For additional information, see CRS Report RL32226, *Highway and Transit Program Reauthorization Legislation in the 2nd Session, 108th Congress*, by John W. Fischer; CRS Report RL33119, *Safe, Accountable, Flexible, Efficient Transportation Equity Act—A Legacy for Users (SAFETEA-LU or SAFETEA): Selected Major Provisions*, coordinated by John W. Fischer; and CRS Report RL31665, *Highway and Transit Program*

Reauthorization, by John W. Fischer; and CRS Report 31735, *Federal-Aid Highway Program: "Donor-Donee" State Issues*, by Robert S. Kirk (available by request from the author).

108 For further analysis, see CRS Report R40451, *The Donor-Donee State Issue: Funding Equity in Surface Transportation Reauthorization*, by Robert S. Kirk.

109 P.L. 111-5.

110 Ibid.

111 U.S. Government Accountability Office, *Federal-Aid Highways: Trends, Effect on State Spending, and Options for Future Program Design*, GAO-04-802, August 2004, p. 3, http://www.gao.gov/ new.items/d04802.pdf.

112 Letter from Raymond C. Scheppach, Executive Director, National Governors Association, Paul E. Lingenfelter , President, State Higher Education Executive Officers, and William T. Pound, Executive Director, National Conference of State Legislatures, to The Honorable Edward "Ted" M. Kennedy, Chairman, Health, Education, Labor, and Pensions Committee, The Honorable Michael B. Enzi, Ranking Member, Health, Education, Labor, and Pensions Committee, The Honorable George Miller, Chairman, Committee on Education and Labor, and The Honorable Howard P. "Buck" McKeon, Ranking Member, Committee on Education and Labor, January 15, 2008, http://www.nga.org/portal/ site/nga /menuitem.cb6e7818b34088d18a27811 0501010a0/?vgnextoid=4a33ae4748977110VgnVCM1000001a01010aRCRD&vgnextchannel=4b18f074f0d9f f00VgnVCM1000001a01010aRCRD.

113 National Governors Association, "NGA Statement on Higher Education Bill," Press release, July 31, 2008, http://www.nga.org/portal/site/nga/menuitem.6c9a8a9ebc6ae07eee28aca9501010a0/?vgnextoid=9d9608b7bda 7b110VgnVCM1000001a01010aRCRD&vgnextchannel=759b8f2005361010VgnVCM1000001a01010aRCR D.

114 U.S. Advisory Commission on Intergovernmental Relations, *Categorical Grants: Their Role and Design* (Washington, DC: GPO, 1978), p. 174.

115 H.R. 491.

116 U.S. Department of Transportation, "Let's face reality on the Highway Trust Fund, not rush comprehensive legislation," Washington, DC, June 18, 2010, http://fastlane.dot.gov/2009/06/lets-face-reality-on-the-highway-trustfund. html. Also see Ray LaHood, Secretary of the Department of Transportation, "Statement Before the Committee on Environment and Public Works, United States Senate," Washington, DC, June 25, 2009, http://epw.senate.gov/public/index.cfm?FuseAction=Files.View&FileStore_id=186af0e4-fa98-49e1-874b-b14d8c3ab270.

117 U.S. Congress, Senate Committee on Environment and Public Works, *Impacts of Expected Highway Trust Fund Insolvency*, 111th Cong., June 25, 2009.

118 House Committee on Transportation and Infrastructure, "The Surface Transportation Authorization Act of 2009: A Blueprint for Investment and Reform Executive Summary," Washington, DC, June 18, 2009, http://t4america.org/docs/061809_STAA_summary.pdf. The draft bill can be viewed here: http://atfiles.org /files/pdf /STransJune22bill09.pdf.

119 P.L. 111-46, To restore sums to the Highway Trust Fund, and for other purposes ($7 billion); and P.L. 111-147, the Hiring Incentives to Restore Employment Act ($14.7 billion). P.L. 111-147 also transferred $4.8 billion to the mass transit account. Earlier, P.L. 110-318, To amend the Internal Revenue Code of 1986 to restore the Highway Trust Fund balance, transferred $8 billion into the Highway Trust Fund. See CRS Report R41512, *Surface Transportation Program Reauthorization Issues for the 112th Congress*, coordinated by Robert S. Kirk.

120 P.L. 111-118, the Department of Defense Appropriations Act, 2010; P.L. 111-144, the Temporary Extension Act of 2010, P.L. 111-147; the Hiring Incentives to Restore Employment Act; and P.L. 111-322, the Continuing Appropriations and Surface Transportation Extensions Act, 2011.

121 The White House, "President Obama to Announce Plan to Renew and Expand America's Roads, Railways and Runways," Washington, DC, September 6, 2010, http://www.whitehouse.gov/the-press-office/2010/09/06/ presidentobama-announce-plan-renew-and-expand-america-s-roads-railways-;. Also, see The White House, "Remarks by the President at Laborfest in Milwaukee, Wisconsin," Milwaukee, Wisconsin, September 6, 2010, http://www.whitehouse.gov/the-press-office/2010/09/06/remarks-president-laborfest-milwaukee-wisconsin.

122 The White House, "President Obama to Announce Plan to Renew and Expand America's Roads, Railways and Runways," Washington, DC, September 6, 2010, http://www.whitehouse.gov/the-press-office/2010/09/06/ presidentobama-announce-plan-renew-and-expand-america-s-roads-railways-. The Administration argued that the establishment of the infrastructure bank "marks an important departure from the federal government's

traditional way of spending on infrastructure through earmarks and formula-based grants that are allocated more by geography and politics than demonstrated value."

[123] Ibid.

[124] Ibid.

[125] Ibid.

[126] P.L. 112-5, the Surface Transportation Extension Act of 2011.

[127] The House Committee on Transportation and Infrastructure's website lists the Committee's priorities for SAFETEA's reauthorization, which include, among others, consolidating and reforming surface transportation programs "so that federal Highway Trust Fund revenues are spent on programs and projects that are truly in the federal interest;" providing states "the flexibility they need to address their unique transportation challenges by establishing innovative financing options" and that "take advantage of private sector expertise and capital;" eliminating "unnecessary bureaucratic red tape so that infrastructure projects can be built in half the time;" and establishing a national transportation plan. See U.S. House of Representatives, Committee on Transportation and Infrastructure, "Subcommittee on Highways and Transit," Washington, DC, http:// transportation .house.gov/subcommittees/Highways.aspx.

[128] David R. Mayhew, *Congress: The Electoral Connection* (New Haven, CT: Yale University Press, 1974), pp. 52-61. The House Committee on Transportation and Infrastructure had 75 members during the 111th Congress.

INDEX

D

E

F

G

H

N

O

P

S

T